Leadership and Personal Development

A Toolbox for the
21st Century Professional

Editors:
Katja Kruckeberg
International Leadership Consultant

Wolfgang Amann
Goethe Business School

and

Mike Green
Henley Business School

Leadership and Personal Development

A Toolbox for the
21st Century Professional

edited by

Katja Kruckeberg
International Leadership Consultant

Wolfgang Amann
Goethe Business School

and

Mike Green
Henley Business School

Information Age Publishing, Inc.
Charlotte, North Carolina • www.infoagepub.com

Library of Congress Cataloging-in-Publication Data

Leadership and personal development : a toolbox for the 21st century professional /
editors: Katja Kruckeberg, Wolfgang Amann, and Mike Green.
    p. cm.
  Includes bibliographical references.
  ISBN 978-1-61735-553-0 (pbk.) -- ISBN 978-1-61735-554-7 (hardcover) --
ISBN 978-1-61735-555-4 (e-book)
  1. Leadership. 2. Success. 3. Maturation (Psychology) I. Kruckeberg, Katja.
II. Amann, Wolfgang. III. Green, Mike, 1959-
  BF637.L4L384 2011
  658.4'092--dc23   2011028161

Printed in the United States of America

CONTENTS

Foreword.. vii

Introduction to Leadership and Personal Development
Katja Kruckeberg, Wolfgang Amann, and Mike Green 1

PART I: EXPLORING YOU IN YOUR WORLD

1. Exploring Your Strengths
   Katja Kruckeberg 15

2. Understanding Your Personality
   Katja Kruckeberg 27

3. Personal and Organizational Values
   Helen Stride 55

4. Discovering Your Emotional Capabilities
   Mike Green 69

PART II: SELF-LEADERSHIP

5. Self-leadership: Circles of Life
   Katja Kruckeberg 89

6. Self-coaching and Learning
   Chris Dalton 111

7. Creating Your Personal Vision
   Mike Green and Katja Kruckeberg 125

PART III: COMMUNICATING MORE CREATIVELY

8. Communicating More Effectively
   Franklin De Vrede and Katja Kruckeberg 145

9. Advanced Facilitation Skills
   Claire Collins 171

v

10. Polish Your Coaching Skills
Patricia Bossons and Denis Sartain 185

PART IV: REFINING YOUR RELATIONSHIP SKILLS

11. How to Build a Network That Works
Didier Gonin 205

12. Building Relationships and Working in Teams Across Cultures
Erich Barthel 223

13. Relational Aspects of Coaching and Communication
Claire Collins 243

PART V: ELEVATING YOUR LEADERSHIP CAPABILITIES

14. Systemic Leadership
Daniel Pinnow 259

15. Stepping into Your Leadership Roles
Mike Green 273

16. Leading in a Virtual Environment
Inger Buus 287

17. Leading More Effectively Through Feedback
Phil Cullen 301

PART VI: LEADING YOURSELF AND OTHERS THROUGH COMPLEXITY

18. Complexity Skills
Wolfgang Amann, Christoph Nedopil, and Shiban Khan 317

19. Crisis Management Skills
Wolfgang Amann, Shiban Khan, and Christoph Nedopil 331

20. Creativity Skills for the 21st Century Professional
Mike Green, Katja Kruckeberg, and Wolfgang Amann 343

21. Key Lessons on Leadership and Personal Development
Katja Kruckeberg, Wolfgang Amann, and Mike Green 357

About the Editors and Authors 365

FOREWORD

Currently, the business world calls for strong personal leadership. This may be where leadership is concerned with keeping talents on board and recruiting new ones at an amazing pace, or where leadership is about dramatic turn-around of large organizations that allow them to survive extremely turbulent conditions.

Whether it is about leaders in the East or in the West, this book addresses an important area by focusing on the link between leadership and personal development. It will help executives mobilize people and provide them with the appropriate skills to meet the fast changing business conditions. Besides having these skills, successful people need to have a much clearer sense of purpose, direction and of how they personally fit into the greater picture.

Professionals seek inspiration on how they should engage with others and make them thrive amidst chaos. This book offers executives and their teams highly relevant practical tools and methods that are indeed inspirational. Real life cases and the latest thinking in this prominent field provide inspiration and applications that can be easily accessed and used on the job.

Specifically, this book offers proven and cutting-edge insights into the leadership domain, such as leading in a virtual environment, systemic leadership, networking skills, and self-leadership. The chapter on complexity skills provides an excellent introduction to preparing for and dealing with crises, including the challenging issues of how to stimulate creativity while maintaining direction.

All in all, this book serves as guide to all those who care about effective leadership in practice, who are guided by a sense of value and a clear vision, and who thrive on leading themselves and others towards well-balanced goals, ambitions, and businesses. This books value lies in not only reading and reviewing leadership and personal development theories, but applying these leadership and personal development skills in practice. It is worth the effort.

August 2011

Jørgen Thorsell, CEO Mannaz Ltd.
Hong Kong, China
Inger Buus, Executive Vice President, EMEA
London, Great Britain

INTRODUCTION TO LEADERSHIP AND PERSONAL DEVELOPMENT

Katja Kruckeberg, Wolfgang Amann, and Mike Green

WHAT IS SPECIAL ABOUT THE BOOK?

This is the first book on leadership and personal development for practising managers and professionals that fully takes into account that the world has changed drastically in the past decades, and continues to do so in ways and at a pace, that few could have anticipated! In some respects, we don't know what the future holds for us, either on the macro-level, or on the micro-economic, political, sociological, and environmental level. However, by concentrating on ourselves, by knowing exactly who we are and what is important for us, by creatively envisioning a future based on our greatest strengths, and by equipping ourselves with key tools and skills, we will cope up well with this level of uncertainty.

WHAT WILL THIS BOOK DO FOR YOU?

First and foremost, it will provide you with new ways of thinking about and behaving toward the changes around us. Since the three authors and editors

Leadership and Personal Development: A Toolbox for the
21st Century Professional, pp. 1–11
Copyright © 2010 by Information Age Publishing
All rights of reproduction in any form reserved.

whole heartedly agree with Einstein's maxim that today's problems cannot be solved by the level of thinking that created them, this book can be considered as an attempt to equip you with new techniques, tools and skills, to make you more effective in managing yourself and others in a variety of contexts. In other words, the book is an opportunity to gain advanced *mental software*.

Secondly, it offers a new approach to leadership and personal development, focussing on the links between these two areas. We recognize that the good old times, of planning one's personal development in a linear, step-by-step fashion over a lifetime, by paying tribute to these areas' current requirements, are over. While recognizing that there are different learning styles and personality types, we urge you to adopt a more proactive, flexible and emergent approach to your leadership and personal development. This modern approach will give you a cutting-edge advantage in our fast changing world.

Thirdly, this book is mostly based on state-of-the-art thinking, and combines the latest research from organizational psychology and management practice. Topics such as sustainability, complexity and creativity are considered the key issues that should play a role not only in developing a positive, future society, but also in refining the current and future you. We also incorporate our experiences, from coaching and training thousands of managers and leaders over many years.

PHILOSOPHY BEHIND THIS BOOK

As mentioned, we are living in the interesting times, in which the tools and techniques that have served us well over the decades of growth and globalization, are not necessarily the ones which will help us thrive or even survive. Not only does the world need to look at different ways of tackling the various crises and challenges it is facing, but we as individuals also need to tackle the impact of these changes with confidence, and the ambition to succeed.

The prime responsibility for the development required to face the future lies with you. One of our strong beliefs is that leadership and personal development are a proactive process that you should lead and initiate. We will offer relevant and modern tools and techniques that are useful to develop a new level of excellence in your field. However, you are ultimately the one who will make the crucial choices, regarding driving and sustaining your development. We can pass the baton to you, but you have to run with it!

Another of our core beliefs is that there is no one right way. We all have different personalities and learning styles. We have, therefore, crafted each section to give you a number of entry points to suit your learning style the best. Whether you start with thinking differently or with acting differently, this is your choice. But, whatever the entry point for each particular journey, our aim is that you should challenge yourself: You should think about things differently, do things differently, and be different. We are also great believers in authenticity, so although we might urge you to change the way you do things we also hope that by the end of the process you will be more yourself, rather than less yourself.

We also encourage you to decide for yourself, whether you want to take a more systematic or a more emergent approach to your development. Your decision will very much depend on your learning style and your personality type. Some prefer a very structured approach. Others might feel more energized by starting with a point of interest and following the flow of thoughts and experiences that will result from the process. Both ways are fine, as long as you connect deeply with the discussed topics. However, we have to emphasize that, as a response to the dramatically changing world around us, all professionals have to be more flexible regarding their personal and career development, to make maximum use of arising opportunities. Someone remarked that career paths currently resemble *crazy paving* rather than a straight line. Adopting a more emergent approach and mindset to development, often allows another slab of *crazy paving* to be laid.

While acknowledging the important contribution of all the psychologies, we do veer towards the stance taken up by positive psychologists. We argue that a strength-based approach should be adapted, as we believe that by focussing on what makes people successful instead of asking what makes them fail in life, you are in a more resourceful position to face today's and tomorrow's challenges.

The idea of sustainable development, applied to leadership and personal development is an important concept. Thinking in terms of the wider system, rather than in terms of an egocentric system, is a potentially valuable approach to personal development. Furthermore, how you deal with your limited resources will determine your level of success and happiness. Focussing on your strengths is one way of making sure, that you work and live economically, while taking a more holistic view of your life is another.

Thinking in terms of complexity and systems goes hand-in-hand with the above ideas. Just as there are different learning styles and ways to approach this book, there are also ways of looking at discrete situations and events, as well as of ensuring that the wider system is factored into the equation. Thinking global and acting local is an often-used phrase that still has immense power when you try to think, be and act with integrity in today's world.

Last but not the least we want to point out that one of the main learning principles of this book is to encourage you, to act with integrity. What does this mean? We strongly believe that you always need to have good answers to very generic questions: What in your life and business really matters to you? How can you make an appropriate contribution to the society, and the world in which you live? And then you must have the courage to act accordingly.

WHY NOW? IDEAS WHICH CAN'T BE IGNORED

There was a time when you may have had some islands of stability in your life. Perhaps your home situation was relatively stable, but you had to change jobs or career. Or work was steady while you were experiencing upheavals in your private life. However, with exponential change happening across the political, economic, social, technological, and environmental systems, its impact on our work and private lives is dramatic. Every day we are directly confronted with information, which will directly impact our lives and our well-being. The list of factors that is changing and affecting our lives seems to be endless. Scanning through the headlines and business literature reveals the following:

- China will soon be the largest "English-speaking" country in the world;
- The top ten in-demand jobs this year, did not exist in 2004;
- The US department of labor estimates that today's children will have had 10–14 jobs by the time they are 38;
- MySpace was a social platform that at one time was as large as the fifth largest country in the world; it became insignificant as fast as it took its competitor, Facebook, to become the largest (at the time this book was finalized!)
- It is estimated that one week's worth of New York Times contains more information than an 18th century person was likely to come across in a lifetime;
- The amount of technical information is doubling every two years.

At the moment, there is little certainty regarding how all these changes will modify the way we live. However, we do know that we can no longer assume that we will be in the same job for many years or, indeed, in the same profession or the same industry; perhaps not even within the same country. We can ensure that we develop transferable skills which can help us cross boundaries and borders, but we will also have to learn new technical and social skills to meet the demands of occupations and situations, which did not exist previously.

The so-called 'psychological contract' between employer and employee has also shifted dramatically. What the employees once assumed about their employment status, the nature of their job, the potential for tenure, the reward mechanisms, the career path, and the opportunities for growth and development, has changed beyond recognition. They can no longer assume that loyalty is given if working conditions are satisfactory. The relationship between employer and employee is now more tentative, more conditional, and more fluid. Both the parties need to manage their side of the contract actively.

The change in the employer-employee relationship has simultaneously seen a change in job demands. The majority of us now live and work in a much more diverse workplace and society. Multiculturalism is a fact of life, presenting a myriad of opportunities, synergies, tensions and conflicts. No longer can we assume that the persons we are, embedded within our particular organizational and national cultures are the predominant culture. Different ways of doing things, different behaviors, and different motivating factors all feed into the heady brew of diversity, and working across organizational boundaries and different geographies and time zones.

Besides the changes we observe in our environment, we can also see changes within the members of our societies, as Table 1 below illustrates. When we examine the different generations of workers, we see a shift in work values and behaviors. Younger people, for example, tend to want more excitement, some sense of community, and definitely a life outside work. They are not as interested in a job for life or a particularly linear career path (even if these were on offer). Understanding the motivating factors for different generations, particularly where you need to work alongside, or provide a service to someone from a different generation – is crucial.

Furthermore, the way the economic system is currently affected by the financial crisis, which started in one country and has now spread throughout world, is simply unbelievable. Our global economy's level of interconnectedness allows change at a pace that is as new as the idea of communicating virtually was, some 50 years ago. A crisis that occurs in one system affects every other system, and at this very moment we simply do not know what consequences this will have for the world's political, social, technological and environmental systems.

And while it was by no means our intention to deliver a complete summary of all the changes we see coming our way, we do hope that this subchapter has given you an idea of how encompassing these changes are going to be, and how much they will affect our lives! Therefore, it is only fair to acknowledge that change seems to be one of the few constant factors in today's society, and in tomorrow's world. For these reasons, this book's core question is:

Table 1. Generational differences

Baby Boomers 1946–1964	Generation X 1965–1977	Generation Y 1978–1987
Organise life around work and work around life	Work to live rather than live to work	High expectations, positive
Value competition	Value development	Value autonomy
Egocentric	Clear goals, value own time	Enjoy diversity
Possibilities and change	Flexibility and adaptability	Optimistic
Work hard	Work hard when it matters	Takes things in their stride

Source: Adapted from Gursoy (2008), p. 451.

"How can we equip ourselves with new ways of thinking and behaving, to fully engage in these changes and stay above the waterline, instead of sinking?"

To answer this most important question that forms the crux of this book, we briefly describe the content and structure of the book.

CONTENT OF THE BOOK

The book presents a number of interesting options from which you can choose; – a buffet of sorts. Overall, we have divided this book into six main parts, and outlined what you can expect from them.

Part 1 of our book, – Exploring you in your world, – offers four chapters with which to start your leadership and personal development journey. Katja Kruckeberg introduces and outlines the book's overarching assumption: You can fight a constant uphill battle, and focus on mitigating your weaknesses, or, as suggested, adhere to a strength-based approach. In the latter, you systematically build on your strengths to gain a competitive advantage, and move more effortlessly through your work assignments. As Katja outlines, the society's fixation with weaknesses and failure encourages employees around the world, to identify their weaknesses in order to become better at their jobs. The corresponding training approach leads the employers to use training as a way to correct shortcomings in their workforce, – often with little success, but at a guaranteed high cost. Katja illustrates business case considerations why such a strength-based approach can offer more. She clarifies different notions (knowledge, skills, and talents) to help you identify your areas of strengths. Activities complement her conceptual and practical input.

Katja then invites you to explore the concept of personality further. With the help of the Personality 5 tool, she enables you to think more systematically about your and other people's personalities, the associated behaviors, and how to make use of this knowledge in the context of your leadership and personal development. Being able to detect fundamental psychological preferences, and learning how to deal with them, are of utmost importance in today's corporate world where, – to an unprecedented degree, – problems are solved in teams. Knowing personalities and having the semantics to communicate this knowledge equip you with a crucial element, to subsequently deal more aptly with a wide range of personalities.

Helen Strides continues your learning journey by inviting you to reflect on your personal values, and the values of the organizations you work for. She aims to raise your self-awareness, to explore your personal value statement, and also to check if you live your life accordingly. This chapter furthermore illustrates how to build effective and ethical organizations that benefit the communities they operate in. Clarifying your values proactively is the key, as in times of crises there may be no time to do so. Having decided for yourself which behaviors are actually acceptable, enables you to avoid certain dilemmas in which sets of conflicting goals would otherwise harm your work performance and, even worse, your health, emotional well-being, and partnerships.

Mike Green closes part 1 by sensitizing you to knowing and managing emotions. Realizing how you feel and why, as well as the ability to change your emotional state and that of others, are currently prerequisites for a high-performance leader and manager. Mike most certainly does not argue against emotions, but is in favor of developing capabilities to understand and manage them better.

Kicking off **part 2**, Katja challenges the reader by posing the question: Who wants to be led by anyone, who is unable to lead his or her own life reasonably successfully? She maintains that self-leadership should always be the start of any leadership development. She therefore outlines six elements of subjective well-being to boost the quality of life, for those on a quest for leadership and personal development. The main message is that we need more balanced personalities; we should not optimize one part of life at the cost of the other parts. Too many managers and leaders ruin their health in the first half of their professional lives in their quest to generate the wealth, which they then have to spend in the second half of their professional lives to maintain or restore a critical level of well-being and health. Why not reflect on balance earlier? She explains that you are the one in the driver's seat. In today's world, waiting for others to fix problems does not only sound strange; – it actually is. Therefore, Katja introduces the Circles of Life tool to enable you to make conscious choices, – before someone else does so with potentially other interests in mind.

As there may be times when coaches are not around and to avoid dependency, Chris Dalton adds to the substance of this book by introducing the principles and processes, embedded in your individual learning journey of coaching yourself. The author writes about the importance of specific types of questions and the role of beliefs in the self-coaching process. These questions intentionally do not direct you to a specific personal development orientation by assuming that one is superior, or the only possible way forward. Instead, the author offers you four main orientations from which you can choose. These orientations, – with the help of the force field analysis concept – also renders you sensitive to how adult and life-long learning have become essential parts of career management.

Mike and Katja follow up with the advantages of forming an attractive vision for your future and personal development. Research suggests that having a clear vision for development is a decisive factor for success.

Envisioning the future helps to interpret lucrative spot-on opportunities, or clear-cut distractions. Mike and Katja also explain the components of a vision, and compare these with a personal mission statement before providing you with activities to embark on your visioning process. Exercises, such as applying the Competency Star to your situation, have proven to be very effective in numerous of our coaching sessions and leadership and personal development programs, at top business schools.

Part 3 shares insights into and the success patterns of advanced communication skills. Franklin de Vrede and Katja Kruckeberg present key thoughts on the barriers in communication. After having worked through this chapter and the corresponding exercises, you will have increased your knowledge on why communicating with others has become more important than ever before. You will have learned about the 'volcano', to mention just one example of the dynamics of conversations. Franklin and Katja familiarize you with the crucial steps of communicating more professionally with others relying on the FIBAR model (facts – interpretations – belief systems – actions – results).

Advanced communication skills are also necessary to effectively develop and apply your facilitation skills, as Claire Collins demonstrates. Facilitation is presented as a key means to manage effective discussions about and deliver outputs for major projects and visions. Facilitation helps overcome barriers in teams that prevent them from achieving their goals. However, Claire shows that facilitation is just one of many means to an end, because although it offers tremendous benefits, it needs to be applied carefully. Claire describes the facilitators' ideal skill profile, as well as different groups' characteristics. On the basis of the attention pyramid, groups can embark on different tasks, depending on their level within this pyramid. In order to complete the facilitation picture, Claire outlines and discusses the actual facilitation process, and how to run such sessions. Before offering two case studies and a set of practise activities, she provides additional advice on how to facilitate more effectively.

Advanced communication skills are useful and necessary when applying your coaching and communication skills, as Denis Sartain and Patricia Bossons illustrate in a typical management conversation. These experts shed light on the role of coaching when managing someone. They explain what coaching is and why it is a useful part of a manager's toolkit. They take you through the GROW model of coaching, which is one of the most effective coaching processes in a performance management context. This model can keep you on track as you make progress through a coaching conversation, and helps you identify how such a conversation differs from a normal management conversation. Finally, the authors look at the key issues for which you need to prepare as you use coaching skills, as part of your management role.

Part 4 focuses on advanced relationship skills. You can, of course, travel through life alone and solve all your problems yourself. But why should you? Didier Gonin introduces networking skills and outlines in which areas they can help you, how you can map and grow your network, and use it strategically. Didier includes considerations regarding your personal and organizational networks. While it is true that 95% of vacancies in the companies are not filled via job ads, but relationships, we emphasize the law of the harvest: One only gets as much out of networks, as one is willing to invest at first.

Networks and working in teams can easily span different cultures, which is why Erich Barthel renders you sensitive to key intercultural do's and don'ts. A long-standing question in academia and business schools is whether management is culture-bound or culture-free. Erich makes you aware of those areas, where at least some culture-bound nature cannot be denied. In fact, he explores the key elements of cultural differences and warns that poor preparation may lead to culture shocks; – times of diminished happiness, and diminished work-related productivity. He compares different degrees of diversity in teams and suggests constructive and proactive ways for dealing with different cultures. Poorly managed diverse teams easily turn into a disaster. They are rapidly outperformed by homogeneous teams. The latter, though, have problems competing with well-managed, diverse teams, especially when the problems at hand, demand creativity and different viewpoints. Erich then invites you to reflect on your current teams' diversity. He outlines a four-phase model to proactively tap into diverse teams' potentials, while mitigating the downsides.

Claire rounds off this chapter on relationship skills with her thoughts on the relational aspects of coaching and communication. Without a well-established relationship between people, – so-called rapport, – working together effectively is impossible. The relationship forms the crux of every good working and coaching relationship. Clair shares her experiences with building relationships by listening actively, showing empathy when building a relationship, and outlines the tools for good bonding.

Part 5 of this book on leadership and personal development invites you to explore your possible leadership skills further. Daniel Pinnow summarizes his extensive experience in the field of leadership development by first juxtaposing older and newer schools of management. He invites you to examine your personal leadership potential, by introducing the systemic leadership concept. Daniel delves deep into various aspects, starting with the crucial call to 'know thyself', as the very first step. However, he clarifies that without a developed ability to lead yourself there is no effective way to lead others. You have to walk the talk, and lead by example. The chapter closes with a set of activities through which you can work on these leadership skills, which are likely to matter even more, the higher you climb organizational hierarchies.

Mike then offers you insights into leadership by offering you a review of five leadership roles: the edgy catalyzer, the visionary motivator, the measured connector, the tenacious implementer, and the thoughtful architect. He leaves no doubt that leadership is indeed situational, – no one role or model fits all occasions. Those able to play the roles flexibly can expect enhanced performance. Mike helps you to reflect on these five roles with guiding questions regarding your situation, and offers you exercizes to practise the roles.

The authors and editors of this book fully acknowledge that, increasingly, our communication work and leadership tasks take place virtually. Inger Buus elaborates on the pros and cons of virtual team work, and what comprizes effective leadership in a virtual environment. However, the essential elements of sound leadership, including trust, purposefulness, cultural sensitivity, balancing priorities, and respecting that we have to work our way forward on a learning curve, remain as valid as they are in the real world.

Phil Cullin closes part 5 of this book by sharing how to lead through feedback; – an increasingly popular method. As he demonstrates, there are good and bad ways of providing feedback, no matter what the actual intentions behind the feedback process is. Our reasons for including aspects of feedback in this book are twofold: The feedback can ensure unseen but high levels of motivation in your subordinates, – or crush their spirits. The same could happen to you, which is why, knowing how to accept and provide feedback is the key. Phil introduces a framework for categorizing messages and discusses four options in detail. More importantly, Phil describes opportunities to create a culture of providing feedback. Such learning loops are essential for personal and team development. Phil shares pointers for better feedback, and warns of barriers to effective feedback. The exercises at the end of this chapter help you practice these conceptual insights.

Part 6 equips you with conceptual insights and training opportunities to enhance your complexity skills. Personal and organizational performance depends strongly on the ability to understand what really drives complexity in today's world, and how to master it. While complexity skills have not yet become the mainstream content of personal development programs, we are convinced they will do so. Therefore, Wolfgang Amann presents a framework of four drivers of complexity and encourages you to train your simplifying skills, as complexity is not the latest management fad, but a reality here to stay.

In a subsequent chapter, Wolfgang depicts key elements of professional crisis management, i.e. providing you with some insights into situations in which complexity may lead to a full-fledged crisis. He shares considerations on mentally preparing for crises-prone times, preventing crises, detecting and understanding crises, and managing crises, which entails a call to rapidly explore the means and ways to turn crises into opportunities.

The latter may require substantial creativity, – the ability to combine inside and outside the box thinking. Mike, Katja and Wolfgang thus close part 6 of this book on personal development with an overview of what creativity means, how to enable more of it and turn it into tangible results. Creativity is thus not something only a few special people can produce. It is a skill to develop and practise, – ideally before the going gets tough!

HOW TO USE THIS BOOK

We feel that there are a number of approaches to maximize the usefulness of this book. When you pause for reflection during the day or night, or when you hit a problem, use the table of contents and index, to identify a section which can help you immediately. When you make time available to think about your leadership and personal development, and want to build a more comprehensive idea of your development, you can approach the book in a more structured way.

Parts 1 and 2 should provide you with a good entry point to assess where you are currently, and to build a vision of where you want to be. Part 3 should provide you with enough tools and techniques, and a variety of important and interesting topics to act as a springboard to many development activities. Feel free to dip into the book at any entry point, or to work through the initial chapters, so that you can get a feel for where you need to be focussed. Each chapter will provide you with an introduction to the topic, will illustrate the ideas with one or more case studies to allow you to understand the area better, will provide you with a simple self-assessment tool, where appropriate, and, most importantly, suggests activities and exercises. Further resources and references are also included.

PART I

EXPLORING YOU IN YOUR WORLD

CHAPTER 1

EXPLORING YOUR STRENGTHS

Katja Kruckeberg

OBJECTIVE OF THIS CHAPTER

The main objective of this first chapter is to encourage you to think in-depth about what you are really good at in life and at work in particular. Therefore, we invite you to (re-) connect with your unrealized and realized strengths so that you can make conscious choices to put those activities that allow you to perform to the best of your ability, and that you enjoy the most, while doing them in the center of your professional life.

INTRODUCTION

In a world of constant change across many areas of your life, it is more important than ever, that you know what you are really good at and what you really enjoy doing, in order to excel at your chosen career field. Knowing your strengths and applying them will not only make you more successful in a highly-competitive, fast-changing labor market, but will also make you resilient enough to face the challenges that constantly come your way. Systematically building on your strengths over your lifetime can guide you through your career, avoiding the necessity to plan it step-by-step in the old-fashioned

Leadership and Personal Development: A Toolbox for the
21st Century Professional, pp. 15–25

way that is no longer effective in today's corporate world. This will almost certainly not only lead to a more successful career, but also to a more contented and happy life—these two states of minds often go together.

We realize, of course, that this sounds almost too good to be true, but there is, nevertheless, a great deal of evidence to support this claim. Wide research has shown that people who are successful and happy in life have one thing in common: They not only pursue enjoyable activities, but also enjoy the actual *pursuit*. It is not only achieving their targets that makes them happy, but the journey itself. Whereas people with a similar level of professional success, but a lower level of contentment, have in common that they do not like their jobs as much, they are obviously good at. Success in itself does not make one happy—fulfilling activities on a day-to-day basis does.

While this thinking seems to be an attractive approach, people have, for many centuries gone for the opposite. Society's obsession with weaknesses and failure has encouraged the employees around the world to identify their weaknesses, in order to become better at their jobs. This converse approach has led the employers to use training as a way to correct shortcomings in their workforce—often with little success.

Today, organizational psychologists who start adopting a *strength-based approach* are focusing on what makes people successful, instead of asking what makes them fail. Rather than looking at what causes dysfunction, why not look at realizing potential? The focus is therefore more on exploring the strengths and virtues that enable the individuals, groups, and organizations to thrive. This recent branch of psychology, called "positive psychology", is currently being widely researched and has attracted the attention of both the individuals and organizations worldwide, due to its amazing practical impact (Snyder & Lopez, 2001).

Raising your self-awareness—getting to know yourself better—is known as the most important first step in any leadership and personal development process. Consequently, we have designed the following chapter in a way that will provide you with opportunities to start this journey with us, by further exploring your strong sides. The consecutive chapters two, three, four, and five will then encourage you to continue this self-reflection journey by offering insights into and ideas, on personality, personal values, emotional capabilities, and your circles of life.

THE BUSINESS CASE, OR: WHY SHOULD I BOTHER?

Many organizations have already adopted a strengths-based approach. Companies like Coca Cola, Yahoo, and Microsoft are currently following this new paradigm in human resource development.

Why are these companies investing loads of money to focus their people on developing their strengths, instead of working on their weaknesses? The answer is simple: Because it is worth it.

The Gallup Institute and other big consultancies' latest research reveals that when the employers focus on performance strengths, there is a significant improvement in a company's performance. Conversely, focussing on weaknesses shows a decline in the overall performance. More specifically, by supporting the development of strengths in the workforce, companies have reduced the employee turnover and increased employee engagement. These findings have furthermore convincingly demonstrated that a company's productivity and profitability also increases (Buckingham, 2004).

WHAT CAN IT DO FOR YOU PERSONALLY?

Linley, one of the most influential UK experts on strengths, argues that most of the successful people attribute their excellent outcomes to having applied their strengths constantly and consistently, throughout most of their lives. Indeed, research has shown that those who use their strengths at work every day are more successful in their career, significantly more engaged, less stressed, and their customers are more satisfied (Linley, 2008).

CASE STUDY 1

Duncan Bannatyne

The views of Duncan Bannatyne, one of Britain's most successful entrepreneurs, on strengths:

"By this stage of the business, I had learned that my strength as an entrepreneur was both my willingness and ability to delegate. [...] My ability to delegate is a major reason why I made it where others did not. I know other entrepreneurs with completely different skills to mine, and completely different outlooks. I know one very successful businessman, who spends millions of pounds developing products he is not sure he can sell. [...] And I know other entrepreneurs who are great at closing deals or motivating their staff. What we have in common is that we have worked out what works best for us. You can run a business any way you like, but you will run it better if you build it around your strengths, and delegation is one of mine.[...] Some of my managers were not great at the job straight away, but by letting them

(Continued)

CASE STUDY 1 (*Continued*)

manage their department as they chose, they got the chance to learn a bit about themselves, and develop their own style. And once they found that out, they could mould their department around their strengths, just as I have built a business around mine. This gave them a chance to become great managers, and that in turn gave them a chance to do what I did best: drive the business forward."

Source: Adapted from Bannatyne, D. (2006). *From an ice-cream van to Dragons' Den*. Anyone can do it: My story. Orion.

FIND YOUR PERSONAL STRENGTH FORMULA FOR SUCCESS (SFS)

In short, the strength formula for success works as follows:

You start with a talent (something innate, which you either have or do not have, rather than something which you can develop from scratch), and you add skills and knowledge (Buckingham, 2001). The most important point is to identify your talent correctly, as it acts as a multiplier in your personal strength equation:

Strength = Talent × (Skills + Knowledge)

This sounds a bit like a cooking recipe, but it is not really that easy. Creating a strength focus in yourself and seriously living up to it is not something that happens overnight. It first takes a lot of reflection, courage and willingness to act, and also time and energy to initiate the necessary internal and external changes. But, eventually it will pay off. One of the greatest advantages of building your life around your strengths is that you will be able to do the same amount that you do now (or more), and feel refreshed afterward instead of drained.

WHAT ARE THE KEY INGREDIENTS OF STRENGTH?

To work with your strengths, you need to have a thorough understanding of all the ingredients that form strength. Let us start by looking at the elements of strengths that we can acquire through learning and practising: knowledge and skills.

Knowledge

There are many ways to define wha t knowledge is. However, for the purpose of strength building, it is important to distinguish between factual and practical knowledge. Factual knowledge is content driven. If, for example, you want to be an accountant, you need to learn the basics of accountancy; if you want to become an information technology (IT) specialist, you need to acquire knowledge of computer software and hardware. Factual knowledge can be learned at school, university, and business school.

Practical knowledge is what you cannot learn from books. Practical knowledge is gained while you are applying your factual knowledge through experiences. You can, for example, learn about presentation skills and techniques from a book. But what you learn when you actually present to a big audience—for example, how an audience reacts differently when you use your voice in different ways—is called practical knowledge. Sometimes, it is also referred to as experiential self-knowledge, which plays an important role when you develop yourself further or, more specifically, when you work with your strengths.

Skills

Skills are sometimes described as the proficiency or facility acquired or developed through training or experience. Skills are the capacity to do something well, for example, a technique. Skills are usually acquired or learned, as opposed to abilities or talent, which are thought of as innate. If you want, for example, to be good at marketing, leading people, selling, or accounting, you will need to learn all the relevant skills required to succeed, besides the knowledge that you need of the chosen field.

Talent

Talent is often defined as a natural, innate ability of a superior quality. Marcus Buckingham, probably the best-known international expert on strengths, defines talent as "a recurring pattern of thought, feeling or behavior that can be productively applied" (Buckingham, 2001). The important point is that we believe that talents—unlike knowledge and skills—are innate, and cannot be easily developed in adulthood. Talents are, for example, your:

> level of empathy when dealing with people,
> preference for lateral, big-picture thinking,
> preference for analytical, detail-oriented thinking,
> ability to talk effortlessly to people in all situations,
> ability to present to big audiences,

    understanding people and their behavior,
    understanding technical problems,
    ability to organize events,
    and so forth.

Of course, everybody can improve in these areas but some people feel more drawn to these activities than others. In short, one could say your talents are the behaviors, feelings, and thoughts you naturally find yourself doing or having, most likely on a daily basis. Marcus Buckingham puts it as follows: "Any recurring patterns of behavior that can be productively applied are talents!"

Sometimes talents are also described as personality preferences. If you read Chapter 2, you will discover more about recurring patterns of behavior and mental processes, that largely determine who you are and what you are naturally good at, all of which are considered a part of your "psychological DNA".

CAN TALENTS BE BUILT DURING THE SPAN OF A LIFE TIME?

Although people do change over the course of their lives, the latest neuroscience research indicates that core patterns of thinking, feelings and behaviors are formed relatively early in life and do not change much after our adolescence. By that time, the human brain has formed a mental network consisting of a unique pattern of synaptic connections that determine how we experience the world. This mental network is unique to each of us, and defines our talents (Rath, 2007). There are dominant synaptic connections, like a talent for speaking to a big audience and feeling energized when doing so, and there are less dominant synaptic connections, which might cause a lack of empathy or a lack of interest in the details of work. Whatever your talents, they are pre-determined by your brain's early development. Furthermore, you should be aware of them, as they determine your success: Only if you combine knowledge, the right skills and *talent,* can you achieve superior performance in any given field. Skill development on its own will never lead you to superior performance. If you do not naturally enjoy communicating with people, you can attend all the sales training in the world, but you will probably never excel at sales.

Your Strengths Portfolio

To build up your strengths portfolio, you need all three key ingredients of strengths: knowledge, skills, and talents. However, the key to excellent performance is, of course, discovering what your talents are, and then starting from there. Talents are your strongest synaptic connections, your mental highways, on which true excellence is built! (Buckingham, 2004).

The question is finding out what your talents exactly are, so that you can take full advantage of them. In the process, you may not become everything you want to be, but you may become the BEST YOU CAN POSSIBLY BE!

The definite sign of strengths and talents is that they give us energy. When you apply your strengths, you feel good while doing so. In addition, using strengths makes you feel authentic, since you are anchored in the core of your personality—in your unique mental networks and preferences. If you follow your strengths, you will feel more engaged and people around you will most likely notice that you are more inspired. This, by the way, differs from applying your weaknesses. While pursuing activities that are not supported by your underlying preferences and talents, you will feel more drained maybe even de-energized. Most likely, people in your environment too, at work or at home, will notice this.

In any one person, there are several strengths, rather than just a few. Linley puts it as follows: "We all have a symphony of strengths that advance into the foreground, or recede into the background as the situation requires" (Linley, 2008, p. 2).

CASE STUDY 2

Changing Career Direction

Bjorn, (29, Swedish), Internal HR consultant, London, UK

I was certain of my strengths as an IT consultant when working for one of the big, global consultancies in London 2 years ago. I was on an impressive salary, proud of my achievements and knew I was recognized for what I was doing. However, despite all this, I felt miserable. I was not motivated to go to work and my doctor noted that my mental and physical health was declining. Since my employer guaranteed a budget for personal development, I decided to obtain the support of an executive coach specializing in strength development. After a few coaching sessions, I realized what was going wrong in my life. I had pursued a career that did not fully support my talents, but exploited the points that I thought I was good at—my IT knowledge and analytical thinking capabilities. Unfortunately, I did not enjoy these. What I really enjoy is interacting with people, listening to their problems and making plans to help them achieve their goals. After talking to my boss and various company stakeholders, I am now in a position where I can apply these talents. Working in the HR department as a mentor and as a coach for young professionals, I feel re-energized and much happier, than I have been for years.

CONCLUSION

We, the authors of this book, hope to have (re-)confirmed the superiority of the strength-based approach for you, the reader, encouraging you to "put all your eggs into one basket" when it comes to focussing on your strengths. This does not mean that working on your weakness is worthless; it should just not be the center of your efforts in the area of leadership and personal development. To ensure you continuously move in the right direction, make sure that you bear the afore-mentioned orientation points in mind. To help you work with your own strengths and eventually build your life around those strengths, have a look at the activities at the end of this chapter. They have been designed to put you on your *personal strengths path*. If you are far off from your strength paths at the moment, this journey can take month and even years, but you can start off by reflecting on your strengths.

Your Activities for (re-) Discovering Your Strengths

Activity 1: What did you do last week that made you feel good and full of energy?

Remember, strengths are not just that which you are good at! Strengths are the points that you are good at, and that simultaneously make you feel good. When exploring your talents, you need to look for activities that you enjoy doing, that have a yearning quality to them, that satisfy you, and allow you to learn quickly (Buckingham, 2007). Now, when thinking over the past week, can you identify any situation or any activity at work, that matches the above criteria? Please write this (these) down in sufficient detail:

1. _____

2. _____

3. _____

Activity 2: Explore your talents by looking at the good times in your life

The most promising way to re-discover your strengths is by remembering your childhood, or your time as a young adult. Led by your brain's dominant synaptic connections, you were most likely using your dominant mental network for activities that felt good and natural to you at these times. Take your time to think about activities that you really enjoyed doing throughout your life; activities that you wanted to repeat again and again; activities that made you feel strong, and brought a smile to your face.

Ensure the most conducive environment for your reflections, whether outside during a short walk or any other place that allows you to gather your thoughts. Capture the outcome of this journey of reflection. What were the activities that made you feel strong?

1. _____

2. _____

3. _____

Summary of Activity 1 and 2: Draw your personal strengths capstone

After having successfully identified some of your talents, it is time to summarize these insights about yourself, and to think how this would work for you, in practice. How could you turn your strengths into practice? How could they form the capstone of your present and future success and happiness? You should concentrate on three of your strengths, which you must describe very specifically. For example, if you have identified a talent for public speaking, what specifically is it that you speak about, and/or who specifically are the people to whom you talk? We encourage you to also reflect on the next possible steps to take them further.

Top level strength:

_____

Medium level strength:

_____

Bottom level strength:

_____

REFERENCES AND RECOMMENDED READINGS

Ban natyne, D. (2006). From an ice-cream van to Dragons' Den. *Anyone can do it: My story*. London: Orion.

Buckingham, M. (1999). *First break all the rules*. New York: Simon & Schuster.

Buckingham, M. (2004). Now, Discover your Strengths. *How to develop your talents and those of the people you manage*. London: Pocket Books.

Linley, A. (2008). Average to A+. *Realising Strengths in yourself and others*. London: Capp Press.

Rath, T. (2007). *StrengthsFinder 2.0*. New York: Gallup Press.

Snyder, C. R., & Lopez, S. (2001). *Handbook of Positive Psychology*. New York: Oxford University Press.

RECOMMENDED VIDEO LINKS

The Martin Seligman presentation on positive psychology (video) at a TED conference
http://www.ted.com/index.php/talks/martin_seligman_on_the_state_of_psychology.html

How the mind works by Steven Pinker.
http://www.youtube.com/watch?v=vuwNfPca_Pw

CHAPTER 2

UNDERSTANDING YOUR PERSONALITY

Katja Kruckeberg

OBJECTIVE OF THIS CHAPTER

The main aim of this chapter is to introduce you to the Personality 5 (P5) tool. This should provide you with a variety of ideas that might help you think more systematically about your and other people's personality, and how to make use of this knowledge in the context of your leadership and personal development.

INTRODUCTION

To introduce the topic, please take a moment to consider the following questions: What does your core personality look like, and how would you describe it? In which manner does your way of being and behaving differ from that of others? Do you have the right knowledge and language to describe these differences systematically and efficiently?

Your personality impacts every aspect of your life and has a direct effect on all your relationships with other people. In order to create a working life

Leadership and Personal Development: A Toolbox for the 21st Century Professional, pp. 27–53

that really suits you, it is vital to know who you are and what your personality looks like. Without a very clear understanding of yourself, you could run the risk of following the demands and needs of others during your career, or merely randomly following the many opportunities that cross your way, without ever harnessing your true self. As we stated in chapter 1 of this book, increasing your self-awareness is the first and the most important step in any leadership or personal development process. Learning more about the facets of your personality, or as we sometimes say, your "psychological DNA," is an important part of increasing your knowledge about yourself and understanding why you behave as you do.

So, let us start by clarifying what we mean with the term personality. Do you know what this word actually represents? If you look at the etymological roots of the word, you see that the term "personality" originates from the Latin *persona*, which means mask. The interesting point is that in the theatre of the ancient, Latin-speaking world, the mask was not used as a plot device to disguise a character's identity, but was rather a convention employed to represent that character, and his personality (Wikipedia, 2011). The burning question is therefore: What is your persona composed of? How can you describe your personality using the language that everybody can follow? To support you in this endeavor, the following chapter has been designed as follows:

In a first step, we will introduce you to the core ideas of the Big Five trait theory and the Meyers Briggs Type Indicator (MBTI[1]), as these are two of the most prominent examples of personality theory. Afterwards, the Personality 5 (P5) tool will be described in more depth. This tool was created on the basis of the Big Five instrument and the MBTI, and provides you with a language framework that you can use in your working environment. It is a tool specifically designed to allow the 21st century professionals to analyze important facets of their personality, and their resulting, daily behavioral patterns. This will provide you with state of the art language that you can use in a management context, to understand and describe your personality type and how it differs from that of the other people. It is easy to understand and apply, while carrying a lot of explanatory power. We will then encourage you to self-assess your personality type according to the P5 concept, which perfectly allows you to start combining this knowledge and insight with your leadership and personal development. You will also understand how studying your personality type through the P5 model might help you understand how you communicate and interact with other people and why they react to you as they do. You might find that certain patterns in either your behavior or in people's reaction to your behavior become much more transparent. But first, a bit of background is needed on the main concepts from which the P5 tool originated.

THE BIG FIVE—OVERVIEW OF THE CONCEPT

Personality psychology is a branch of psychology that describes personality and individual differences. Its main objective is to construct a coherent picture of a person and his or her major psychological processes and different forms of behavior. There is no consensus on the definition of *personality* in psychology. Theorists generally agree that a) traits are relatively stable over time, b) traits differ in individuals, and c) traits influence behavior. Lewis Goldberg proposed a five-dimension personality model, nicknamed the "Big Five" (Srivastava, 2011), which is the most common model in this field:

1. **Extraversion**: This broad dimension encompasses more specific traits, such as being talkative, energetic, and assertive, the tendency to be sociable, fun-loving, and affectionate, versus retiring, sombre, and reserved.

2. **Openness to Experience** (sometimes called intellect or intellect/imagination): This includes traits like the tendency to be imaginative, independent, and interested in variety, versus practical, conforming, and interested in routine.

3. **Conscientiousness**: This includes traits like being organized, thorough, and full of planning the tendency to be organized, careful, and disciplined, versus disorganized, careless, and impulsive.

4. **Agreeableness**: This includes traits like being sympathetic, kind, and affectionate, the tendency to be soft-hearted, trusting, and helpful, versus ruthless, suspicious, and uncooperative.

5. **Neuroticism**: This includes traits like the tendency to be calm, secure, and self-satisfied versus anxious, insecure, self-pitying, tense, and moody.

As you can see, the Big 5 encompasses important dimensions of personality and explains a great deal of behavior that people exhibit on a daily basis. However, although the Big 5 is a solid and scientifically validated concept of personality, it has not proved to be useful in a management context. On one hand, the managers think that it is inappropriate that they are *assessed*, with regards to their personality (ultimately, people feel that the tool distinguishes between better or worse traits) and, on the other hand, the dimension neuroticism is related to mental illness, which is not an adequate aspect of personality to measure in a work context.

THE MBTI—AN OVERVIEW OF THE CONCEPT

Another theory of personality is widely known under the name *psychological type*, and aims to describe and explain normal differences in behavior between *healthy people*. Based on many decades of research and observations, the influential Swiss psychiatrist Carl Jung came to the conclusion that differences in behavior mainly result from people's inborn preferences to use their minds in distinct ways, which he describes in detail in his work. This theory was later used by the American mother-and-daughter team of Katharine Briggs and Isabel Briggs Meyer for the development of the MBTI Instrument, which made Jung's theory accessible and applicable to millions of people, over the last 6 decades.

In essence, the MBTI instrument works on the assumption that a huge part of the personality can be described using four psychological dimensions. In simple terms, these four dimensions explain "how people are energized," "how they make decisions," "how they like to organize the world around them" and "what kind of information they naturally notice and remember." As it becomes apparent, each of these four dimensions deals with frequent facets of everyday life, which is why understanding your MBTI type, can give you valuable insights into your and other people's behavior.

For an initial understanding of the concept *personality type* (Myers Briggs, 2000, 2003), it is useful to imagine each of these eight dimensions as a continuum between the opposite extremes. The first dimension tells us something about "where people get their energy from" and is called the extroversion–introversion scale. This scale is based on Jung's insight, that people either tend to be energized by the external world (of events, activities, people, and so forth) or by the internal world (of ideas, memories, emotions, and so forth).

The second dimension deals with the way people absorb information. Jung observed that when people's minds are active and awake, they are involved in one of the two mental activities: They are either absorbing information or they are organizing, evaluating, and assessing this information. He identified two different ways of absorbing, or as he put it, perceiving information: Either by using the five senses, which is called sensation or sensing, or by mainly using intuition.

The third dimension provides insight into the second group of mental activities mentioned above: How people evaluate the information they absorb, how they come to a conclusion, and how they make decisions. Jung again distinguished between the two different ways of assessing information, which he called feeling and thinking.

And last but not the least, the MBTI contains a 4th dimension which gives an indication of how people prefer to live and organize their lives. The two poles of these dimensions are called judging and perceiving. And they provide answers to the questions whether people like to live their life in a planned and organized way, or in a more spontaneous and flexible way.

Within this body of theory, it is believed that people's preferences are innate and that people fall within one section, in each of these four dimensions. This generates 16 possibly different types into which we all fit. The philosophy behind the MBTI maintains that all preferences are equally important, valuable, and necessary.

Thoughts on the MBTI

The MBTI Instrument is without a doubt, the most widely used psychometric instrument in the world, and an estimated three million people—mostly managers—have their MBTI profile established every year, and thus have a better understanding of their personality and their day-to-day behavior. Having coached and trained thousands of managers and leaders ourselves, we observed certain distinct disadvantages of using the MBTI in a management context. One is that there is a risk of stereotyping people in organizations, if managers use this instrument without taking the time and interest to become expert at it.

Although it is emphasized that people should not use this knowledge to put labels on people, or use it to excuse one's own behavior, this is what often happens in practice.

Another potential pitfall is that the language the MBTI offers to describe the different dimensions of the MBTI instrument can be confusing (for example, in real life we use the words judging and perceiving differently from the way it is used in this context, the same is true of sensing and intuition). As the meanings of these words differ from the day-to-day language, they are particularly difficult to remember. The same applies to the 16 four-letter types. Often, when professionals return from a leadership workshop where they were introduced to the MBTI concept, they struggle to apply it for these reasons which make the effort of organizing an MBTI feedback, not as rewarding as it could be in some cases. Even people who have been introduced to the concept several times during the course of their careers struggle with the MBTI language because it is so removed from their work context.

HOW TO WORK WITH YOUR PERSONALITY IN THE 21ST CENTURY?

In an attempt to overcome the potential disadvantages of the MBTI described above, we have developed the P5 tool, depicted in the Fig. 2.1 below. Building on our experience and integrating some of the Big Five and the MBTI's thinking, we propose five dimensions that allow you to analyze the important aspects of your personality and your daily behavior.

As you will see, there are lots of similarities with the tools already introduced. However, the P5 tool will primarily provide you with the language that you can take home, that you can remember, and that you can use in normal conversations with other people without having to rely on the somewhat strange psychological terms that are not a part of your working context's day-to-day language.

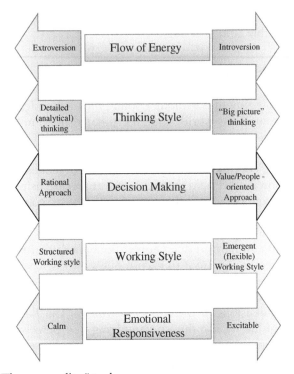

Figure 2.1. The personality 5 tool

WHAT IS MY PERSONALITY AND HOW DOES IT IMPACT MY BEHAVIOR?

In the following pages, you will find more information concerning each of these five dimensions of personality. This is followed by a table summarizing the characteristics that, based on our observation and research, are frequently associated with these categories of human behavior. While reading through this pool of information, start asking yourself what category of each personality dimension describes you more than others. Which kind of behavior do you show most often? You should answer these questions thoroughly, without jumping to conclusions too quickly! Try to understand the concept first, and then reflect on how this relates to you. It is perhaps advisable to note your reflections before you start reading and understanding the next dimension of the P5 tool.

FLOW OF ENGERY: EXTRAVERSION VERSUS INTROVERSION

The least controversial dimension of personality, observed as far back as the ancient Greeks is simply extraversion and introversion. People who are more extraverted, are described as outgoing and physical stimulation oriented, whereas people, who are more introverted are described as quiet and physical stimulation averse. In practice, this means that people who "score" high on extraversion, often opt for a highly interactive social life. Typically, they like to arrange active weekend breaks with friends and family. In their work life, they deal well with open-door policies, and big office spaces. When spending time with other people, they often feel re-energized instead of drained, like some of their more introverted colleagues feel. Very extroverted people feel comfortable in any type of gathering and will often walk right into them, becoming acquainted with everybody very easily. Those people feel that a pause in a conversation is an invitation to speak up. People in this category are also quite ready to share their feelings, personal history, and opinions with others. They tend to seek two-way conversations about feelings, and might feel offended if others do not join in.

People who "score" high on introversion usually enjoy peace and quiet in the weekend. They prefer intimacy with a trusted friend to popularity within a group. Having a few deep friendships is as important to them as being popular and having a wide circle of friends are to the more extroverted person. In their work life, they can come across as rather reserved and they definitely prefer quieter workspaces, which allow them to think and work effectively. Work processes that do not allow for internal dialogues are not effective for very introverted people. Furthermore, introverts are often very happy to communicate with others in writing and reading, rather than phoning.

If this dimension is regarded from a strength perspective–as introduced in Chapter 1–we could say that some people's strength lies in focusing their energy externally, while others' strength lies in focussing their attention on their internal processes.

This dimension is similar in content and language to the first dimension of the Big Five concept, as well as to the first dimension of the MBTI. The key point is to be aware of the difference in the personality in these dimensions, in order to provide a working environment that allows the people to perform to the very best of their abilities. In Table 2.1, you will find a quick summary of the characteristics of those, who fit either extraversion or introversion.

Table 2.1.   Depiction of Flow of Energy

Extroverts	Introverts
Express their thoughts readily	Reflect in silence
Think in public	Think first and speak out afterwards
Action oriented	Reflect more before acting
Like social gatherings	Often prefer smaller gatherings or one-to-ones
Express their feelings and share personal stories	More contained

THINKING STYLES: DETAILED THINKING VERSUS "BIG-PICTURE" THINKING

When you look at the kind of information to which people generally pay attention, it is easy to see that some people focus primarily on the world's tangible, concrete aspects, where as others are more attracted to ideas and abstractions. Some people are interested in detailed information, while others immediately start to think about how these details fit into the bigger picture. This is a very important distinction when examining how people's personalities differ, as it has multiple consequences for the way we interact with our environment. In the context of the P5 tool, we therefore differentiate between people who gather and process information from a "detail" perspective (known as analytical, sequential thinking), and those who primarily gather and process information from a "big picture" perspective, looking for patterns and connections within any given data (known as "big picture" thinking). Or, in other words, there are people who either apply an analytical thinking approach or a "big picture" thinking approach to make sense of the information they are absorbing and processing, from the inside and the outside world.

Detailed (analytical) thinking follows the scientific approach to problem solving. People who use this approach first and intuitively, when gathering and processing information fall into this category of information processing. These people are very observant about the details of what is going on around them, and are especially attuned to practical realities. In organizations, the majority of the people working in finance, operations, production, or project management roles demonstrate this preference, when it comes to absorbing information from the outside world, as this is probably one of the reasons why they were attracted to these professions in the first place. These professions have in common that they entail a lot of expert knowledge (facts), and require a practical outlook on life. People who like to focus on concrete information, like to know the specifics and details about what exactly is needed in a given situation. They like to know how things worked in the past and they need to have a realistic picture of the future, which should show continuances of the present and the past. Usually, they prefer clarity regarding objectives and roles, and value real responsibilities.

"Big picture" thinking is said to be a right-brained activity. People, who focus first on abstract, "big picture" information usually examines this information in their minds, by observing relationships between facts. They want to explore patterns and connections, and are especially excited if they observe new options for the future. In most organizations, you find that majority of people working in Human Resource (HR), marketing, and law, as well as those in general management position are good at abstract thinking and are often known to be *big picture* people.

In the MBTI language, these dimensions are described by using the terms sensing and intuition. The statistics of how these two preferences are spread among roles, show that the majority of business executives have an innate preference for detail-oriented information processing (sensing). Nevertheless, when moving up in the organization, executives need to strengthen their conceptual and visionary skills, which fall into the "abstract information processing," big picture category. This is an important requirement for the different transition stages of leadership development. The higher you move up in the organization, the more important it becomes to sharpen and polish your cognitive thinking skills. One of the key prerequisites for successfully navigating through these career transition points is that your thinking systems and lateral thinking techniques should become more agile.

As mentioned before, if you compare this dimension of the P5 tool with the MBTI, you notice that it is similar to the sensing and intuition dimensions. Also, if you consult the Big Five instrument again, you will find some similarities with the factor "openness to experience," which is sometimes called the intellect, or intellect/imagination factor. However, the P5 model's logic has no preferences. To be a fully rounded executive and leader, you need to develop both the sides of these dimensions. People, who are good at connecting dots ("big picture" thinking) might sometimes not sufficiently consider, the practicalities of a situation. In real life, you will find that successful people always present both sides of the dimensions. In Table 2.2 you will find the characteristics of people who focus on either "detailed," sequential information or on "big picture," abstract information when absorbing and relating to information.

Table 2.2. Depiction of Thinking Styles

Analytical thinking: process information from a "detail" perspective	*"Big picture" thinking: process information from a "big picture" perspective*
Good at analytical, sequential, and logical thinking	Good at lateral, holistic, systemic thinking
Focus on the challenges of the present	Focus on future oriented solutions
Details, factual	Bigger Picture, conceptual
Focus on what is real	Focus on patterns
Understand ideas and theories through practical applications	Want to clarify ideas and theories before putting them into practice
Trust experience	Trust conceptual insights

DECISION MAKING: RATIONAL APPROACH
VERSUS VALUE/PEOPLE-ORIENTED APPROACH

When it comes to assessing information, people consider different kinds of information. Some people are rather fact oriented when assessing information to make a decision, while others first want to consider the impact of decisions on people first, and ascertain how these decisions are aligned with their internal value system.

People who fall into the first category of this dimension, want to examine the logical consequences concerning their choice of action. Usually, they attempt to remove themselves mentally from any given situation to examine it objectively. If all the matters are internally consistent and logical, they are regarded as correct. If not, the topic at hand must be incorrect. Treating people fairly is seen as equal to treating everybody the same, regardless of their different backgrounds or personalities. Fact-oriented executives believe in rules that should be applicable to everybody. It is only in a second mental process that they consider a decision's impact on the other people, and how the outcome of their analysis and decision making process is aligned to their values and core beliefs in life.

On the other hand, those who are primarily value-oriented and people-oriented in decision making processes want to consider the impact of any decision on other people first. In a second mental process, they then consider the logical and factual implications. Typically, they attempt to mentally place themselves into any given situation, to understand the situation. They strive to identify with the people involved so that they can make decisions that make sense for both the sides. They feel good about respecting and supporting others. Their goal is to treat each person as a unique individual.

This dimension is again very similar to the MBTI instrument's thinking, and feeling the dimension. It also shows some similarities with the Big Five's agreeableness factor. People, who care about value alignment when evaluating and assessing information tend to strive for harmony and are satisfied when they can assist groups, so that everyone gets along well. People, who use mainly a rational approach to decision making, however, can come across as very competent but aloof, since they try to distance themselves for a better understanding of a situation. By stepping back, they try to observe what is going on from the outside, thereby gaining a better understanding of what is happening. To extract the most information from any given situation, it would, of course, be best to apply both the mental activities: stepping in and stepping outside, applying logic, and analysis and assessing this against one's own value system to empathize with the players of the situation.

Bill Gates, Margaret Thatcher, and Alfred Einstein are examples of well-known people, who showed a dominant rational approach to decision making. Mikhail Gorbachev and Martin Luther King are examples of people, who primarily cared for value alignment when evaluating and assessing information.

However, if you look at Bill Gates' current activities, you see that people's profiles develop even more over the course of their lives, if they are interested in their development and have the freedom to do so. Nowadays, Bill Gates dedicates most of his fortune and his working time to charitable causes, for clearly value-based reasons. He is still applying his fine intellectual capabilities in the best and the most efficient way. Please read the extract from Bill Gate's Annual Letter 2010 below; this gives insight into his work in the charity sector through the Bill and Melinda Gates Foundation. Look for evidence of his personality with regard to the above-described P5 dimensions.

CASE STUDY 1

Example for Personality Type Development

Extract from Bill Gate's Annual Letter 2010.

This is my second annual letter. The focus of this year's letter is innovation, and how it can make the difference between a bleak future and a bright one.

2009 was the first year my full-time work was as co-chair of the foundation, along with Melinda and my dad. It has been an incredible year, and I enjoyed having lots of time to meet with the innovators working on some of the world's most important problems. I got to go out and talk to people making progress in the field, ranging from teachers in North Carolina, to health workers fighting polio in India, to dairy farmers in Kenya. Seeing the work firsthand reminds me of how urgent the needs are, as well as how challenging it is to get all the right pieces to come together. I love my new job and feel lucky to get to focus my time on these problems.

The global recession hit hard in 2009 and is a huge setback. The neediest suffer the most in a downturn. The 2009 started with no one knowing how long the financial crisis would last, and how damaging its effects would be. Looking back now, we can say that the market hit a bottom in March, and that in the second half of the year the economy stopped shrinking and started to grow again. I talked to Warren Buffett, our co-trustee, more than ever this year, to try to understand what was going on in the economy.

(Continued)

CASE STUDY 1 (*Continued*)

Although the acute financial crisis is over, the economy is still weak, and the world will spend many years undoing the damage, which includes lingering unemployment and huge government deficits and debts, at record levels. Later in the letter I will talk more about the effects of these deficits on governments' foreign aid budgets. Despite the tough economy, I am still very optimistic about the progress we can make in the years ahead. A combination of scientific innovations and great leaders, who are working on behalf of the world's poorest people, will continue to improve the human condition.

One particular highlight from the year came last summer, when I traveled to India to learn about the innovative programs they have recently added to their health system. The health statistics from northern India are terrible—nearly 10% of the children there, die before the age of 5. In response, the Indian government is committed to increasing its focus and spending on health. On the trip I got to talk to Nitish Kumar, the chief minister of Bihar, one of the poorest states in India, and hear about some great work he is doing to improve the vaccination rates. I also got to meet with Rahul Gandhi, who is part of a new generation of political leaders, focused on making sure these investments are well spent. The foundation is considering funding measurement systems to help improve these programs. Rahul was very frank in saying that right now a lot of money is not getting to the intended recipients and that it would not be easy to fix. His openness was refreshing, since many politicians would not say anything that might discourage a donor from giving more. He explained how organizing local groups, primarily of women, and making sure they watch over the spending, is one tactic he has seen make a big difference. The long-term commitment to measuring results and improving the delivery systems that I heard from him and other young politicians, assured me that health in India will improve substantially in the decade ahead. In India, just like everywhere else we work, the needs of the poor are greater than the resources available, to help them solve their problems. It is important to get more money, but that alone will not solve the big problems. This is why Melinda and I are such big believers in innovations that allow you to do a lot more for the same cost.

Source: Adapted from Gates Foundation's 2010 Newsletter as found on http://www.gatesfoundation.org.

Table 2.3.   Depiction of Decision Making

Rational approach to decision making	*Value-oriented approach to decision making*
Analytical	Empathetic, holistic
Strong belief in logic	Strong internal value system
Focus on the internal consistency of an approach first	Consider the impact of a decision on people first
Objectivity	Do not believe in objectivity as a guiding principle
People should be treated equally	Consider individual cases and background information

For a quick check of your own and others' orientation on these dimensions, see Table 2.3 that describes the characteristics of people, with primarily either a fact orientation or a people/value orientation, in the decision making processes in business.

WORKING STYLES: STRUCTURED WORKING STYLE VERSUS EMERGENT (FLEXIBLE) WORKING STYLE

People differ very much in the way they approach their work. In essence, some prefer a structured approach to work, while others operate more efficiently by applying a more flexible, emergent approach to work. People with a structured approach usually like to organize their work and tasks, in a systematic and structured way. They often prefer a clear plan of action with defined outcomes. They like to have timeframes, prefer things to be planned, and do not necessarily like surprises, as they like to regulate their projects. Decisions are needed to achieve closure, which allows them to move on. Usually, these people prefer to make an early start to projects as they do not feel comfortable with too much last-minute pressure. In times of organizational change, they have a strong need for information about the case for change, and how the change will specifically impact their lives. If they do not get this information, it creates a lot of stress and insecurity.

People with an emergent working style prefer to work in a more flexible and spontaneous way. They like open-ended plans with flexibility and options. They prefer to have opportunities to explore different possibilities, and readily adjust plans as the process continues. They are usually open-minded and willing to trust the process. They seek experiences when working. The emphasis is on understanding work rather than controlling it. They would feel confined if they were exposed to too much structure and time limitations. In general, they like the working process and the solutions to *emerge* and they perform well under stress, as many of them are pressure-prompted. Adapting to new circumstances comes quite naturally, and, in times of organizational change, they often fall into the early adopters' category as change is a normal way of working for them.

In most of the organizations, there is a strong tendency to foster a structured approach to work. However, this is currently changing. With organizational change widely recognized as one of the few constant factors in today's business world, the executives increasingly acknowledge the necessity for people to be more flexible and adaptable. The importance of planning is definitely being challenged by the necessity to react to the moment. Today's executives, with an innate structured approach to work, must challenge their ability to be flexible and more spontaneous. Professionals with an emergent approach need to show a strong ability to be organized, as well as to plan and forecast to be successful. This applies to all the dimensions of the P5 tool: to become a mature, rounded person you need both the approaches.

This dimension is very similar to the Big Five model's conscientiousness factor and the MBTI model's 4th dimension—judging versus perceiving. However, unlike the MBTI dimension judging versus perceiving, this dimension of the P5 model is limited to explaining work-related behavior.

For a further understanding of the behavioral implications of both the approaches, you can find two examples of highly successful businessmen below. One of these men favored a more planned approach to life, while the other favored a more emergent approach, to the way he managed his career development.

CASE STUDY 2

Jack Welch

Jack Welch – a famous example of a structured approach to career development.

Welch joined General Electric (GE) in 1960. He worked as a junior engineer in Pittsfield, Massachusetts, at a salary of $10,500 annually. Welch was displeased with the $1,000 raise he was offered after his first year, as well as the strict bureaucracy within GE. He planned to leave the company to work with International Minerals & Chemicals in Skokie, Illinois. However, Reuben Gutoff, a young executive two levels higher than Welch, decided that the man was too valuable a resource, for the company to lose. He took Welch and his first wife

(Continued)

CASE STUDY 2 (*Continued*)

Carolyn out to dinner at the Yellow Aster in Pittsfield, and spent 8 hours trying to convince Welch to stay. Gutoff vowed to work, to change the bureaucracy to create a small-company environment. *"Trust me,"* Gutoff remembers pleading. *"As long as I am here, you are going to get a shot to operate with the best of the big company and [with] the worst part of it pushed aside."* "Well, you are on trial," retorted Welch. *"I am glad to be on trial,"* Gutoff said. *"To try to keep you here is important."* At daybreak, Welch gave him his answer. *"It was one of my better marketing jobs in life,"* recalls Gutoff. *"But then he said to me–and this is vintage Jack– 'I am still going to have the* [goodbye] *party because I like parties, and besides, I think they have some little presents for me.'"* Some 12 years later, Welch would audaciously write in his annual performance review that his long-term goal was to become chief executive officer (CEO). Welch was named the vice president of GE in 1972. He moved up the ranks to become the senior vice president in 1977, and vice chairman in 1979. Welch became GE's youngest chairman and CEO in 1981, succeeding Reginald H. Jones.

Source: http://en.wikipedia.org/wiki/Jack_Welch.

CASE STUDY 3

Steven Paul Jobs

Steven Paul Jobs, a famous example of an emergent approach to career development.

Steve Paul Jobs is an American business magnate and inventor. He is well known for being the co-founder and (CEO) of Apple. Jobs also previously served as the chief executive of Pixar Animation Studios; he became a member of the board of The Walt Disney Company in 2006, following the acquisition of Pixar by Disney.

In the late 1970s, Jobs, with Apple co-founder Steve Wozniak, Mike Markkula, and others, designed, developed, and marketed one of the first commercially successful lines of personal computers, the Apple II

(Continued)

CASE STUDY 3 (*Continued*)

series. In the early 1980s, Jobs was among the first to see the commercial potential of the mouse-driven graphical user interface, which led to the creation of the Macintosh. After losing a power struggle with the board of directors in 1984, Jobs resigned from Apple and founded NeXT, a computer platform development company specializing in the higher education and business markets. Apple's subsequent 1996 buyout of NeXT brought Jobs back to the company he co-founded, and he has served as its CEO since 1997.

Jobs' history in business has contributed much to the symbolic image of the idiosyncratic, individualistic Silicon Valley entrepreneur, emphasizing the importance of design, and understanding the crucial role aesthetics play in public appeal. His work, driving forward the development of products that are both functional and elegant, has earned him a devoted following. Jobs is listed as either [the] primary inventor or co-inventor in over 230 awarded patents or patent applications, related to a range from actual computer and portable devices to user interfaces (including touch-based), speakers, keyboards, power adapters, staircases, clasps, sleeves, lanyards, and packages.

Source: http://en.wikipedia.org/wiki/Steve_Jobs.

If you look at Jack Welch's career, you notice that he made the decision to be successful within GE very early in his career, whereas Steve Jobs' career was much less foreseeable. Both approaches worked out just fine for these two influential business people. However, considering today's business world, it is questionable whether the good old traditional career path—working oneself up the career ladder of one particular organization—is still a road to success. With 80% of the organizations around the world experiencing major restructuring activities at this very moment, this traditional career path, like the one Jack Welsh chose, is probably outdated or simply not feasible for the majority of the workers. Nowadays, people have to be more flexible, and have to work on expanding their professional network and employability to prepare themselves for the business rules and principles that are the norm in our fast changing times. Again, to quickly check your and others' personality, read through the following table that presents the characteristics of people who prefer either a structured or an emergent approach to work.

Table 2.4.   Depiction of Working Style

Structured approach to work	*Emerging approach to work*
Planned, structured	Spontaneous, flexible
"Project management approach"	Creative approach to work
Systematic and methodical	Casual approach to time and task
Goal oriented	Goal can be modified
Prefer short-and long-term plans	Emergent strategy to work and career
Like to conclude things	Like to have options until the last minute
Like to finish without inappropriate haste	Pressure prompted

Emotional Responsiveness

This dimension asks people to reflect, on how strongly they usually react to any external stimuli. People, who are immune to external stimuli, are emotionally stable and less reactive to stress. They tend to be calm, even tempered, and less likely to feel tense or rattled. Though they are usually low in negative emotion, they are not necessarily high on positive emotion. Individuals who fall into the immune category (particularly those who are also high on extraversion) generally report more happiness and satisfaction with their lives. People, who are more easily excitable, often show high scores with regards to both negative and positive emotions. When they are convinced of a project, they really tend to go for it. They are very enthusiastic people who are able to inspire others. However, their responsiveness can also make them vulnerable in times of confusion, or when too many organizational change efforts are taking place.

This dimension has no equivalent in the MBTI instrument, but shows some similarities to the Big Five model's 5th factor. It is very important to be clear regarding where you stand, regarding this personality dimension, as it very strongly determines the degree to which other aspects of your personality shine through. For example, people who are more excitable usually bring a lot of energy to the table and are often regarded as inspiring. On the other hand, people who show a weak emotional response to external stimuli can usually be very strongly relied on in times of change, constant stress, or in crisis situations. If you belong to the more excitable category of people, you have to watch yourself carefully. You need to invest your energy wisely throughout your career, as you might have a tendency to burn out. Know which battles are worth fighting! On the other hand, if you belong to the less excitable category of people, you need to consider that people tick differently, which you, as a leader, should take into consideration to protect your employees. Some of the most talented people source their passion and inspiration from their readiness to react

Table 2.5.   Depiction of Emotional Responsiveness

Immune	*Excitable*
Weak response to external stimuli	Strong response to external stimuli
Limited emotional variety	Wider emotional variety
Calm	Enthusiastic
Even tempered	Higher variation in temper

emotionally to their surroundings; nevertheless, overplaying this side of oneself usually leads to uncomfortable situations.

HOW TO USE THE P5 TOOL IN A PROFESSIONAL CONTEXT

The P5 tool should be used to analyze your and other people's behavior in order to gain a deeper understanding of the psychological factors, involved when working on your personal and leadership development. Unlike the MBTI, however, the P5 tool does not differentiate between 16 different personality types. The P5 tool only attempts to explain work-related behavior.

It is important to remember that most of the senior professionals demonstrate behavior from both sides of each P5 dimensions. Nevertheless, one side will feel more comfortable, which is usually the side for which you have a natural preference, where you operate more smoothly.

Also keep in mind, that all of the behaviors in the P5 tool's different dimensions have advantages and disadvantages. Whether it is one or the other, depends on the circumstances in which we operate.

The activities at the end of this chapter will guide you through a process to make the best use of the P5 tool. But before you go there, read how one of our clients has used the tool to first increase her self-awareness, and to then become a more rounded, mature leader in her working environment.

CASE STUDY 4

A Spanish Chief of Marketing on Working with the P5 Tool

Ana, (46) Spanish, Chief of Marketing in a global electricity company, Hong Kong, China.

What can knowing your personality do for you? In my case a lot! I was first introduced to the P5 tool by my executive coach in 2008. I used it as a reflective tool to think more systematically about my personality. It was really interesting to see the patterns emerging behind

(Continued)

CASE STUDY 4 (*Continued*)

my day-to-day activities. Sometimes we know that we tend to behave in similar ways again and again, even if we do not want to, but in many cases we do not know why this happens. This has partly changed since I have worked with the P5. For me, it was the key to understanding that I could describe a central part of my personality using easy language. As a result of my self-reflection process, I understood that I am an extroverted big-picture person, who is very much people and value oriented, when it comes to decision making processes, who uses an emergent approach to work (and I mean emergent to the extreme), and who is highly emotionally responsive to any external stimuli. This insight explained a great deal about both the successes and failures, in my working life so far. And building on this made a major difference, in the way I experienced myself as a leader of a team of eight senior people in my field. All of a sudden I was able to explain many of the conflicts I had had with them so far, and the kind of misunderstandings that sometimes hindered the development of our relationships. From my perspective, dimension 3 (process information from a "detail" perspective versus "big picture" perspective) and dimension 4 (structured approach versus emergent approach to work) have the most explanatory power. Nowadays, I know that, as a leader, I have to think about and act in all of these ways, to compensate for the differences in personality traits. I am the one who gets paid for managing the relationships with the members of my team in such a way, that they can perform to the best of their abilities. In my case, my emergent approach to work caused many problems in the Chinese environment in which I am currently working. I still have not figured out how much of this can be explained by culture, and how much by differences in personality. However, I know that I have become as successful as I am, because I am a creative person who can live with a great deal of insecurities. In order to be a successful leader NOW, however, I need to provide the right working environment for people who differ in their personality type. By incorporating a more planned approach into my leadership style, my working relationships have improved a great deal, and I have also received feedback from my employees (though I have to admit that I really had to push for this feedback as you do not get this easily in Asia).

My recommendation is to put a copy of the P5 on the wall of your office–as a reminder of how different people are, and how these differences shape up the way we interact with one another and with the world around us. It helps us appreciate these differences instead of suffering under them.

CONCLUSION

As shown in this chapter, working with your personality does have a number of advantages. The more you know, the more often you will be able to make suitable decisions for yourself. If you create a life that suits your strengths and your personality, you will have much more energy available than people who do not. You will know how to develop yourself into more senior roles, and become the mature professional you wanted to be. Being able to use this knowledge to interact with other people in a better manner will be a positive side-effect, if you dedicate some of your attention to working with your personality.

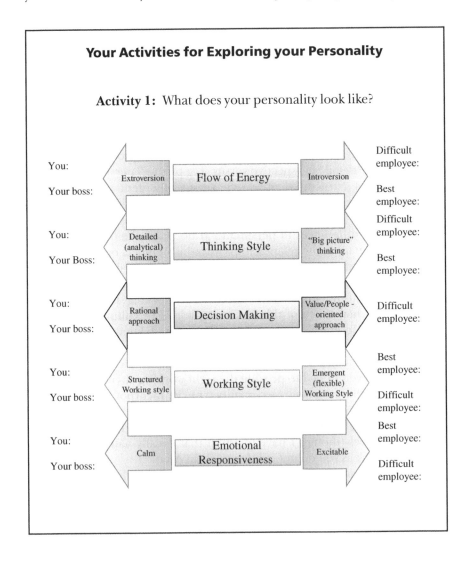

Your Activities for Exploring your Personality

Activity 1: What does your personality look like?

Now try to apply the knowledge gained in this chapter, and with respect to each dimension of the P5 tool, carefully decide which category describes you more.

Energy orientation: Are you more of an extroverted type or an introverted type?

Thinking Style: Do you gather and process information intuitively from a "detail" perspective (analytical thinking), or a "big picture" perspective ("big picture" thinking)?

Or in other words: do you usually apply an analytical thinking approach or a "big picture" thinking approach to make sense of the information you are absorbing from the inside and outside world?

Decision making: Do you give more weight to factual analysis or to your internal value system?

Working style: Do you have a structured or an emergent approach to work?

Emotional responsiveness: Would you describe yourself as a rather calm person, or a rather excitable, enthusiastic person who reacts quite vividly to external stimuli?

Now use the P5 template presented above if you want to.

Just remember: We are able to demonstrate behavior from both sides of the P5 tool. The key is to gain an increased awareness of what mental process we usually access FIRST and what behavior we show most often.

Activity 2: Analyze the personality of the people you work with.

Please revisit the P5 tool template presented in Activity 1, and try to analyze the personality type of your superior, your best employee (the one with whom you get along the best), and your most difficult employee (that you get along with the least). Make notes using the template.

Now try to apply the knowledge gained in this chapter, and with regard to each dimension of the P5 tool, ask yourself which category describes you the most?

Energy orientation: Is your boss/best employee/difficult employee, an extroverted type, or an introverted type?

Your boss

_____

Best employee

_____

Difficult employee

_____

Information processing: Does your boss/best employee/difficult employee gather and process information primarily from a "detail" or a "big picture" perspective?

Your boss

_____

Best employee

_____

Difficult employee

_____

Decision making: Does your boss/best employee/difficult employee give more weight to rational analysis, or to his/her internal value system?

Your boss

_____

Best employee

_____

Difficult employee

_____

Working style: Does your boss/best employee/difficult employee have a structured or an emergent approach to work?

Your boss

_____

Best employee

_____

Difficult employee

_____

Emotional responsiveness: Would you describe your boss/best employee/difficult employee as a rather calm person or a rather excitable, enthusiastic person who reacts quite vividly to external stimuli?

Your boss

_____

Best employee

_____

Difficult employee

_____

Activity 3: Use this knowledge to improve your relationships.

Having carefully reflected on your own and other people's behavior and personality, can you make use of this knowledge to explain some of the things that happen to you at work?

_____

_____

Does it help you to re-think your leadership style, in order to accommodate other people's personality preferences?

_____

_____

Activity 4: Does your personality match your career ambitions?

Understanding your personality can assist your career development in a number of ways.

Please take time to reflect on the outcome of your analysis, and relate it to career-related considerations.

Does your personality actually fit with your current role requirements?

_____

_____

Does your personality type fit with your envisioned career direction?

_____

_____

Should you consider changing the direction of your career slightly, to fit your personality better?

_____

_____

Activity 5: Reflect on your personal maturity.

This is an activity for people who would like to think about personality development beyond the P5 tool. Please read the following contribution on "Ego Development: a key aspect of personality development" and start asking yourself how this knowledge relates to you.

Ego Development: A Key Aspect of Personality Development

Have you ever experienced working with a manager for whom it seems easy to integrate differing perspectives, who is able to deal well with ambivalence without trying to wish it away, who is self-reflective and allows himself to be questioned, without feeling as if he is being personally attacked?

If so, then you have probably noticed a key dimension of personality development: maturity. This is an aspect of personality that psychologists also characterize as ego development, a subject that has been intensively researched over the last 50 years. The significant difference in this aspect is that it is not about stable dimensions on which people's personality differs, but it is more about the development of the personality as a whole. The good news is that while most of the characteristics (for example, temperament, intelligence) are fixed, one can develop this aspect throughout one's life. The following graphic shows how this type of development can be envisioned.

Often, what is described as development refers to the acquisition of knowledge, further competencies and new experiences. However, the basic way in which a person relates to and interacts with the world remains the same (horizontal development = learning).

In contrast, a more differentiated and integrative view of oneself and the world is associated with a qualitative shift (vertical development = ego development). With this shift, one becomes more able to effectively deal with complex contexts, different people and novel situations. In particularly stressful times, a temporary regression to earlier ego development stages may occur, and the person is likely to be able to reflect on this.

Personality maturity can be measured in more than 10 different stages of ego development. Vertical development through these stages shows a progressive movement towards greater self-reflection, increased awareness, and agility. Most managers are in the middle stages. They are therefore, far from the level at which they are able to effectively deal with complex and contradictory situations. To date,

Developmental Directions

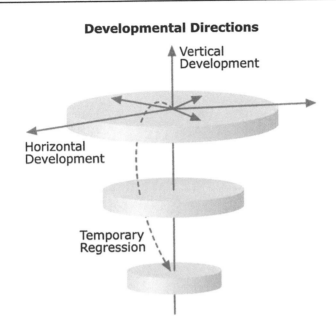

Vertical
Development

Horizontal
Development

Temporary
Regression

numerous studies have demonstrated that a manager's ego development stage has a significant influence on his success. Compared to stable personality traits, ego development stages are harder to see, yet their impact is unmistakable.

In this regard it can be extremely helpful to receive feedback on the stage one has reached, and, hence, to what degree this will influence one's perceptions, self-definition, and actions. With this, one can better identify the associated possibilities and limitations, and can approach one's development in a more focused and encompassing manner.

Source: Based on Thomas Binder & Jason Kay, systemic consulting group, Berlin, www.E-D-Profile.net.

REFERENCES AND FURTHER READING

Briggs Myers, I. (2000). Introduction to type. (6th ed). Palo Alto: CPP Inc.

Briggs Myers, I., Mccaulley, M., Quenk, N., & Hammer, A. (2003). *MBTI manual*. Mountain View: CPP Inc.

Engler, B. (2006). Personality theories. New York: Houghton Mifflin Press.

Srivastava, S. (2011). *Measuring the Big Five Personality Factors*. Retrieved 25.07.2011 from http://www.uoregon.edu/~sanjay/bigfive.html.

Wikipedia (2011) – http://en.wikipedia.org/wiki/Personality.

CHAPTER 3

PERSONAL AND ORGANIZATIONAL VALUES

Helen Stride

OBJECTIVES OF THE CHAPTER

The main objective of this chapter is to help you continue to raise your self-awareness and explore your own "values statement." In addition you will be challenged to explore what role values play in the relationships you have with others, especially in terms of building trust with the people you manage. And last but not the least, this chapter is about understanding the relationship between leaders' values and organizational effectiveness.

WHY ARE VALUES IMPORTANT TO YOU AS A LEADER?

Never have the values of leaders in organizations been as important, as they are today. Various commercial crises from Enron, to the credit crunch, to BP's environmental disaster in the Gulf of Mexico, have revealed a need to reject business as usual. The public—and also the governments—are demanding that organizations stop placing the individual needs of share-holders and board members above everything else, and accept their duty to

Leadership and Personal Development: A Toolbox for the 21st Century Professional, pp. 55–68
Copyright © 2011 by Information Age Publishing

be responsible citizens. In order to restore the public's trust in the commercial sector, the leaders must demonstrate that they have integrity, and are focused on collective values such as protecting the environment, rather than on individual values such as power and personal achievement. After all, the values of leaders impact not only their immediate circle, but have more far reaching consequences.

Do your values live up to these ideals? How can you find out? Your values are important not only for the sake of society, but also for your ability to serve as an inspirational leader, and for the effectiveness of your organization.

This chapter begins with a brief definition of what values are. The next section will discuss in detail how values are used to build trust and influence people. Then, the links between leaders' values, and the values of the organizations they lead, are discussed. Finally, we will provide you with a few exercises to help you establish which values are really guiding your behavior. This will not only help you to increase your self-awareness, but will also assist to ensure that your leadership style is authentic and inspiring.

Value and Values

The terms value and values are often used interchangeably, especially in business literature. Although the terms are related, there are fundamental differences that need to be explored.

We are all familiar with the idea of something being of value to us. With tangible items such as a car or an item of clothing, value is normally considered in economic or monetary terms. Value can also be applied to intangible items such as an experience or friendship. When we value a particular standard or principle such as justice, freedom, loyalty, or ambition, we tend to take these on as our own, so they become "our values" or criteria, for how we want to live our lives. Values, as criteria or standards, play a very important role in everyone's lives. Before we consider values as criteria in more detail, we need to briefly explore the on-going debate of whether values have a moral dimension, or are simply a preference for behaving in a particular way.

Values and Morality—"should" or "are"

> *"Human life is—and has to be—a moral life, precisely, because it is a social life.....In common sense terms, morals are socially agreed upon values relating to conduct"* (Kluckhohn, 1951, p. 398).

One of the enduring debates about values is whether they are linked to how things "should" be, or to how things "are". Should the way we behave be driven by a desire to create a better society, or should it simply be driven by our own needs and desires? Kluckohn (1951) suggests that human life has to be a moral life, because we are dependent upon each other for our survival. In other words, human beings should agree on a set of socially agreed principles or values for getting along together. Values, should therefore, act as a restraining influence on "selfish" behavior and be in the interest of everyone. The opposing view is that the selection of values is an emotional response based on an individual's feelings of pleasure. We can see from Rokeach's definition in the 1970s (see below) when he introduces the idea that values can be related to a personal preference for behaving in a certain way, as well as a social preference.

What is your view? Do you believe that society needs a set of agreed values for how we behave, or is it acceptable for the behavior to be driven by individual need?

Values as Criteria—Standards for How We Behave

Let us now return the discussion to the idea that values are criteria, or standards of behavior. Some of the most influential work on values as criteria has been conducted by psychologist and marketer Rokeach, who defines values as:

"..an enduring belief that a specific mode of conduct or end-state of existence is personally or socially preferable, to alternative modes of conduct or end-states of existence" (Rokeach, 1973, p. 5).

As criteria for how we conduct ourselves, values are a code of conduct for how we live our lives. In particular, they drive us in how we behave in social situations, and how we interact with others. As such, they play a crucial role in determining the sort of person we are, and how we are viewed by others. A person who highly values ambition and being capable, for example, is likely to behave very differently, and to be perceived differently, to someone, who values forgiving and being helpful. Values also impact our "end state of existence" or our global goals such as freedom, equality, or protecting the environment.

Rokeach argues that the values' discussion should avoid the "should" or "ought" debate, and instead, focus on preferences that people have for conducting themselves and for living their lives. Rokeach's taxonomy includes values that are driven by individual want (for example, pleasure and ambition), as well as values driven by a sense of duty (for example, forgiving and polite). While Rokeach (1973) defines values as being personally as well as socially preferable, it is the work of Schwartz (1992) that clearly divides values into those that are in the interest of the individual, and those that have more of a collective focus.

In Table 3.1, the values types on the left-hand side are driven by individual need (self-direction, stimulation, hedonism, achievement, and

Table 3.1.   Values Types

Values Type	*Values Type*
Self-Direction	Benevolence
Stimulation	Conformity
Hedonism	Tradition
Achievement	Universalism
Power	Security

Source: Adapted from Schwartz, 1992.

power), while those at the top of the right-hand side are driven by the needs of the group (benevolence, conformity, and tradition). Universalism and security-type values can have either an individual or collective focus. For examples of the individual values in each category, please see Appendix 1.

Although it is argued that values remain fairly constant throughout our lives, we do observe people living by different sets of values at different life stages. For example, having become the richest man in the world, Bill Gates of Microsoft now devotes much of his time and wealth to philanthropic activity, as shown in Chapter 2. When we manage to transcend our own needs and desires in this way and live by values that connect us to others, values appear to have an inspirational quality. One of the reasons that Barrack Obama's inaugural speech was so powerful was because it communicated with our collective identity. It was about how we could improve things together.

Do you agree with the above statement? Do collective values such as social justice and consideration inspire you? If not, what types of values inspire you?

Values and Personal Development

Values not only inspire, they also underpin our identity or sense of self, which is critical to our self-esteem. They are the essence of who we are. Because values are an abstract concept, however, we are not always aware of which values are guiding our behavior. We may be driven to get the next promotion at work, spend our holidays paragliding, or visit the local shelter for homeless people at Christmas, but we may not realize that it is our values that are underpinning each of these different behaviors. So we may find ourselves behaving in a particular way, and not really understand the significance of what we are doing. Or we may feel angry about a situation, and not realize why? For example, if we find ourselves in a situation which compromises our values, we will feel uncomfortable and this may elicit a wide range of emotions. It is not uncommon in Western society for people to be involved in certain social circles (for example, the organization for which they work for) which espouses a set of values that they themselves do not entirely embrace.

Raising awareness of what our values are is therefore important in helping us gain a better understanding of ourselves. With the growing interest in authentic leadership, values' questionnaires are often at the heart of leadership and executive development, because leadership forces us to reflect, on what we really value in life.

CASE STUDY 1

On Paul's Values

Paul (40), English, Editor and Senior Manager, London, UK.

Paul is a 40-year-old editor of adult non-fiction. Until quite recently he had a senior management position at a successful, family-run publishing company. We will call the company Wilcox and Sons, to protect Paul's anonymity. Having worked as a journalist in the cut-throat world of international media, Paul was attracted by Wilcox's reputation for traditional family values, such as fairness and integrity. The culture of the organization encouraged open, honest dialogue, and the views of everyone were respected. Staff development was also taken very seriously. As a part of Paul's development, he and I would have weekly coaching sessions to help him plan for his future. Following the sudden and unexpected death of the founder, however, everything changed.

The board of directors believed that the company needed to adopt a more commercial approach and appointed a chief executive officer (CEO) from business. The culture began to shift almost over-night. A small group of supporters, loyal to the new CEO was put into position of responsibility, and those whose face did not fit were invited to seek employment elsewhere. Paul felt outraged by these new changes, and challenged the CEO and the management team. It soon became clear that the CEO would not tolerate dissension. How could the loyal and capable employees be treated so shoddily, Paul would ask in our weekly sessions. Although Paul continued to fight the new regime, his values were being seriously compromised, and anger soon started to turn to stress and anxiety. Eventually, Paul reluctantly resigned from Wilcox and Sons.

Paul is now the CEO of another publishing company. When I asked Paul what he had learnt from his experience at Wilcox, he said,

(Continued)

CASE STUDY 1 (*Continued*)

"I learnt two key things: one, to believe that it is only your view that counts, is the road to tyranny. And, in this society that is unacceptable. Second, in this business people are everything; so we need to create an environment where people feel respected, and can trust those who have power over them. It is my job as a leader, therefore, to create this type of environment." Wilcox and Sons did not survive as an independent entity. It was taken over in 2009.

Shared Values, Trust, and Cooperation

This brings the discussion to values, and their role in building trusting relationships and influencing other people. We will consider this from the perspective of managers and leaders. The old adage is that we do not leave an organization, we leave our boss. So what makes people want to work for someone, be prepared to go the extra mile? We know that the most important factor in any strong relationship—whether it is between two individuals or an individual and an organization—is a high level of trust between the two parties. While trust, like values, may seem an abstract, nebulous concept, we now have a good understanding of what trust is and how we can build it. We also know what the enormous benefits of a trusting relationship are. Each of these issues will be considered, in turn.

Trust is defined as "confident expectations and a willingness to be vulnerable" (Lewicki, 2006, p. 191). This means, that when we trust someone we feel confident that they will behave towards us in a trustworthy manner—although we know that there is always some risk that they will not! Human beings seem to know instinctively that it is better to trust, than not to trust. So, even when we have no prior experience of someone, it is unlikely that the level of trust is zero. There are two main reasons for this: first, trust leads to cooperation, which is a good thing, and second, research has shown that trusting behaviors are reciprocated. If we act in a trusting way towards another person, he or she is much more inclined to act in a trusting way towards us. However, while to trust is our natural default, the extent to which we are prepared to risk trusting someone when we first meet, will also be determined by factors such as our personality, and the culture from which we come. In addition to cooperation, research also shows that trust is strongly correlated to commitment to another person— and a desire to maintain the relationship at all costs! So what has this got to do with our values?

There are three key factors that help us to build trust, and all of them are related to the values that we have. Following an initial encounter with someone, the extent to which we are prepared to trust them is determined by the experiences we have of them, both directly and indirectly. In order to trust someone, we are looking for experiences that demonstrate that they have integrity, that they are competent and that they have benevolent values. These types of experiences are keys, in helping to build trust with others. For example, do they do what they say they will? Is he or she competent at his or her job? And, do they demonstrate loyalty, helpfulness, and friendship? (see Schwartz's benevolent type values in Appendix 1). In addition to these direct experiences, we also build an idea of other's trustworthiness from what other people say about them—or their reputation.

The final issue that drives trust between people, and between people and organizations, is the concept of shared values. Shared values are defined as "social factors in inter-personal attraction, liking, and loving: similarities—shared values and beliefs" (Schachter, 1959). This returns us to the role that values play in helping us to define who we are. Having built a sense of self, based on our values, we are then attracted to people and organizations, whose values and beliefs are the same or similar to ours. We understand how people like us see the world, and, as a consequence, are much more tolerant and forgiving of them. While we may be attracted to people who value ambition, wealth, and social recognition (because these are what we value or aspire to), trust, of course, still requires that we act with integrity, and behave in a forgiving and helpful way.

CASE STUDY 2

On Maria Costa's Staying Focused

Maria Costa (42), Portuguese, Executive Coach, Lisbon, Portugal.

At the end of each year, I tend to think deeply, and make up a type of balance sheet of my achievements in the year that is about to end. I do not precisely remember when this custom started, but over the last 4 years, with the countdown of the days toward the end of the year, an intention, a topic, a value starts to take shape inside me. It can comprise any issue such as "organization," "friendship," "family" or "love."

Every year, I therefore dedicate to choosing a value to focus on. An interesting point is that the topic's impact does not show immediately. At the start, it is only an intention, always present, hardly

(Continued)

CASE STUDY 2 (*Continued*)

noticed, but growing stronger as the year progresses. And after some time, everything starts to make sense in the light of this value. Decisions produce actions and effects, and results start to appear. The value acts as a common ground binding all the areas of my life, giving shape to thoughts, plans, and actions.

To give an example, if the topic is "family," which it was in 2009, some of my normal daily reflections could be: "What impact does this decision have on my family? How can it affect us? What will I do to strengthen the bonds? How will I organize my day or weekend?" I started to organize evenings and events together, and as a result, my family grew closer, and friends were integrated closer into our family activities. New relationships were formed, and became part of our lives. It was amazing, how by having the value "family" at the forefront of my decision making, transformed my family life.

Always having this intention in the present, helps me to stay focused and aligned with my beliefs and decisions. My intention for the next year is to align my business activities around a certain value that I hold most dear in my life. I am curious about the kind of changes that will come my way. However, I am already sure these changes will mostly be positive, even if they may sometimes be challenging.

Organizational Values: From Effective to Values Based Organizations

In the recent years, there has been considerable interest in the importance of values in developing effective organizations. It is suggested that there is a relationship between an organization having a set of shared, identifiable values, and corporate success. Like individual values, organizational values are standards against which individuals decide what is right, or are at a preference for taking one course of action rather than another. They are important because they determine group behavior and form part of the organization's identity, which acts both as a guide for the group, and as an inspiration. Shared organizational values are also said to be important in terms of employee commitment—an important factor in relation to absenteeism, turnover, and job satisfaction. In fact, organizational commitment is said to be a "strong belief in and acceptance of the organization's goals and values" (Porter *et al.*, 1974 from Finegan, 2000). Collins and Porras (2000) go as far as to say that it is not only the values per se that are at the heart of visionary companies, but particular types of values—values that have a likeable or humanist quality. These values are similar to Schwartz's benevolence and universalism value types that have a collective rather than an individual focus.

With a few exceptions, for example, Body Shop and Apple—most of the commercial organizations do not have a clear, strong set of values that they live by, and that are shared by the employees. One of the reasons for this is that there is often a disparity between the values that companies would like to have or "espouse," and those that actually drive behavior. All too often, companies will claim in their values, statements to believe in fairness, staff involvement, integrity, and so forth, while being autocratic and focused solely on driving the bottom line. So, what's going on here? There is quite clearly a tension between how organizations think they "should" be behaving, and how they "are" behaving. Even though writers such as Kay (1998) argue, that business is unsustainable unless it operates according to the same values as society, research suggests, that with the exception of "visionary" organizations, the values that predominate in the commercial sector are values such as power and wealth. But what, you may ask, has this got to do with you as a practicing manager or leader? To answer that we must turn to Schein's (1992) work on the role of leaders in creating the values, that under-pin the organization within which they work. Organizational values, he argues, originate from either the organization's leader or its founder and are adopted by the group once it becomes clear that such values will help the organization to achieve its objectives in the external environment. In the case of Body shop and Apple, both have or had charismatic leaders with sets of clear, personal values, which underpinned both their behavior and that of their organizations.

In the recent research conducted in Scandinavia (Pruzan, 2001), a significant discrepancy was found between the values that the members of staff said were important to them, and those they believed to be important to the organization. While the staff valued good health, honesty, they believed that the organization for whom they worked valued only success and efficiency. Pruzan argues that values with such a strong individual focus may not even reflect the values of the leaders. He suggests that leaders arrive at work, hang their own values on a hook outside their office, and don an entirely different set of values for the day. It is this discrepancy between the types of values espoused by leaders, as important for achieving commercial success, and the staff values that are problematic in an organization. This type of schizophrenia, Pruzan continues, is not sustainable, and is unhealthy for both the individuals and organizations. The objective of an organization, therefore, should be to identify the values with which all the staff members identify, and which reflect the underlying values systems of the organization's members; values that are likely to reflect those of the society.

CASE STUDY 3

On Celia's Values and Priorities

Celia (48), English, Manager at UK Charity, Bath, UK.

Celia worked for a UK development charity, which we will call One World to protect her anonymity. The primary objective of One World was to alleviate poverty in some of the world's poorest regions. Although the charity was founded by the Church, it had long since been multi-denominational, working with people of all faiths, and those of no particular faith. Celia is not a practicing Christian, but was drawn to the principles which One World lived by. "There was a culture of cooperation and empowerment with staff being positively encouraged to contribute views and ideas regarding a broad range of organizational decisions," Celia told me. While, not all the views could be acted upon, the management team recognized the need to justify why it had made the decisions it did. The strong sense of equality within One World was reflected in the pay structure. The principal's salary never exceeded three times that of the lowest-paid person. This value of moderation extended to all aspects of the charity's operations; personal calls were frowned upon, taxis were never used and staff stayed with colleagues when working away from home. Celia continued, "The charity felt that it could not justify the slightest extravagance when it was spending donated money, and when its beneficiaries lived in abject poverty."

For Celia, however, the rewards far outweighed any sacrifice that she made. The culture of benevolence and universal values was inspirational, and created a strong bond and collective identity amongst the staff. Trips to see partners overseas were often deeply humbling. During one trip, an Ethiopian woman walked 5 miles from her village with a farewell meal she had prepared for Celia. Such displays of human kindness, Celia told me, bring into sharp focus the meaninglessness of so much that is valued in the West. Needless to say, the staff's commitment levels were high, and those who left did so reluctantly. "Like so many of the friends I made who have since left," Celia concluded, "no organization I have worked in since has felt so like 'coming home.'"

Concluding Comments

A recent survey showed that 99% of the UK population believes that company directors are overpaid. And there are lots of similar survey results that show that this is also the case in USA, in many European countries, as well as in many Eastern countries. So is there a moral crisis in the boardroom? Is it about time that leaders behave according to the standards, that the rest the society is encouraged to conform to as well? Our answer to these questions is a definite yes. As leaders, it is of utmost importance to consciously consider the values that you live by – not only for your own development, and for the future of your organization, but also for the future of the society.

Your Activities for Clarifying Personal and Organizational Values

Activity 1: Conduct your own values audit.

We would like to ask you to conduct your own values audit. Using values from Schwartz's taxonomy (please see Appendix 1), identify 10 that are most important, as "guiding principles" in your life. If a friend or colleague were to witness you acting according to each of these values, what behavior would they see? How do these behaviors impact the response you get from other people?

1. _____

2. _____

3. _____

4. _____

5. _____

6. _____

7. _____

8. _____

9. _____

10. _____

Now reduce the list of values to 5. You want to write each of your 10 values on a piece of paper, and remove those which are less important one by one, until you are left with your 5 core principles. Finally, are these core values grouped according to the values types, or are they split across Schwartz's 10 values types? Have any of the results surprised you? Does your current lifestyle allow you to live according to the values that you have identified?

Activity 2: How do your values influence your relationships with other people?

Think about a person in your life whom you trust (for example, a colleague, a family member) Why do you trust this person? How do you behave toward this person? How do you think you are perceived in terms of whether you are trustworthy? How do you think you are perceived in terms of your values?

Activity 3: Explore the values of the organization you work for.

Using Schwartz's list, identify the 5 values which you believe are the guiding principles for the organization you work for. To what extent do these match the organization's espoused values? Where are the gaps? To what extent do these values match the values of the organization's various stakeholder groups? What impact does this congruence or incongruence have?

What are these 5 values?

_____

Where do they match or show a gap with your organization's value?

_____

What impact does this match/mismatch have?

_____

How do these values match the organizational stakeholder's priorities?

_____

What impact does this congruence or incongruence have?

_____

REFERENCES AND FURTHER READING

Collins, J., & Porras, J. (2000). *Built to last* (3rd ed.). New York: Random House.

Finegan, J. (2000). The Impact of Person and Organisational Values on Organisational Commitment. *Journal of Occupational and Organisational Psychology, 73*(2), 149–169.

Kay, J. (1998). The Role of Business in Society. www.johnkay/society/133.

Kluckhohn, C. (1951). Values and Value-orientation in the Theory of Action: An Exploration in Definition and Classification. In T. Parsons & E. A. Shils (Eds.), *Toward a General Theory of Action* (pp. 388–433). Cambridge, MA: Harvard University Press.

Lewicki, R., & Gillespie E. (2006). Models of Interpersonal Trust Development: Theoretical Approaches, Empirical Evidence and Future Directions. *Journal of Management, 32*, 991–1022.

Pruzan, P. (2001). The question of organizational consciousness: Can organizations have values, vitues and visions? *Journal of Business Ethics, 29*(3), 271–284.

Rokeach, M. (1973). *The Nature of Human Values*. New York: Free Press.

Schein, E. (1992). *Organizational Culture and Leadership*. San Francisco: Jossey-Bass.

Schachter, S. (1959). *The psychology of affiliation*. Stanford: Stanford University Press.

Schwartz, S. (1992). Universals in the content and structure of values: Theoretical advances and empirical tests in 20 countries. *Advances in Experimental Social Psycholgy, 25*, 1–65.

APPENDIX 1

A Selection of Values from Schwartz Value Survey (SVS) (Schwartz, 1992, p. 29)

Power
Authority
Wealth
Preserving My Public Image
Social Recognition

Achievement
Successful
Capable
Ambitious
Influential

Hedonism
Pleasure
Enjoying Life

Stimulation
Daring
A Varied Life
An Exciting Life

Self-Direction
Creativity
Curious
Freedom
Choosing Own Goals

Universalism
Protecting the Environment
A World of Beauty

Social justice
Wisdom
Equality
A World at Peace

Benevolence
Helpful
Honest
Forgiving
Loyal
True Friendship
Meaning in Life

Tradition
Devout
Accepting Portion in Life
Humble
Respect for Tradition

Conformity
Politeness
Obedient
Self-discipline

Security
Social Order
Family Security
Healthy
Sense of Belonging

CHAPTER 4

DISCOVERING YOUR EMOTIONAL CAPABILITIES

Mike Green

OBJECTIVE OF THE CHAPTER

The main focus of this chapter is to introduce the concept of emotional intelligence, and deal with how becoming more aware of our internal state of being can impact our effectiveness, in both our professional and personal lives.

INTRODUCTION

As you progress through the organizational hierarchy, you will find that your technical, professional, and specialist functional skills need to be supplemented and complemented by inter-personal skills. In order to take on people management roles and leadership activities, you will come to recognize the need for increased self and social awareness. You will need the necessary skills to manage yourself well and to interact and influence others in the organization, and beyond. The higher the level, the less work one

Leadership and Personal Development: A Toolbox for the 21st Century Professional, pp. 69–86

actually does, but more the primary responsibility shifts to managing the people who actually do the work. Emotional intelligence (EI) is the "royal path" to achieve this. If you were to eschew the corporate life and prefer to be entrepreneurial, you would discover, once again, that the skills necessary for networking, for business development, and for getting your message across are all underpinned by emotional intelligence.

In this chapter, we first give you an idea of how the concept developed, and explore the thoughts from the leading experts in the field. We then go on to look at the components of emotional intelligence, and some of the competencies that contribute to it. We specifically look at how developing emotional intelligence can contribute to your workplace and leadership effectiveness. In addition, we examine the different emerging perspectives on the concepts of optimism, happiness, and well-being. We describe three case studies, and suggest a number of activities to help develop emotional intelligence.

HISTORICAL BACKGROUND OF THE EMOTIONAL INTELLIGENCE CONCEPT

The concept of emotional intelligence aims to describe the ability, capacity, skill, or a self-perceived ability to identify, assess, and control one's emotions, those of others, and of the groups. Different models have attempted to explain this concept. However, there is still no consensus up to now, on how the term should be applied. Despite this, emotional intelligence has attracted a massive amount of attention from many parts of the society around the globe, including the field of management education.

The subject first appeared in the beginning of the last century. Researchers of human intelligence started to acknowledge the importance of the non-cognitive aspects of intelligence. Thorndike (1920) used the term social intelligence to describe the skill in understanding and managing other people.

Another example is David Wechsler (1940) who mentioned the impact of non-cognitive aspects on intelligent behavior. He pointed out that the research on human intelligence would be distorted and would fail to reveal the whole pictures, as long as these non-cognitive, emotional factors were not explored further. Gardner (1983) was the first to come up with the idea of multiple intelligences, which included both *inter-personal intelligence* (the capacity to understand the intentions, motivations, and desires of others) and *intra-personal intelligence* (the capacity to understand oneself, to appreciate one's feelings, fears, and motivations).

However, the first use of the term "emotional intelligence" is usually attributed to Payne's doctoral thesis in 1985. Then, in 1990, the work of

Mayer and Salovey was published in two academic journals. They were attempting to develop a way of scientifically measuring the difference between people regarding their emotional ability. They proved that some people were better than others in certain aspects, such as recognizing their emotions, recognizing the emotions of others, and tackling the problems involving emotional issues. As nearly all of their writing was of an academic nature, their names are not widely known outside the academic world.

Instead, the person most commonly associated with the term emotional intelligence is a New York writer and consultant named Goleman. In 1995 Goleman's book came out under the title *"Emotional Intelligence"*. The book made it to the cover of *Time Magazine* in the USA, and Goleman began appearing on American television shows such as *The Oprah Winfrey* and *The Phil Donahue*. He also began a speaking tour to promote the book, which became an international best-seller. It remained on the *New York Times* best-seller list for almost a year. In 1998 Goleman published a book called *"Working with Emotional Intelligence"*. In this book, he widened the definition of emotional intelligence, mentioning that it consisted of 25 "skills, abilities, and competencies". Since then there have been many definitions of emotional intelligence and many claims made about it (Hein, 2010). We find the following two complementary definitions, particularly useful.

> *Emotional intelligence is "An innate ability, which gives us our emotional sensitivity, and our potential for learning healthy, emotional, management skills. To explain this more, I believe each baby is born with a certain, unique potential for emotional sensitivity, emotional memory, emotional processing, and emotional learning ability. It is these four inborn components, which I believe, form the core of one's emotional intelligence. I also believe it is helpful to make a distinction between a person's innate potential, versus what actually happens to that potential over their lifetime."* Hein (2005).

> *"Emotional intelligence is the ability to sense, understand, and effectively apply the power and acumen of emotions, as a source of human energy, information, connection, and influences."* Cooper & Sawaf (1997).

ELEMENTS OF THE EMOTIONAL INTELLIGENCE ACCORDING TO GOLEMAN (2000)

According to Goleman (2000), emotional intelligence is about knowing what you are feeling, and being able to handle those feelings; being able to motivate yourself to get jobs done, be creative and perform well, sensing what others are feeling, and handling relationships effectively.

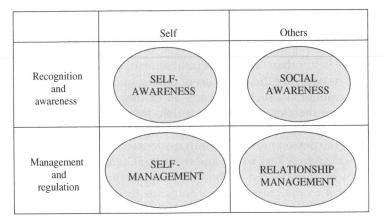

Figure 4.1. The four elements of emotional intelligence
Source: Adapted from Goleman (2000).

As portrayed in the Fig. 4.1, emotional intelligence has four elements or capabilities. Clearly, the first step is to develop high levels of awareness and recognition about yourself as well as the people around you, and then work towards managing and regulating those emotions, in order to achieve high levels of performance—your own, and that of those around you.

These four elements can be understood and described as follows:

- **Self-awareness:** Probably the most essential of the emotional intelligence competencies: the ability to read your emotions. It allows people to know their strengths and limitations, and feel confident about their self-worth.
- **Self-management:** This is the ability to control your emotions, and act with honesty and integrity in reliable and adaptable ways.
- **Social Awareness:** This includes the key capabilities of empathy and organizational intuition. Socially aware managers do more than sense other people's emotions, they show that they care. They are experts at reading office politics.
- **Relationship Management:** This includes the ability to communicate clearly and convincingly, disarm conflicts, and build strong personal bonds.

Let us take a look at a brief case study of a Dutch Chief Executive Officer (CEO).

CASE STUDY 1

The Troubled CEO

Jan (52), Dutch, CEO, currently located in Rotterdam, Netherlands.

Jan was a highly intelligent and capable manager who had risen through the ranks of his organization, and had a sense of purpose and passion for delivering excellent service. The only problem was—for others—that no one ever knew what mood he would be in when they saw him, whether at a one-to-one meeting, or a team meeting.

On a good day, you could go to him for a project update and discuss all sorts of creative and innovative approaches for the future. On another day, Jan would be in a foul mood after a previous difficult meeting. In these meetings, he would grill you, in detail about the previous months' facts and the figures. Any slight anomaly would be seized upon and scrutinized. Either you or your staff would be blamed.

Over the course of time, people began to prepare for hours before their meetings with Jan to ensure that the project update covered all of the possible eventualities that Jan could call into question. There would be little time for blue-sky thinking about the future, and little desire for a spontaneous, easy meeting. These meetings became a trial, rather than a joy. Jan began to complain that nobody produced creative ideas any longer.

Jan's main development areas were his lack of self-awareness and self-assessment of his inner emotional state. This resulted in an inability to exhibit self-control and management of those emotions. This was in turn, accompanied by a lack of insight into the behaviors of those around him, and an inability to enable his staff to relax enough in his presence so that they could jointly deal with the nitty-gritty details of the updates, and with the more creative generation of future options. Goleman contends that although there is a genetic component to emotional intelligence, research, and practice clearly demonstrates that it can be learned and developed further.

COMPETENCIES OF EMOTIONAL INTELLIGENCE

In turn, each of the four areas of emotional intelligence capability is composed of specific sets of competencies. These are outlined in Table 4.1 and their respective definitions are provided.

Table 4.1.   Competencies Within the EI Concept

Self-awareness	*Accurate assessment of own emotional state, competencies, personality, and the impact on others*
Emotional Self-awareness	The ability to read and understand your emotions, as well as recognize their impact on work performance, relationships, and so forth
Accurate Self-assessment	A realistic evaluation of your strengths and limitations
Self-confidence	A strong and positive sense of self-worth
Self-management	*Ability to use one's self-awareness to impact positively on the external world with others*
Self-control	The ability to keep disruptive emotions and impulses under control
Trustworthiness	A consistent display of honesty and integrity
Conscientiousness	The ability to manage yourself and your responsibilities
Adaptability	The skill to adjust to changing situations and overcome obstacles
Achievement Orientation	The drive to meet an internal standard of excellence
Initiative	A readiness to seize opportunities
Social Awareness	*Accurate assessment of others' emotions, interpretation of individual, and group behaviors, and a willingness to engage with them*
Empathy	The skill of sensing other people's emotions, understanding their perspective, and taking an active interest in their concerns
Organizational Awareness	The ability to read the currents of organizational life, build decision networks, and navigate politics
Service Orientation	The ability to recognize and meet customers' needs
Relationship Management	*Ability to use one's self-awareness, self-management, and social awareness to impact positively in the external world*
Visionary Leadership	The ability to take charge and inspire through a compelling vision
Influence	The ability to wield a range of persuasive tactics
Developing Others	The propensity to bolster the abilities of others, through feedback and guidance

Relationship Management	Ability to use one's self-awareness, self-management, and social awareness to impact positively in the external world
Communication	Skills to listen and send clear, convincing, and well-tuned messages
Change Catalyst	Proficiency in initiating new ideas, and leading people in a new direction
Conflict Management	The ability to de-escalate disagreements, and orchestrate resolutions
Building Bonds	Proficiency at cultivating and maintaining a web of relationships
Teamwork and Collaboration	Competence in promoting co-operation and building teams

Source: Adapted from Goleman (2000).

Let us have a look at another case study to illustrate our message.

CASE STUDY 2

Development of Communication and Relationship Skills

Nathan Hobbs (British), organizational psychologist, London, UK.

When I first graduated in the 1980s with my head full of books and theories, I was particularly naïve for a psychologist, and insensitive to my impact. Not only did I fail to listen and would constantly interrupt colleagues, I just did not get the more subtle undercurrents in a social situation, and was jealous of my own wife's abilities in this area. I had come home from work and talked about my day, and she had strung together coherent points of view of what was going on around me, the office politics and so on.

I had to do something about this quickly if I was not to derail later on, and therefore spoke with a wide range of colleagues and network contacts to ask for advice. The first thing I learned is that *there is hearing and then there is listening*; this was a revelation, which made perfect sense. I could accurately repeat what others had said several minutes later, even when I had interrupted, or not actually understood them. Strangely, part of my brain worked as a reasonably accurate voice recorder, yet I was not actually processing the information in a useful way.

The second thing I learned was that as a rational intuitive person, and an extrovert at that, I needed *a conceptual framework to help create internal representations of the world*, in a way that would make sense of it.

(Continued)

CASE STUDY 2 (*Continued*)

My new-found mentor taught me Transactional Analysis, for which I remain forever grateful. I have since learned several other useful frameworks that help me take sense of the world around me; systems psychodynamics has probably been the most useful of these, in that it is in essence a "theory of everything."

Now, if this sounds overly scientific or cybernetic in outlook, the key factor missing in my story so far is that *empathy complements and strengthens social awareness.* Although I received a lot of feedback from my boss about my social insensitivity, she liked me, which was just as well. Somehow, there is a separation between being "in the moment" and reflective understanding. I learned to test my intuitions on those around me, seek feedback and, through this critique, hone my awareness. Nowadays, I find that I mostly get away with occasional insensitivities as clients see that I care a great deal and work hard to help solve their problems. Looking back, this was an important realization for me: *if you care about your clients and their challenges, they forgive you if you do not always listen.* Later, as a manager of fellow consultants, I learned that listening is also a core leadership skill, essential for being understood, as well as for understanding and identification with colleagues. Simply showing an interest in other peoples' attitudes and perspectives provides a strong platform for leadership adaptability and in turn, they are more open to listening and support.

In my observations and interactions, voice tone and non-verbal communication became particularly important ways of accessing meaning, which is where some readers might feel I should have begun my story. I did put in some basic groundwork to learn about non-verbal communication in sales situations, as I was by now a sales coach; however, I quickly realized that without strong inquiry I was still not listening effectively and learned that *ego becomes a barrier to listening, if you focus too much on what is going on inside your head.* A more pragmatic colleague gave me feedback just recently that I am still somewhat over-inclined to share representational models directly with clients. When I stop and think about this, I know this is true, and work hard to keep my modelling "backstage," so to speak; this works when I have a strong grasp of the context in which I am working, although I may appear to regress at times. I am also learning that story-telling between communicants, allows people to draw meaning without pushing a direct point of view or emphasis.

EMOTIONAL INTELLIGENCE AND LEADERSHIP ROLES

Daniel Goleman was one of the first thinkers to bring the term "Emotional Intelligence" to a wider management audience. In his research at nearly 200 global companies, he found that while the qualities traditionally associated with leadership, such as intelligence, toughness, determination, and vision are required for success, they are insufficient. Really effective leaders also have high levels of emotional intelligence.

Research by Cameron and Green (2008) identified five leadership roles which leaders need to step into, if they are to be truly effective. These five roles are briefly explained in the Table 4.2. However, as these leadership roles have proven to carry such explanatory and practical power in leadership development today, we have dedicated a whole chapter in this book to this topic. Returning to the concept of emotional intelligence, we can clearly state that in our experience of working with leaders and professionals, different configurations of emotional intelligence competencies contribute to each of the roles.

Table 4.2.   Five Leadership Roles and EI Competencies

Leadership Role	Purpose	EI competencies
The Edgy Catalyzer	Focuses on creating discomfort to catalyze change	Drive to achieve, initiative, self-control, service orientation
The Visionary Motivator	Focuses on engagement and buy-in to energize people	Self-confidence, visionary leadership, change catalyst, adaptability
The Measured Connector	Focuses on sense of purpose and connectivity across the organization, to help change to emerge	Self-control, organizational awareness, building relationships, communication
The Tenacious Implementer	Focuses on projects plans, deadlines, and progress to achieve results	Collaboration, team leadership, influence, conflict management
The Thoughtful Architect	Focuses on frameworks, designs, and the complex fit between strategies and concepts, to ensure that ideas provide a sound basis for change	Initiative, organizational awareness, communication, change catalyst

Source: Cameron and Green (2008).

The following interview aims to illustrate the role that emotional intelligences plays in leadership development.

Per Geisler Hansen (56), Danish, International Expert on Leadership Development, Copenhagen, Denmark.

Per, based on your many years working as an international expert in the area of leadership and personal development, do you think that the concept of emotional intelligence is still important in today's business life? If so, why?

For centuries, a lot of emphasis has been put on certain aspects of intelligence, such as logical reasoning, mathematic skills, spatial skills, and the like. However, when academic performance, professional performance, and personal success in life were examined, it became obvious that intelligence alone could not be used to explain these phenomena. Some of the so-called high potentials—people with extraordinary intellectual skills—seem to be doing poorly in life and business, and researchers started to explore this further. They found that some of these high potentials with great intellectual skills were missing out on opportunities, by behaving and communicating in a way that damaged their chances to succeed.

As was later proven soundly, one of the main factors explaining success in life and business is emotional intelligence: People's ability to manage their emotions, their ability to connect, and communicate with others, their ability to understand their and other people's emotions. Famous academics made the concept popular. Their research proved that people with high emotional intelligence are more successful in life, than people with low emotional intelligence. It is said that emotional intelligence is twice as important as IQ, with regards to career success!

Our experience has shown that introducing the emotional intelligence concept as a topic in leadership workshops is often not successful as people feel it is a difficult topic to tackle. Do you have any ideas why this is so?

The emotional intelligence is often dealt with as an isolated topic in leadership workshops and this is wrong. If I, for example, look at the table of contents of the book you are writing, it is safe to say that every single chapter dealt with, in the context of leadership and personal development is underpinned by emotional intelligence. Do you not agree?

Developing your emotional intelligence is part of a life-long journey—as is leadership and personal development. People who expect a quick fix should not even start thinking about these topics, as this is just not doable.

What kind of experience have you had working with emotional intelligence in executive coaching? Can people actually develop a higher level of emotional intelligence?

Yes, they certainly can. However, increasing your emotional intelligence is not a task for a weekend workshop, but is, rather like Leadership Development, a life-long learning. If you think of emotional intelligence as consisting of self-awareness, self-management, social awareness, and relationship management, it becomes obvious that we can all increase our emotional intelligence.

In my experience, managers participating in leadership development often become increasingly interested and curious the more they work with the softer issues of leadership development—like emotional intelligence. That is also a sign that they seem to widely accept that this is the key to improving their management skills and their performance as managers. This curiosity also increases with age—as self-insight increases. The more you know, the more you want to know.

The first step in any leadership workshop or executive coaching is usually to work towards increasing people's self-awareness and knowledge of themselves. Of course, at a certain stage in people's life, when they have reached a certain management position, they do know their strengths and weaknesses to a certain extent, but that is usually not sufficient if your aim is to achieve excellence in the area of leadership. And again, if you look at the other three categories of emotional intelligence, you can see that there are also many possibilities to work towards increasing your skills and knowledge in these areas. However, there also seem to be components of emotional intelligence that are inherited and more difficult to develop, like empathy, which is a key ingredient for building good relationships. The latest research has identified the neurons in our brain that determine our capability to feel and sense the emotions of others. Thus, some are born with more of these neurons and some are born with fewer, just as some are more skilled at thinking analytically or are better at mathematics. Making a conscious effort to improve and develop ourselves applies to all four areas of emotional intelligence. However, if you do this success is almost guaranteed.

EMERGING THEMES—OPTIMISM AND HAPPINESS

The Emotional Quotient Inventory developed by Bar-On (2000) highlights two areas which have specific links to our general well-being, and are linked to a number of other key concepts in this book. In his definition of emotional intelligence, Bar-On includes an element called General Mood EQ, which is further specified as optimism and happiness. The *Oxford English Dictionary* defines optimism as "hopefulness and confidence about the future or success- ful outcome of something; a tendency to take a favorable or hopeful view." In his book "*Learned Optimism*," Seligman (2006) shows that although there may be some innate disposition to feeling optimistic (or pessimistic), there are strategies that you can develop to help you learn to be more optimistic. There are two sides to being either an optimist or a pessimist: When things are gen- erally going well in your life, this can reinforce your positive world view, which in turn creates a virtuous circle of increased confidence that can create the conditions to operate at a more optimal level. Conversely when things go wrong, one can either see this as a confirmation that the world is a bad place and out to get you or one can see this as a temporary setback, and reframe it as such. It is really the difference between having self-limiting beliefs and an inner resolve to believe, that the future is indeed exciting and positive.

There are a number of simple practices that can develop optimism; these include reframing, being solution focused, and developing a sense of a positive future (see resources section below). "Happiness is a state of mind or feeling characterized by contentment, love, satisfaction, pleasure, or joy" (Cambridge Advanced Learners Dictionary). Seligman (2002) describes three aspects of happiness:

- **The Pleasant Life:** Where one can deal graciously with the past, bring a sense of mindfulness and acceptance to the present, and use strategies of learned optimism to engage with the future;
- **The Good Life:** Which is the embodiment of one's strengths and six notable virtues of wisdom and knowledge, courage, love and human- ity, justice, temperance and spirituality and transcendence; (See also Chapter 1 on Exploring your Strength); and
- **The Meaningful Life:** Which is one where meaning and purpose are actively pursued through attention to creativity, and a sense of giving to the world in the form of altruism.

CONCLUSION

As Goleman demonstrated in his research on effective leadership, many of today's effective managerial and leadership behaviors are underpinned by a heightened emotional intelligence capability. It is not the hard skills alone that result in effective leadership. The differentiating factor between average and highly functioning leaders is emotional intelligence. We have an innate disposition towards some of the EI competencies, but they can all be developed. The emotional intelligence is therefore, a concept of increasing importance for your career advancement. What got you to your current position, may not necessarily take you further. It is likely that your emotional intelligence needs to be honed further. If you are already at an advanced level, ensure you keep it a step ahead of what might be needed. Have a look at the set of activities below to get started.

Your Activities to Enhance Your Emotional Capabilities

Activity 1: Self-assessment of your emotional capabilities.

You may wish to undertake the following self-assessment questionnaire to see how you score in terms of your levels of emotional intelligence. Having read through the competencies and their corresponding traits, rate yourself in terms of how regularly you show each competence in your day-to-day work (1 = Rarely, 2 = Occasionally, 3 = Quite Regularly, 4 = Usually, 5 = Always).

Self-awareness	1	2	3	4	5
Emotional Self-awareness					
Accurate Self-assessment					
Self-confidence					
Self-management	1	2	3	4	5
Self-control					
Trustworthiness					
Conscientiousness					
Adaptability					
Achievement Orientation					
Initiative					
Social Awareness	1	2	3	4	5
Empathy					
Organizational Awareness					
Service Orientation					

(Continued)

Relationship Management	1	2	3	4	5
Visionary Leadership					
Influence					
Developing Others					
Communication					
Change Catalyst					
Conflict Management					
Building Bonds					
Teamwork and Collaboration					
Additional Emotional Capabilities	1	2	3	4	5
Optimism					
Happiness					

Having completed the assessment you may wish to:

- Check out how you rated yourself with one or two close working colleagues, and see whether their perceptions are similar.
- Reflect upon the areas where you consider yourself to be less developed than you would wish. What action do you need to take?
- Take the opportunity to plan specific actions and incorporate them into your personal action plan.

Activity 2: Improve your emotional capabilities.

In some ways, the whole emotional intelligence concept is based on the idea that you have some self-awareness of who you are, and what you are doing. Therefore, it is crucial that you begin to deepen and broaden your sense of self. This activity encourages you to experience all the four dimensions of the emotional intelligence quadrants—self-awareness, self-management, social awareness, and relationship management—and to increase your competence in each, by committing to certain actions. You can use this exercise to either "do finger exercises" at any time of the day or the week, or to use it as a possible resource when you are faced with a difficult situation that you need to handle. There is a full page template at the end of the chapter for photocopying and recording.

Emotional Intelligence Competency	Self-coaching Questions	Implications	Next Action
Self-awareness			
Emotional Self-awareness	What am I thinking? What am I feeling? What am I doing?		
Accurate Self-assessment	What knowledge and skills do I need in this situation?		
Self-confidence	How do I need to frame issues to myself to succeed?		
Self-management			
Self-control	Which of my emotions do I need to be managing better?		
Trustworthiness	How can I maintain honesty and integrity in this situation?		
Conscientiousness	What actions do I need to take to improve this?		
Adaptability	How and when might I need to adapt my style?		
Achievement Orientation	What would an ideal job look like?		
Initiative	How can I be proactive in this situation?		
Social Awareness			
Empathy	How do those affected really feel about this?		
Organizational Awareness	Who are the key stakeholders, and how do I engage with them?		
Service Orientation	How do I deliver a world-class service?		
Relationship Management			
Visionary Leadership	What is my compelling vision and how do I articulate it?		
Influence	Which influencing style do I need to adopt?		
Developing Others	Where and what are the coaching opportunities?		

(Continued)

Emotional Intelligence Competency	Self-coaching Questions	Implications	Next Action
Communication	Who should I be listening to, and what and to whom should I be communicating?		
Change Catalyst	What behaviors and attitudes need to be changed?		
Conflict Management	Where are the tensions and how can I ensure an adequate resolution?		
Building Bonds	How do I deepen my stakeholder relationships?		
Teamwork and Collaboration	Am I investing enough time, effort, and energy in the team?		
Optimism	Am I building on strengths and reframing issues, and problems positively?		
Happiness	Am I spending time on developing the Pleasant Life, Good Life, and Meaningful Life?		

RESOURCES

Much of this personal development book essentially concerns increasing your self-awareness, self-management, social awareness, and relationship management skills. In order to further develop some of these emotional intelligence competencies, we suggest you turn to the relevant chapters:

Emotional Intelligence Competency	Relevant Chapter
Self-awareness	
Emotional Self-awareness	Chapter 4
Accurate Self-assessment	Chapter 1, Chapter 2, Chapter 5
Self-confidence	Chapter 1, Chapter 6
Self-management	
Self-control	Chapter 4, Chapter 5
Trustworthiness	Chapter 3, Chapter 16
Conscientiousness	Chapter 3, Chapter 6
Adaptability	Chapter, 6, Chapter 18, Chapter 19, Chapter 20
Achievement Orientation	Chapter 7
Initiative	Chapter 5, Chapter 6, Chapter 7
Social Awareness	
Empathy	Chapter 12, Chapter 13
Organizational Awareness	Chapter 3, Chapter 14, Chapter 16
Service Orientation	Chapter 8, Chapter 9
Relationship Management	
Visionary Leadership	Chapter 7, Chapter 14, Chapter 15, Chapter 16
Influence	Chapter 8, Chapter 14, Chapter 15, Chapter 16
Developing Others	Chapter 10, Chapter 17
Communication	Chapter 8, Chapter 9, Chapter 10
Change Catalyst	Chapter 7, Chapter, 15
Conflict Management	Chapter 9, Chapter 14
Building Bonds	Chapter 11, Chapter 12, Chapter 13
Teamwork and Collaboration	Chapter 12
Optimism	Chapter 4, Chapter 1, Chapter 5, Chapter 7
Happiness	Chapter 4, Chapter 7

REFERENCES AND FURTHER READING

Arya, A., & Green, M. (2007). *Emerging leadership* London: I&DeA.
Bar-On, R., & Parker, J. (2000). *Handbook of emotional intelligence*. San Francisco: Jossey-Bass.

Bar-On, R. (2006). The Bar-On model of emotional-social intelligence (ESI). *Psicothema, 18*, suppl., 13–25.

Cameron, E., & Green, M. (2008). *Making sense of leadership: Exploring the five key roles used by effective leaders.* London: Kogan Page.

Cooper, R., & Sawaf, A. (1997). *Executive EQ.* London: G. P. Putnam's Sons.

Gardner, H. (1983). *Frames of mind.* New York: Basic Books.

Goleman, D. (1998). *Working with emotional intelligence.* London: Bloomsbury.

Goleman, D. (2004). What makes a leader? *Harvard Business Review, January 2004.*

Goleman, D. (2000). Leadership that gets results. *Harvard Business Review, April 2000.*

Goleman, D., Boyatzis, R., & MeKee, A. (2001). Primal leadership: The hidden driver of great performance. *Harvard Business Review, December 2001.*

Hein, S. (2005). *Introduction to emotional intelligence.* http://eqi.org/history.htm

Hein, S. (2010). *Practical guide to emotions and emotional intelligence–Volume 1,* www.eqi.org.

Levey, J., & Levey M. (2005). *The fine arts of relaxation, concentration and meditation: Ancient Skills for Modern Minds.* USA: Wisdom Publications.

Mayer, J., Salovey, P., & Caruso, D. (2008). Emotional Intelligence: New ability or eclectic traits. *American Psychologist, 63*(6), 503–517.

Payne, W. (1985). *A study of emotion: Developing emotional intelligence,* doctoral thesis.

Seligman, M. (2002). *Authentic happiness.* New York: Free Press.

Seligman, M. (2006). *Learned optimism.* New York: Vintage Books.

Smith, M. (2002). "Howard Gardner and multiple intelligences", The Encyclopedia of Informal Education, downloaded from http://www.infed.org/thinkers/gardner.htm on October 31, 2005.

Thorndike, R. (1920). Intelligence and its uses. *Harper's Magazine, 140*, 227–335.

Wechsler, D. (1940). Non-intellective factors in general intelligence. *Psychological Bulletin, 37*, 444–445.

PART II

SELF-LEADERSHIP

CHAPTER 5

SELF-LEADERSHIP: CIRCLES OF LIFE

Katja Kruckeberg

OBJECTIVE OF THIS CHAPTER

The objective of this chapter is to introduce the six elements of subjective emotional well-being (SEW), and to describe how they influence the generic quality of your life. With the support of the circles of life tool, you will be encouraged to quickly and graphically assess the current status quo of your overall well-being, and to define a more desired outcome. Subsequently, you can transform these insights into a positive program of action that will allow you to lead your life successfully.

INTRODUCTION

Who wants to be led by anyone who is unable to lead his or her own life reasonably successfully? The answer is probably no one. Self-leadership is not only a key ingredient of a life well lived, a life that feels good, a life that we can be proud of, but also a key ingredient of leading others. It seems difficult to follow people who are not good at life itself, and it is also not

Leadership and Personal Development: A Toolbox for the
21ˢᵗ Century Professional, pp. 89–109
Copyright © 2011 by Information Age Publishing

easy to be a good leader if you are not good at life itself. It somehow seems to go hand in hand. Daniel Pinnow–an expert in systemic leadership development will explore this second theme—the question of how self-leadership is intertwined with the leadership of others–further in a later chapter.

For now, we invite you to think about your own life in a new, perhaps more holistic way than you usually do. We invite you to define success, not only with regard to professional success and status, but to carefully take other important areas of your life into consideration as well.

Let us start by looking at this chapter's central concept: your SEW. The SEW is a measure of an individual's perceived level of life's satisfaction and happiness. This thinking has its philosophical roots in Aristotle's concept of *eudaimonia*, the life well lived. Nowadays, concepts that are similar to SEW are frequently assessed in surveys, by asking the individuals how satisfied they are with their own lives. The Mental Health Foundation offers a useful definition of emotional well-being: "A positive sense of well-being, which enables an individual to be able to function in the society and meet the emotional demands of everyday life" (Carpenter, 2010).

Recognizing the subjectivity of well-being is a key to understanding this construct. The SEW reflects the difference between peoples' expectations and their present experience. Humans' ability to adapt to new circumstances is such that life expectations are usually adjusted to lie within the reach of what the individual perceives to be possible. This enables people in difficult circumstances to maintain a reasonable well-being. By using statistical techniques, such as factor analysis, psychologists have shown that a number of factors contribute independently to the overall level of SEW. These factors include professional well-being, financial well-being, values well-being, physical well-being, social well-being, and community well-being. To benefit from a relatively high level of well-being, you need to make sure, that at least your basic needs are met in all areas of your life.

However, when you are busy and all of your energy is focused on a special project, it is easy not to pay enough attention to important areas of your life, and consequently, you may find yourself off balance. And this is okay—you need to have drive and focus if you are going to get things done. Nevertheless, taking this too far can lead to intense stress and poor health. And as a result, your overall well-being will suffer.

If this resonates with you, be assured that this is a very common scenario for high-achievers, and any ambitious people striving for success. Sometimes, you probably just need to keep your head fully in the game to achieve pockets of excellence in your career or in other areas of your life. However, if you strive for long-term success and a life well lived, you need to have a more holistic approach to life.

To bring things back into balance, you have to take a helicopter view and examine yourself systematically at least once in a while. This is where the circles of life tool can help you. It supports you to, in turn, take six important areas of your life into consideration and assess what is off balance. This will allow you to make a few smart decisions about how to move on the best with your life.

THE CIRCLES OF LIFE

In the following, we will introduce the six elements of the circles of life tool, describe its main characteristics, and show how they influence your perceived level of happiness with your life: your SEW. At this point, we have to stress that this tool is relevant mainly for people with a reasonable level of emotional and psychological health. It does not aim to explain conditions like depression or other severe psychological and emotional health problems, nor do we claim that this instrument can help you to heal such conditions.

Also, please keep in mind that nobody has to strive toward perfection in these six, central areas of life. This tool should only help you to think more systematically about your life to bring you into the position to initiate changes in a thoughtful and deliberate manner. However, due to our different life interests, personality types, values, and so forth, all of us will place a different importance to these areas, which is perfectly fine. Positive changes in one area may produce positive ripple effects in other areas, as all circles of life are highly inter-connected as illustrated in the Fig. 5.1. If you are, for

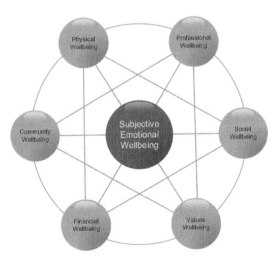

Figure 5.1. Circles of Life

example fully content with your professional, social, and community life, you might get away with some bad eating habits and a low or non-existing level of exercise, as these strong areas of your life may compensate for investing less time and energy in another area of your life. As human beings we are not perfect nor should we strive to be. Thus, while reading through the following chapters look how the information offered resonates with you, so that you can assess afterward the status quo of your circles of life from your individual perspective.

PROFESSIONAL WELL-BEING

If you examine how you spend the waking hours of your life, you will probably notice that you invest the majority of this precious time at work, which is very common for people between 18 and 65. Thus, how you experience this time is of the utmost importance. A common research finding is that job satisfaction is correlated with life satisfaction. This correlation is reciprocal, meaning people who are satisfied with life tend to be satisfied with their job, and people who are satisfied with their job tend to be satisfied with life. Evidence from a variety of sources shows that people's perceptions of how well they are functioning in a working context, and the extent to which they perceive their job-related activities as having meaning, are central to an overall sense of well-being (Seligman, 2002).

If you are truly unhappy with your job, this will significantly affect your overall well-being. Thus, the question is: What can you do if you think there is room for improvement, regarding your satisfaction with your overall job situation? What can you do to maximize your professional well-being? Based on professional career specialists' research (Dawis, 1992) and our own experience, we offer the following seven recommendations:

1. The first recommendation is to increase your self-awareness and to get to know yourself better. If you have worked your way carefully through the first chapters of this book, you now know more about your strengths, your personality, and the values you hold dear in life. Now, continue to consider the kind of work-related activities you are most attracted to. Be clear, about what you expect from or require of a job.

2. Explore different ways forward in your career—start thinking about alternatives. During each leadership and management transition ask yourself if where you are heading, is actually in line with your

overall idea of a life well lived. Remember this life is not a rehearsal. We only have one shot at living a good life.

3. Consider working with an executive coach to explore the possibilities for your further development. Working with a coach can be an eye-opener and a source of motivation, which is sometimes needed in times of personal change and development.

4. Check and manage your expectations. Overall job satisfaction is a trade-off. Even the best jobs in the world usually include aspects that might be irritating or annoying.

5. Severe job dissatisfaction should not be tolerated for long! Research has unequivocally established that severe job dissatisfaction leads to anxiety, tension, interpersonal problems, and even depression in the long run. Thus, it is important to seek a solution if your job is a strain on you, rather than being a source of inspiration.

6. Examine the kind of work you are doing separately from the conditions of work (pay, supervisor, co-workers, company, and physical working conditions). If you are becoming increasingly discontent with the kind of work you are doing, explore new options. If you are discontent with the conditions of work, you could set matters right by re-negotiating these with your boss or your colleagues, or by changing your job.

7. Attend networking events with professionals in your field. Networking (see Chapter 11 on networking) is a great way to get exposure, to practice presenting your unique professional interests, and to refine them.

You can find the seeds for a passionate professional life within you and your working life experience. The next steps are to give this area of your life ongoing attention, and to even make unconventional decisions in order to bring these seeds to fruition.

SOCIAL WELL-BEING

Extensive research has shown that the quality of interactions with others influences all aspects of health and well-being. For example, it is well known that social isolation is strongly associated with illness, while social support has a strong positive relationship with physical and mental health, and healthy lifestyle. Keyes (1998), who intensively investigated the relationship between social well-being and overall life satisfaction, proposes five dimensions of social well-being: social integration, social contribution, social coherence, social actualization, and social acceptance. Building on these insights, you will now find questions that can help you to reflect upon the quality of your social well-being.

Social Integration

- How satisfied are you with your relationship with your partner?
- How satisfied are you with your relationships with your immediate family?
- Would you like to have more/stronger relationships with other people? If so, with whom?

Social Contribution

- How often did you help other people in the past 6 months?
- If you help someone, do you expect help in return?

Social Coherence

- Do you feel part of a larger network of people?
- Do you feel that you really belong to these networks?
- Do they represent who you are?

Social Actualization

- To what extent do you feel that you get the recognition you deserve for what you do? (At work, at home, outside the home, in your leisure activities, and so forth.)

Social Acceptance

- To what extent do you feel that people treat you with respect?
- To what extent do you feel that people treat you unfairly?

Physical Well-being

Physical well-being is one of the most important parts of the circles of life tool, as it strongly influences how you experience your life as a whole. In previous years, physical well-being was commonly described as the absence of illness. However, this definition does not take into consideration that the physical well-being concept is highly subjective, nor does it consider the human ability to adapt to new circumstances. Somebody in a wheelchair, for example, can have much greater physical well-being if he or she has adjusted well to this situation, than somebody who has not. What you consider physically fit, others may not. You may be proud of your daily 5 km run, but professional endurance athletes would not consider this an achievement.

To take this aspect into consideration, we define physical well-being as a subjective measure of the body's ability to function efficiently and effectively in the chosen field of work and leisure activities, and to feel healthy and energetic enough to carry out the day's activities, without suffering undue fatigue. According to current research, physical well-being is most enhanced by regular exercises, good nutrition, good quality sleep, and relaxation. (see Fig. 5.2)

Now let us have a look at how you approach each of these areas of your physical well-being, to improve your overall fitness level.

Quality Sleep

If you are totally satisfied with the quality of your sleep, you might as well skip this part and continue reading about healthy nutrition in the following part of this chapter. However, if you are one of the millions of people who suffer from a sleep disorder, take some time to read the following recommendations on how to improve the quality and the quantity of your sleep.

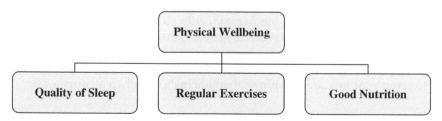

Figure 5.2. Components of Physical Wellbeing

Deciding to stick to a regular sleep schedule is the first step to take if you have serious sleeping problems. If your bedtime fluctuates greatly, your biological clock is probably negatively affected. An activity you could undertake to set things right is to introduce a regular schedule so that the brain and your body know what is expected of them. This is a kind of conditioning and works extremely well. You will experience the positive impact within a matter of days and weeks.

Another activity that you could undertake is to establish a bedtime routine. The habit of following a certain pattern of events every night before you go to bed will let your brain and body know that it is time for sleep. A soothing ritual lets you blank out your daily worries, and helps you to ease into sleeping mode. For some people this means listening to a certain kind of music, while for others it might mean taking a shower at the same time each evening.

Activities that excite you too much and over-stimulate your brain should be avoided 2–3 hours before you go to bed. Are you very sure that watching certain movies or surfing the Internet does not prevent you from easing into sleeping mode?

Also start establishing the right eating habits. Try to stop eating at least 2 hours before you want to go to sleep. There are certain foods that should be avoided altogether in the evening if you have a sleeping disorder or do not feel refreshed throughout the day: no fatty, sugary food. Eating fresh fruits and vegetables, drinking coffee and alcohol will also contribute to disturb your sleep patterns.

In order to reduce the amount of sleep you need per night, we recommend checking out your breathing patterns. Go to the recommended resources at the end of this chapter, and check out the literature and other materials on the Buteyko breathing method invented by a Russian scientist, to prepare the Russian astronauts for short periods of sleep during their stay in the outer space.

Without sufficient quality of sleep you will never be able to tap into your full well-being potential. Thus, if you are serious about improving your overall well-being, you first need to move good quality sleep to the top of your agenda if you are not doing well in this area, and re-organize all of your other priorities. When you start replacing unhealthy sleep habits with a solid sleep schedule, you will find that your energy and enthusiasm will increase on an almost daily basis. Personal change is of course, never easy and overcoming sleeping disorders or day-tiredness will take time and a lot of self-control. However, your new sense of physical well-being will make it all worthwhile.

Good Nutrition

Good nutrition is extremely important for almost every aspect of your physical well-being. It influences your skin, your brain, all of your organs, and your immune system. Without good nutrition you are probably unable to enjoy your full physical well-being potential. A good nutrition provides the body with all the micro- and macro-nutrients it requires. If these nutrients are not correctly balanced, your body will adapt and suffer unwanted long-term damage.

What is a good nutritional balance? Scientists are still debating over this and will probably continue to do so. There are so many different "schools" and fads, that it becomes hard not be overwhelmed. Some suggest watching blood sugar levels, others warn of carbohydrates, others in turn suggest not combining proteins and carbohydrates as different digestive juices are required. Some in turn warn not to cause negative body chemistry by worrying too much, and instead merely focus on balanced meals. In the meanwhile, we have to make our choices based on our current knowledge.

One way of making sure that you eat healthily is to balance your food in keeping with the Harvard Healthy Eating Pyramid, which is a simple, trustworthy guide to choosing a healthy diet. It recommends eating sparingly from the top level of the pyramid: red meat and sugar. At the second highest level, you find dairy products from which you should not eat more than one to two servings per day. On the next level, you find white rice, bread, pasta, potatoes, sugary drinks, and sweets and salt, from which you should also not eat more than two or three servings. Then come nuts, beans, tofu, fish, poultry, and eggs, which you can use to enrich your diet. And the group from which you should eat the most contains fruit, vegetables, whole grains, and healthy oils. At the bottom of the pyramid, you find the recommendation to exercise daily, and to control your weight regularly (see Fig. 5.3).

For more information about The Healthy Eating Pyramid, please see *The Nutrition Source*, by the Department of Nutrition at Harvard School of Public Health (http://www.thenutritionsource.org), and *Eat, Drink, and Be Healthy*, by Walter C., Willett, M. D., and Patrick J. Skerrett (2005).

Good nutrition is definitely one of the cornerstones of physical well-being. However, we believe that there is no "one size fits all" answer when it comes to nutrition, and that the answers will vary across different cultures.

The important point is that you acknowledge the importance of this topic when reflecting on you circles of life. If you identify this part of your physical well-being as a potential obstacle to your overall well-being, it is definitely time to do something about it. Bad nutrition can make you feel unhealthy very quickly, as demonstrated in the documentary nominated for an Academy award, "Super Size Me" (2004), in which a healthy young man went on an extreme McDonald diet for a month. Not only was his physical health at seriously risk after a month–his liver and heart were no longer functioning normally, and the doctors advised him to stop the diet immediately—but his psychological health was also suffering. He felt highly addicted to eating and started suffering mood dips after every

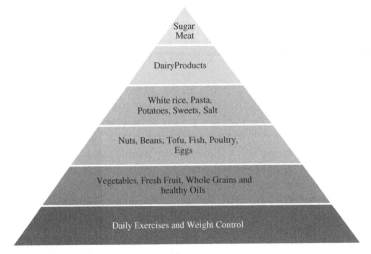

Figure 5.3. The healthy eating pyramid

meal. Psychologically, he felt better only while eating, but physically he felt drained out all the time. Although he had been very sporty and energetic before he started the diet, he felt in a very poor physical state after 3 weeks, with insufficient energy to fulfil his day-to-day tasks.

So, if you are unsure about your current nutrition and how it affects you start observing yourself. Do you actually feel that the food you are consuming makes you feel good? Is it an energy resource, or a drain on your physical and psychological health? If the latter, we recommend you move this topic to the center of your short-term development goals, as it might also prevent you from achieving your goals in other areas of your life. Visit a doctor to discuss this topic, go to a library and do some relevant reading, or talk to friends who know about good nutrition. But do not let this situation go unsolved for too long. Nutrition should support, not prevent you from achieving your goals!

Regular Exercises

There are different kind of exercises that build up your endurance capabilities, your overall strength, and your flexibility. In the following, you find short descriptions of these different areas of physical fitness training.

Cardiovascular endurance comes from aerobic exercise. The goal is to build cardiovascular efficiency, which is your heart's ability to pump blood through your body. Although the heart is a muscle, this does not mean that it can be exercised directly, like most of your other muscles. The only way to train it is through exercising the large muscle groups, particularly your leg and arm muscles. That is why exercises like swimming, nordic walking, biking, cross-country skiing, and jogging are so powerful.

Flexibility training refers to developing a wide range of movement in a series of joints. Flexibility training has long been underestimated, and perhaps overlooked by health-care professionals. The quality of life is considerably enhanced by improving and maintaining a good range of motion in the joints. Flexibility can be increased by stretching exercises and helps the muscles to relax, which helps the body to rest and achieve high-quality sleep.

The purpose of **strength training** is to build physical strength and endurance. When properly performed, strength training can provide significant functional benefits and improvement, in overall health and wellbeing. Training commonly uses the technique of progressively increasing the muscles' force output through incremental increases in weight, elastic tension, or other resistance, and uses a variety of exercises and types of training equipment, to target specific muscle groups. Strength training is primarily an anaerobic activity (De Mello, 2004).

According to the present state of scientific knowledge, to promote and maintain physical wellbeing and health adults need moderate-intensity aerobic activity for a minimum of 30 min on two days each week. In addition adults will benefit from performing activities that increase muscular strength for a minimum of 20 minutes on two days each week focusing on the core muscles (back muscles and stomach muscles). And last but not least, adults should perform activities that maintain flexibility for a minimum of 10 minutes on two days each week. This recommended amount of activity is in addition to routine activities of daily living (e.g., shopping, walking around in the office, etc.). Thus, to promote your overall physical wellbeing you need to invest 2 hours a week. That is not too much to ask for, is it?

FINANCIAL WELL-BEING

Financial well-being is about managing your economic life effectively. Financial well-being is about having the financial means to enjoy a gratifying lifestyle achieved through your ability to manage your finances in a smart way, which is (almost) independent of the income you generate.

> "*People with high financial well-being manage their personal finances well and spend their money wisely. They buy experiences instead of just material possessions, and they give to others instead of always spending on themselves. At a basic level, they are satisfied with their overall standard of living. Their successful strategies result in financial security, which eliminates daily stress and worry because of debt. This financial security allows them to do what they want to do, when they want to do it. They have the freedom to spend more time, with the people they like to be around.*" Rath (2010, p. 154).

We cannot of course, provide you with a thorough guide on how to handle your finances. When it comes to financial well-being however, we have made the following observations: From a certain point onward, financial well-being does not seem to correlate significantly, with the level of income people generate. Only when people fall behind a certain wage minimum is the relationship between financial well-being and the level of income or money available clearly proven.

However, people with high financial well-being seem to have three factors in common:

1. **People with high financial well-being handle their finances consciously by following the very basic economic principle of not spending more money than they earn.** Even if you are a person with an emergent approach to life, having a pretty good idea of your finances is advisable. You should, at least, develop a realistic budget for the short- and long-term, so that you know what you need to spend on necessities and what you will have left over for the fun stuff. Look at the timing of when bills are due and make sure your cash-flow meets those bills. Budget some fun money each month and once it is gone, the fun has to be free. Keep track of your spending sensibly, and last but not the least, borrow sensibly. Remember, any money you borrow now must be repaid later, and—even more important—any money borrowed will decrease your overall level of happiness if you have to worry about repaying it.

2. **People with high financial well-being make smart decisions regarding the added value that each pursuit contributes to their overall emotional well-being.** If for example, it is just within your financial reach to buy a Porsche—which would, by the way, make you very happy as you really love this car—then you should ask yourself the question: Is it necessary to buy a new Porsche, or would a 3-year-old Porsche do as well? How much more value would a new Porsche add to your overall emotional well-being, than a 3-year-old one? The answer is probably not very much more, but a new Porsche will cost twice as much as the 3-year-old one!

3. **People with high financial well-being spend money on buying experiences rather than material things.** They also tend to spend money on others and not just on themselves. A good life can also be regarded as the sum of the good moments you have enjoyed in life. If you look at it this way, this third point becomes rather obvious. So start thinking about how you can spend your money most wisely, by rather pursuing many good moments.

Another, perhaps little bit more philosophical approach to thinking about your finances is to consider that most people are not happier, because they have more money. We all know stories of people who won in the lottery but after 5 years are not reported to have a higher perceived well-being, than before. Ask yourself what you find important before you start focusing too much on just increasing your income to live a happier life. What is it that really matters to you? Usually, there are other values that are more important than finances. Therefore, even if you really want to boost your financial well-being, we recommend that you first assess whether your professional well-being, your social well-being and your physical well-being are thriving. It is commonly agreed upon and research evidence widely supports the suggestion, that financial well-being has a much smaller influence on our overall subjective emotional well-being than is generally believed.

COMMUNITY WELL-BEING

Community well-being is a concept that refers to an *optimal quality of healthy community life*. From an individual perspective, it is about the sense of involvement that you feel with the area in which you live. Rath (2005) and his research team at Gallup organization describe individual community well-being as follows:

> *"Community well-being starts with some of the basics. While you might not think about the quality of the water you drink or the air you breathe every day, a lack of security about these fundamental needs can cause a significant concern over time. Feeling safe walking alone at night in your neighborhood and having confidence that you would not be harmed or assaulted is another primary necessity. [...] While the things that make a community perfect will be different for everyone, people use common themes to describe ideal communities. One of the most important factors is aesthetics [....]. Another key differentiator is social offerings or places where people can meet, spend time with their friends, and enjoy the nightlife. The third quality that distinguishes the near-perfect communities from the rest is a general openness to all types of people, regardless of race, heritage, age, or sexual orientation. However, just living in the right place is unlikely to create thriving community well-being. This requires active involvement in community groups or organizations. [...] Thriving community well-being is about what we do, to give back to our community."* Rath (2010, p. 93–95).

Based on Gallup's research and our own observation, it is fair to say that community well-being has a major impact on people's overall perceived level of emotional well-being. This is interesting, as this concept is not as well known as the others, and probably does not come to mind initially, when reflecting on one's satisfaction with life. However, if you look at it from a historical point of view, this might not be as surprising. We know that human beings have always lived in social settings, and have been a part of close social networks over thousands of years. The degree of individualization in our societies is still very new, and our biological needs have not yet adapted to this new situation. It has been clearly proven that our hormone systems cannot work efficiently under conditions of social isolation and our level of productivity drops significantly. Thus, being part of a good community and being actively engaged in it, provides us with an environment for which human beings were designed.

By subsequently taking Gallup's research and our idea of community well-being into consideration, we can refer to the following factors that contribute to this concept:

1. Security
2. Fresh air, water, and—level of pollution
3. Green areas (parks, forests, and so forth)
4. The noise level
5. The aesthetics of the surroundings
6. The recreational/cultural/social offerings
7. The infrastructure
8. Schools and other educational institutions
9. Our level of engagement

As you can see, factors one to eight describe the characteristics of the community itself. Most of us probably share a common striving for a certain level of security and trust in the environment. For a healthy life we also need fresh air, clean water, and a non-polluted environment.

To what extent factors three to eight matter to us depends on our individual needs, values, and preferences, which illustrates that community well-being is a highly subjective concept, and will differ greatly from person to person.

If you are buying a house or renting an apartment, you should look out for the right community as well as the right characteristics for your house. If your finances do not allow you to have it all, and then decide very carefully on a healthy compromise.

However, if you look at the 9th factor contributing to community well-being, you notice quickly that this factor has little to do with the community's external characteristics, but rather with your personal level of engagement.

Community well-being is largely about pro-social behavior which is specifically shown when you integrate yourself into your immediate environment. Broad evidence shows that by building the social capital actively, your overall well-being will improve significantly (Helliwell, 2005). An appropriate slogan could be: well-being through well-doing.

And if you think of it, this is probably not so far removed from your experiences. Many people observe that their well-being significantly improves when they are engaged in helping others (Luks, 2001). Ninety-five percent of those surveyed indicated, that helping other people, and doing voluntary work on a regular basis gives them a warm feeling and increased energy. This is also known as the "helpers' high," which is a euphoric feeling, followed by a longer period of calm experienced after performing a kind act, and has been well researched. Doing good, brings great satisfaction and pleasure to the giver.

Many of you probably care a lot about your immediate community. However, even if your value system places a high value on community activities, appropriate activities may not be a part of your life. This is very natural as there is always a gap between someone's values and lived values due to the many demands we face. The following questions help you to assess the aspects of your lived pro-social behavior:

- To what extent do you feel that you are engaged in the area you live in?
- Do you feel close to the people in your local area?
- How often do you contribute to your community (the school or kindergarten that your children attend, any other institutions, street events, and so forth)?

If you notice that you are not as engaged in your community as you would like to be, then start thinking of ways to change this in the near future. And ask yourself: What can be better than increasing your level of happiness, by increasing other people's happiness too? It sounds a bit naive, but it actually works.

VALUES WELL-BEING

Much research has shown that overall life satisfaction and emotional well-being is strongly related to living in harmony with one's most important values, and having a sense of meaning or purpose in life (Seligman, 2002). Since we regard this as the foundation of any well-lived life, we have dedicated a whole chapter to this topic to support you in reflecting on the guiding values of your life, and on the possibilities to integrate these values into your daily activities. In order to assess and reflect on your values and belief systems and to write your personal value statement, revisit Chapter 3 on personal and organizational values, which Dr. Helen Stride, a leading expert on this topic, contributed.

CASE STUDY 1

French Executive Producer on the Circles of Life Tool

Sophie, (41) French, Marketing Director, Consumer Good Company, Paris, France.

I do this exercise once a year!

I was introduced to the circles of life tool by my company, which sponsored a coach 3 years ago, and I was immediately taken by it. Since then, I devote a full day in January to undertake this very valuable reflection exercise. I also recommend it to everyone I know. I found it particularly interesting that some of the areas that I cared about most in my life were simultaneously the areas with which I was the most discontent, and on which I spent the least amount of energy. I was very dissatisfied with my level of physical well-being and my social life. My poor state of health—I was not ill, just not feeling well—diminished my level of satisfaction with all the other areas as well. I therefore worked on this circle first. I made it a top priority to become fitter and to just feel better physically throughout 2007. First I thought it was time consuming, but these newly adopted sets of behavior have now become second nature. I eat slightly differently, have established some bedtime routine, and do exercises twice a week (some running and some exercises), which is all it took. It is fair to say that I have not felt so well in 10 years. I then bravely attacked the second circle in 2008—equally successfully. I did quite a few things in this area to feel more connected to the people I really like. Interestingly, when I started to work on this circle, I focused strongly on my private relationships, but my new attitude—I call it to give more than you take attitude—quickly spilled over to my working relationships, which was great. The last 2 years I have been doing minor refurbishment work, as my life is running quite well at the moment. I focused a lot on re-organizing my working life by working more efficiently. Next year however, is dedicated to a value that I have neglected for too long: adventure! I am curious to know what is going to happen next. The most interesting part of working with this tool is that I have realized how much I can influence the direction of my life. I have to steer my life in a direction that I want, and I now know how much each area of my life impacts on others–both positively and negatively.

CONCLUSION

When it comes to your overall well-being, it is argued that the whole is greater than the sum of the parts, which means for example, that a positive change in one area will probably result in positive changes in other areas as well. A clearer understanding of the inter-relationship between various facets of well-being, offers an opportunity for improved analysis of your life's causes and effects, and the chance to have a greater impact on interventions. Pay attention to the possible synergy effects!

The circle of well-being is a great tool to help you improve your life's balance. It helps you to quickly and graphically identify the areas in your life to which you want to devote more energy, and helps you understand where you might want to cut back. The challenge is to transform this knowledge and your desire for a more balanced life, into a positive program of action.

Your Activities for Reflecting on Your Circles of Life

Activity 1: Reflect on your circles of life.

The approach suggested in this book assumes that you will be happy and fulfilled if you can find the right, individual, well-being balance in the different areas of your life. This does not mean that all of these areas should be equally important to you, or that you should dedicate equal amount of attention and energy to them. It just means that each circle's basic needs must at least be met, as this is the pre-requisite for having an overall, relatively high level of emotional well-being. The rest is up to your personal liking, values, and preferences.

Taking into consideration your reflection on the six main aspects of well-being, ask yourself: How satisfied am I with each area of my life on a scale of 0 (low) to 5 (high)? We suggest, you fill the outcome of this thought process into the Fig. 5.4 .

Figure 5.4. Circles of Life: Self-Assessment

Now have a look at your circle of well-being. Does it look and feel balanced? What thoughts are crossing your mind?

_____

_____

_____

Activity 2: Desired level of satisfaction with your circles of life in 1 year's time.

Now, think 1 year ahead. What would be a desired score for each area of your life at that time? A balanced life does not mean getting five in each life area; some areas need more attention and focus than others, at any one time. And inevitably, you will need to make choices and compromises, as your time and energy are not unlimited!

Revisit your circles of life and plot the desired scores around your life wheel too. Remember to be optimistic, but simultaneously realistic.

Activity 3: Gap analysis of the status quo
and desired outcome.

Now you have a visual representation of your current life balance and
your desired life balance. What are the gaps? What areas would you
like to pay more attention to?

_____

_____

_____

_____

And remember that gaps can go both ways. There are certainly areas
that are not getting as much attention as you would like to give. However, there may also be areas where you are putting in more effort
than you would ideally like to. These areas are sapping energy and
enthusiasm that may be better directed elsewhere.

Activity 4: Formulating an action plan.

Once you have identified the areas that need attention, it is time to
plan the actions needed to work on regaining a balance. Starting
with the neglected areas, what do you need to start doing to regain a
balance? Make a commitment to these actions by writing them
down.

_____

_____

Now start thinking about the areas you are particularly pleased with. Are you investing too much time and energy in this area? Could you maintain your satisfaction with these areas of your life, if you paid them less attention? What will you stop doing? What will you re-prioritize? What will you delegate? Make a definite commitment to these actions by writing them down.

RECOMMENDED VIDEO LINKS

How to sleep well using the Buteyko breathing method:
http://www.5min.com/Video/How-to-sleep-well-145258543

How to use the Buteyko breathing method:
http://www.5min.com/Video/How-to-Use-the-Buteyko-breathing-method-145258239

RECOMMENDED WEBSITE

Our health is truly dependent on the quality and quantity of the water we drink. Dr. B's pioneering work shows that Unintentional Chronic Dehydration (UCD) contributes to and even produces pain and many degenerative diseases that can be prevented and treated by increasing water intake on a regular basis. For more information visit: http://www.watercure.com

On this website you will find recommendations how to improve your quality of sleep:
http://www.better-sleep-better-life.com/healthy-sleep-habits.html

If you are interested in finding out how people's subjective level of well-being differs around the globe, visit the following website: http://www.nationalaccountsofwellbeing.org/explore/indicators/zsocial

If you are interested in career coaching, visit the following website: http://www.careerkey.org/asp/getting_started.html

REFERENCES

Carpenter, B. (2010). http://www.ssatnet.net/events/inetinternationalconference/speakers/professorbarrycarpenter/emotionalwellbeing.aspx. Retrieved January 11, 2011.

Dawis, R. (1992). Job satisfaction. In L. Jones (Ed.), *Encyclopedia of career change and work issues* (pp. 142–143). Phoenix: The Oryx Press.

De Mello Meirelles, C., & Gomes, P. (2004). Acute effects of resistance exercise on energy expenditure: revisiting the impact of the training variables. *Rev. Bras. Med. Esporte. 10,* 131–138.

Helliwell, John F., & Putnam, R. D. (2005). "The social context of well-being." In A. Huppert, N. Baylis, & B. Keverne (Eds.), *The Science of Well-Being* (pp. 435–459). Oxford: Oxford University Press. http://simple.wikipedia.org/wiki/Flexibility_training. Retrieved January 10, 2011.

Keyes, C., & L. Lee (1998). Social Well Being. *Social Psychology Quarterly.* Washington: American Sociological Association.

Luks, A., & Payne, A. (2001). *The Healing Power of Doing Good–The Health and Spiritual Benefits of Helping Others*. New York: iUniverse.com..

Rath, T. (2005). *How Full Is Your Bucket? Positive Strategies for Work and Life*. NY: Gallup Press.

Rath, T. (2010). *Wellbeing: The Five Essentials Elements*. New York: Gallup Press.

Seligman, M. (2002). *Authentic Happiness: Using the New Positive Psychology to Realize Your Potential for Lasting Fulfillment*. New York: Free Press.

Willett, W., & Skerrett, P. (2005). *Eat, Drink, and Be Healthy*. NY: Free Press.

CHAPTER 6

SELF-COACHING AND LEARNING

Chris Dalton

OBJECTIVE OF THIS CHAPTER

The aim of this chapter is to consider ways in which you can take responsibility for self-development and learning. By examining some of the principles that underpin coaching and considering what it means to develop an identity and good habits as a learner, you can go about setting development goals and managing the first steps in directing your learning.

INTRODUCTION

A lot of who we are is established early in life, and we seem to function perfectly smoothly without needing to acknowledge or reflect on our identities. However, when we come back to learning later in life, with all the experience we have gained, it pays to pause and reconsider the ways in which we construct our identity. Most of us would agree with the idea that we are social

---

Leadership and Personal Development: A Toolbox for the 21st Century Professional, pp. 111–124
Copyright © 2011 by Information Age Publishing
All rights of reproduction in any form reserved.

animals, and that depending on the situation, we may take on a spectrum of identities—parent, colleague, spouse, consultant, friend, commuter, and so on. You could say that as a learner you have an identity too. Is this identity private, controlled, and determined by you, or is it public, formed, and defined by the world around you? Each viewpoint reflects a differing belief, and before you plan a change, you will be in a much stronger position if you first examine the rules you have for yourself about how you live, and what has brought you to a point where you are considering a change.

This chapter offers some thoughts on adult learning and identity, and prepares you for coaching yourself in your learning and development. First it suggests that you spend some time understanding your learner identity by looking at the self-coaching process. Here, the term "learner identity" refers to the ways in which you understand, as a learner, your relationship to the social world, how that is constructed over time and space, and how it might evolve in the future. Then you will examine how to generate your development goals, feedback, and reflection, as part of your personal development planning (PDP). The latter is a structured and supported process undertaken by the learners to reflect upon their learning, performance or achievement, and to plan for their personal, educational, and career oriented development.

The definition above captures several key features of PDP in today's world. The most common approach to managerial development in the recent years has been to see it as a fairly linear process involving the identification of appropriate competences, skills and experiences, and the subsequent modification (using reflection) of behaviors for change at a personal level. In a mechanistic and process-driven view of the world, this seems to make sense. However, new research suggests that a consideration for the individual's well-being and contexts within which he or she finds himself or herself (organization, community, society, and so forth), which are non-linear and holistic, is often missing from this.

COACHING—POSITIVE INTENT AND ASKING THE RIGHT QUESTIONS

Coaching is an intentioned process of helping people by placing them and their needs at the centre of attention and inquiry. To do so, coaches need to deliberately put aside their own wishes and agenda, and explore a new perspective. The coach may use a toolkit of varied skills and devices to this end, but the key requirement in all coaching is the attitude of positive intent the genuine desire to help. This might seem self-evident when you are coaching yourself. After all, who would want to sabotage his/her own learning?

However, learning and change in adulthood often involve carefully examining and even questioning long-held assumptions about ourselves and our beliefs, that we so easily take for granted. And once we have uncovered these, changing such long-held positions can require taking risks and dealing with loss.

Joseph O'Connor (2004), a top coach clarifies that our beliefs are indeed rules about life, which can be empowering or limiting. Behind every limiting belief is a positive intent. We hold on to them for so long because of that. Part of your personal development will be identifying and finding ways to replace temporary, limiting beliefs with permanent, empowering ones.

At the heart of coaching and learning are questions. In coaching, being able to frame questions that open the possibility for new ways of thinking, is crucial. Sometimes these are the difficult ones to ask, but such questions can get to the heart of the matter because they are hard, or have never been asked, and therefore they make you stop and think. You may be able to recall events from your experience where learning was triggered or a problem reframed, by someone just asking the right question.

Self-coaching

Working with a coach is a way of achieving a fresh perspective from another person, on an important issue. When coaching yourself, you are of course, the only one in the equation. There are however, plenty of principles, tools and techniques employed by executive coaches that you can use to powerful effect for yourself.

A coaching intervention always begins in the middle of something, not at the beginning. Learning feels episodic, either because it comes in short, planned projects, or because we must react to something unplanned that suddenly happens. But learning is always part of a wider context. For example, it is likely that there is a story behind your decision to be reading this, and asking yourself the following basic coaching question is an excellent place to start:

What has brought you here?

Establishing your answer to this now, before you go any further, will increase the chances that whatever you do next will succeed. The story you have, the emotions and attitudes that you bring—in short, the person you are—all result from very complex and well-established patterns, which influence how you behave in the world. At the heart of this, often taken for granted, are your beliefs and the values they are based on.

The Role of Beliefs in Learning

A belief is a guiding principle for action and behavior, and most beliefs are there to promote and protect values. Usually established early in your development, values are moral principles and are basic to your identity. Beliefs are habitual and usually, only rarely questioned. Beliefs serve as short-cuts that allow us to act efficiently in our lives. A useful presupposition for learning is that all your beliefs, even the ones which are self-limiting ("I am not good at remembering names" is a typical example) are there for a positive reason. When you know what those are, it becomes possible to change them.

A good way to kick off a reflective learning process is by examining your own self-beliefs, about how you are or who you are. For example, you surely have a sense of self, but where do you think that identity comes from?

- Is identity defined by what sets you *apart* from other people, or by what you have in *common* with them?
- Is self-learning equal to the *"revealing"* of a potential, attributes, and qualities that were always there? Or, is the person you are, the emergent product of your continuous social interaction, and does learning about yourself equal *"inventing"* a story with others as you go along?

The Fig. 6.1 contrasts these two sets of beliefs about identity and learning, and gives four orientations to personal development. You may feel an affinity to one or, on reflection, that the truth is a combination. In any case, the action of asking the question will allow you to think about beliefs you hold, and values you base those beliefs on.

Adults and Learning

How old were you when you became an adult? What does being an adult mean to you? Is there an end-purpose to adult life? Think about the important development tasks or goals you have in your life, and consider whether they arise from any one of the following drivers:

- Your biological maturity.
- Your role in a society grouping (family, community, nation, and so forth).
- Personal choice.

A common way of understanding these and other questions has been by looking at life in terms of stages. For example, Erik Erikson's (1994)

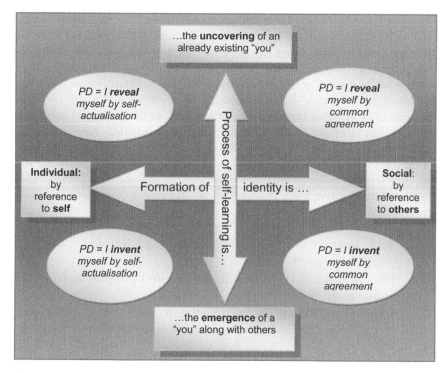

Figure 6.1. Four Orientations in Personal Development (PD)

eight-stage model of development presented development as cumulative stages throughout life, each stage containing a task, or crisis that must be resolved for healthy progression to the next. The early and middle adulthood occupy the 6th and 7th stages. Love is the main theme in stage 6, from about 20 years onward, when the choice is between *intimacy*—compromise with, and commitment to another person—and isolation—if that intimacy threatens the hard-won independence and identity of adolescence. The 7th stage Erikson labelled as "maturity", from age 35–65, where the crisis is between *"generativity";*–caring about what you will leave for the next generation—and *"stagnation";*—turning the same virtue of care inward and focusing on the self at the expense of others. In many societies, mid-life is typically a period of transition from busy building and acquisition to reflection and assessment. For all its challenges, becoming a learner again at a later stage in life can therefore also be very rewarding.

Learning

Some theories favor the idea that learning as an adult is about what changes as you mature, while others concentrate on what stays constant.

For most of us, adulthood is a complex interplay of the two. So how you deal with upheaval and stress in your adult life and how you make sense of what happens to you in your story are the real starting points for learning in personal development. Both are very closely linked to learning.

How we learn has occupied philosophers for thousands and scientists for hundreds of years. Not surprisingly then, there are many theories and speculation about learning in adult life. Most definitions of learning, whether they refer to it as a process, a product, or a function, have in common the idea of change or transformation as a result of experience. Experiential learning is therefore, often seen as an essential part of learning for managers.

When adults learn, the following can be assumed according to Malcolm Knowles:

1. Adult learners need to know **why** they are learning something before they undertake it.
2. They find it crucial to be self-directed and responsible for their decisions about their learning.
3. They can and will use their experience in their learning and change even if that experience contains some beliefs which are very hard to shift.
4. They learn when they need to cope with life situations, or overcome real problems. The value of learning is judged by how it can be immediately applied.
5. Over time, the motivation to learn comes increasingly from within and is done for its intrinsic value.

These are all assumptions about adults as individuals. If you believe that learning is essentially all about self-discovery and fulfilling your innate potential, then this will probably resonate well with you. These days learning theories also remind us however, that learning is a social process and without an environment supportive of change, private attempts at learning tend to run into difficulty.

Aside from the characteristics above, being an adult learner means being an active learner. Active learning means several things. First, it is the habit of asking questions to check the assumptions being made by you or others. It is important that you practise your skill in asking reflective and critical questions. Reflection balances introversion and quiet retreat with extroversion, and interaction with the world around you. Being critical means you are not just interested in seeking understanding, but also in change, which links very nicely to action, new behaviors and goals.

CASE STUDY 1

Interview with Sharon Varney on Reflections on Adult Learning

Sharon Varney, organizational consultant and Doctoral candidate at Henley Business School

What is learning for you?

For me, learning is an on-going, social process of becoming ourselves. As human beings, we are naturally inclined to learn, but habitual patterns of behavior can get in the way. That is why it is often easier to learn when things go wrong than when they go right.

What do you mean by "becoming ourselves"?

For me, thinking about learning as a social process of "becoming ourselves" highlights a number of important facets of learning. First, it highlights the generative nature of learning. It emphasizes that learning can help us to create new knowledge and insights, not merely to acquire them. Second, it draws attention to learning being embedded in human experience rather than being a detached and cerebral activity. Finally, it gives a nod to the idea of exploring many "possible selves", which illuminates learning as being, at least in part, a process of making choices.

Personal Development Goals

As we have seen, knowing *why* one has come to learn is an important first step. Focusing on *what* and *how*, the goals of learning, comes next. In coaching the conversation often revolves around the articulation and achievement of goals, so this is a great place to begin your learning. Do not forget that, as a self-directed learner, your goals can and will evolve, adapt, and lead to further goals *as* you learn, so goal setting, rather than only being the finite *end*, can also become a fluid *means*.

It helps to have a developmental goal that is expressed positively as something to be moved toward, not away from. It will be important that any goal you set is manageable. Writing your development goals in the form of S·M·A·R·T objectives is an idea developed from the work of influential management thinker Peter Drucker. S·M·A·R·T usually stands for:

- Specific: Succinct and definite
- Measurable: Knowing what evidence, perhaps in the form of what you will feel or hear, will tell you that you have hit your target
- Achievable: You have, or can get, the resources you need
- Relevant: Achieving the goal is in harmony with the bigger picture, considering the impact of your goal on your family, work and community
- Time-bound: Without a *"by when?"* your development goal just remains a nicely worded dream.

Finally, after refining the details of your goal, adding a short motivating headline, or creating a positive mental image, helps make it shine.

Force-field Analysis

A very simple but effective tool for working towards a goal comes from the work by Kurt Lewin (1943), a pioneer of social psychology and group dynamics with an interest in how human behavior is influenced by the world around us. A force field analysis shows the dynamic relationship between where you are now (current state), and where you want to be (desired state).

Some things will be pushing away from your current situation, while others will be hindering, restraining, or preventing that goal from being reached. Depending on you and your history, the drivers will vary in intensity, clarity, and importance, but understanding both the sets will help formulate what to do next. It helps to look at this model graphically, as shown in Fig. 6.2.

Some driving forces create their own restraining forces. For example, if your goal was "to complete the London and New York marathons by the time I am 42", and one of your driving forces was "my best friend has the same goal", you need to consider whether that driver is balanced by a restraining habit, or belief to do with the competition.

Life-long Learning and Active Learning

The "Life-long learning" is a general term that applies to many different situations, ranging from an individual's informal interest in a topic to

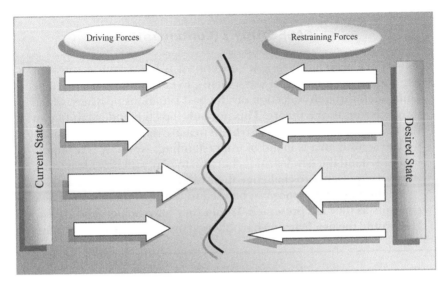

Figure 6.2. Force-field analysis.
Source: Based on Lewin 1943.

CASE STUDY 2

Interview with Peter Mayhead on Reflections on Adult Learning and its Application

Peter Mayhead, a former chief financial officer (CFO) and full-time Executive MBA candidate at Henley Business School

How is your learning structured?

An important part of this process is to create an environment in which the education can be "played with" to allow the deeper understanding to be found. Furthermore, it is vital to be able to understand which tools to apply in each situation.

You are an experienced manager returning to full-time education. How do you go about using your experience in your learning?

(Continued)

CASE STUDY 2 (*Continued*)

As you are introduced to new concepts, it is important to use your experience in a number of ways. Firstly, to enable the learning to be embedded through reflection on the past situations or issues, which were relevant to the theory. This not only aids the understanding of the new concept or idea, but also helps to make the theory less abstract.

The second area is in aid of understanding. Not only is it important to ground the new learning, but also to play with new ideas using the past experience to challenge their validity.

Finally, past experience can be used to test the application of new concepts as they are presented. Would they have helped in the past? How would the new learning have allowed me to change the outcome?

---

state-sponsored programs of interventions, designed to bring about social change or enhance quality of life.

For our purposes, it might be useful to think of life-long learning as a state of mind, where questions continually lead to new questions and where you are using past experience to train yourself in critical thinking. This way, even formal, structured learning can become a rewarding process that you control. This may contrast with the memories of learning as the acquisition of knowledge, or the memorizing of information. Active learners deliberately look for evidence of their learning and for feedback from others, and they tend to find ways to integrate, not isolate, learning into their social life.

This feedback is essential, although for a host of reasons, the adult learners are often wary of sharing their thoughts and experiences with others. Sharing happens in different ways in different cultures, but having an audience is what makes learning authentic and a two-way process.

CONCLUSION

Ultimately, coaching yourself in learning is about achieving clarity and focusing on the events and influences that have led up to this point, and the articulation of developmental goals that lead you where you want to be in the future. Your development goals are your *statements* about learning. They are propositions. Any proposition only has meaning in the context of the question it answers, so asking good questions is the foundation of learning. Undertaking activities to become self-aware and to find out what your goals are will improve your meta-skills and abilities, in thinking about thinking and learning to learn. The more you do them, the better you become.

Your Activities to Enhance Your Self-coaching Skills

Activity 1: Freefall writing—put your self-development
in context.

Freefall writing is a powerful technique developed by Barbara Turner-Vesselago (2009). In Freefall, as the name suggests, you are encouraged to let yourself go and write on a topic or question using whatever comes to mind. With practise, the technique is used to approach ever-more difficult topics, and can help tremendously with personal development.

Write the coaching question "What has brought me here?" at the top of the box below.

Start writing and continue to write for 3 minutes. Time yourself. Do not stop to think about what you are writing, or what you have just written. Write whatever comes into your mind in respect of this question. You may wish to relate your thoughts to Erikson's life-stages model mentioned above.

Activity 2: Mining for goals.

What is important for you *now?*
    After having reflected on the circles of life in Chapter 5, ask your-self again what is important for you now?

_____

_____

_____

_____

Looking at the six areas of the circles of life tool, what are your main objectives for the near future? Without rushing, make a list below of the first five things that come to mind, using the categories above, to prompt you if needed.

1. _____

2. _____

3. _____

4. _____

5. _____

Activity 3: Forming a SMART goal.

Choose one of the statements you wrote in answer to the question in Activity 2 and translate that into a goal using the S·M·A·R·T criteria. Take your time, and come back to it several times, if necessary. When you are done, create a motivating headline or image for yourself, which summarizes this goal.

_____

_____

_____

_____

Activity 4: Force field analysis.

Taking your goal from Activity 3, use the force field analysis model to list the things which are pushing you away from your current state towards your desired state, on a piece of paper. Then list the things which are pushing back from the goal or desired state. You can indicate the relative strength or intensity of each factor by the length or shape of your arrows. *Tip*: Working with another person, or a group, on an exercise such as this can be very helpful and rewarding, so feel free to ask someone else's opinion.

RECOMMENDED VIDEO LINKS

To place your learning in a systemic context, try taking a look at Matt Ridley's up-beat and thought-provoking presentation, at the TED conference held in Oxford in July 2010: http://www.ted.com/talks/matt_ridley_when_ideas_have_sex.html

For inspiration and a positive role model for learning and change, the seminal speech made by the Rev Martin Luther King in Washington D.C. in 1963, is worth repeated viewing. This is the full version on YouTube: http://www.youtube.com/watch?v=PbUtL_0vAJk

REFERENCES AND FURTHER READING

Erikson, E. (1994). *Identity and the life cycle*. NY, San Francisco: Norton.

Fisk, M., & Chiriboga, D. (1990). *Change and Continuity in Adult Life*. Jossey-Bass.

Hardingham, A. (2004). *The Coach's Coach—Personal Development for personal developers*. London: CIPD.

Lewin, K. (1943). Defining the "Field at a Given Time." *Psychological Review*. Vol. 50, pp. 292–310. Republished in *Resolving Social Conflicts & Field Theory in Social Science 1997*. Washington, D.C.: American Psychological Association.

O'Connor, J., & Lages, A. (2004). *Coaching With NLP*. London: Element Books.

Turner-Vesselago, B. (2009). www.freefallwriting.com

CHAPTER 7

CREATING YOUR PERSONAL VISION

Mike Green and Katja Kruckeberg

OBJECTIVE OF THIS CHAPTER

The aim of this chapter is to present the idea of working out a compelling vision, and how to draft one for ourselves. Having such a guiding star has proven to be a truly helpful tool for professionals.

INTRODUCTION

The idea of having a personal vision is not new. Throughout the ages, the movers and shakers of history have had a clear vision of what needs to be done—either for them or for the society at large. Organizations too, have visions which have been created, and—to paraphrase Charles Handy—they add a point and purpose to people's lives. Visions are lofty and strategic. That is, they provide an inspirational overview of where you are heading. Connecting to your personal vision or the organization's shared vision can be a powerful motivating force. When you are clear about what you stand for in life (see Chapter 3 on values), you have the basis of a

Leadership and Personal Development: A Toolbox for the 21st Century Professional, pp. 125–142
Copyright © 2010 by Information Age Publishing

personal system which will add a point and purpose to your life and indeed, will make things like decision-making and contemplating complex and difficult challenges much easier to handle.

This chapter discusses the importance of having a personal vision by showing how critical it is within your organizational and business life as well as for your personal benefit. It will examine some of the components of a vision, and help you build your own vision statement by guiding you through various activities. It also includes two case studies demonstrating how people with a vision can have a tremendous impact, not only on the place of their work, but also on their lives.

VISIONARY LEADERSHIP IN LIFE AND BUSINESS

In Chapter 15 on leadership roles, you will see that the visionary motivator role is the key to facilitate change, whether it is on an organizational, departmental, or individual level. By connecting to your personal vision and creating a vision for your part of the organization, you will become a more effective leader and change agent. Our research (2008) found that the most effective leaders use the visionary motivator role. It was also a popular choice for line managers, and most of the employees want more visionary leadership in organizational life. We have also examined what makes the most effective sales-people so effective. Unsurprisingly, it is their strong entrepreneurial spirit underpinned by a clear personal vision, linked to extensive personal goals. These characteristics promote success, regardless of what the organization's goals happen to be. With such characteristics, you can produce a win-win culture for yourself and those around you.

The Visionary Motivator

The Visionary Motivators articulate a compelling picture of the future and enlist others in the journey. They give purpose to people in their day-to-day roles. The Visionary Motivators begins by suggesting a possible future and rapidly engage others in this. The vision itself tends to be a reflection of the followers' needs and wishes, and creates interest and excitement, without being prescriptive or narrow.

These leaders are very effective motivators and enablers. They connect with people quickly and easily, and their desire to move towards

(Continued)

The Visionary Motivator (*Continued*)

achieving things for everyone is infectious, while at the same time they are able to use their interpersonal skills to affirm, encourage, and excite the colleagues and followers. They hold the vision long enough and strong enough, for others to step into it. In that sense they can be described as motivational coaches, working with individuals to help them understand the future, and see a clear part for themselves in it.

An important element of the Visionary Motivator's natural approach is that they role-model what it is like to be motivated and inspired. They are energetic and relentlessly upbeat, and have the vitality and passion to draw people along in their wake. They have clarity of purpose and the dynamism to go with it. The Visionary Motivators win the respect and trust of the followers by inviting them to believe that they can achieve more, than they ever thought was possible.

Richard Branson is a good example of someone who uses the Visionary Motivator role when he can. He is very good at promoting himself and his brand, and is full of big bold ideas, and convincing grand plans. He is tirelessly energetic and always full of stories of success. However, when asked for details on failures or pitfalls he has been quoted as saying he does not really remember his mistakes, and certainly does not dwell on them.

Source: Extracted from Cameron and Green (2008).

COMPONENTS OF A VISION

So, what are the components of a vision? According to Stewart Friedman, Professor of Management at the Wharton School, the four key components of a vision are:

1. A compelling story of the future is engaging; it captures the heart, and forces you to pay attention. Those who hear it want to be a part of it. And they are moved.

2. What does your future look like—what is the image? If others could travel into the future with you, what would they find? A well-crafted leadership vision is described in concrete terms that are easy to visualize and remember.

3. The story of your future should be a stretch, but it must be achievable too. If it was not achievable, you would have little motivation to even bother for trying.

4. Finally, future simply means out there—some time from this moment forward, but not so far away that it is out of reach.

(Friedman 2008).

CASE STUDY 1

Howard Schultz

Howard Schultz joined Starbucks in 1982 as a marketing director. He tried to persuade them to have coffee shops like the ones in Italy, where they were more of a community institution rather than just a place to buy coffee. When they refused to go in his direction, Schultz decided to follow his passion and set up his own coffee shop, only to buy the Starbucks retail outlets in 1987! He then used his personal vision and business acumen to expand the company rapidly, into a worldwide phenomenon.

In his autobiography, "Pour your heart into it" he illustrates this beautifully by saying, "Again and again, I have had to use every ounce of perseverance and persuasion I can summon, to make things happen. Life is a series of near misses. But a lot of what we subscribe to is not luck at all. It is seizing the day and accepting responsibility for your future. It is seeing what other people do not see and pursuing that vision, no matter who tells you not to. When you really believe—in yourself, in your dream—you just have to do everything you possibly can to take control and make your vision a reality."

Schultz said that he wanted to build a "company with soul." He did just that. Not only did he have the vision and pursued it relentlessly, he actively used his personal vision to engage his employees and his customers—being one of the first employers in the US to offer comprehensive health coverage and also an employee stock-option plan. His vision was real to him, and he focused on engaging others in making it happen.

BENEFITS OF A PERSONAL VISION

Having a personal vision for your life, or your career, is a motivating force which will get you through difficult and turbulent times. It can aid you in making key career decisions when you are at a crossroad. By remembering your vision, you will stay connected to your purpose, and have a sense of purpose and clear direction in life—a route map and a compass.

All the major time and life management philosophies and methodologies, stress the importance of being clear about where you are heading. Stephen Covey's hugely successful book *"The Seven Habits of Highly Effective People"* (1990) stresses the importance of vision, and of always beginning something with the end in mind—or, as Lewis Carol mischievously pointed out, "If you do not know where you are going, any road will take you there". Covey linked this with the need to be proactive and to prioritize by "putting the first things first". Of course, if you have a motivating vision for yourself, you will be much more likely to be motivated to do something, and what you will do is aligned with what is important according to your vision.

In his book *"Getting Things Done: The Art of Stress-Free Productivity"* (2001), David Allen puts great emphasis on the next action. What is it in your daily life which you need to do next? His whole system is a methodology for getting things done in the moment. And yet, although a fantastic personal productivity tool, it would not be as immensely popular—or as effective—without his imperative to have a life vision. He charts the linkages between the very next action, one's current actions, current projects, areas of responsibility, 1–2 year goals, and the criticality of having 3–5 year visions and life vision.

Putting a man on the moon

A workman was seen diligently sweeping the floor of one of the hangars at Cape Canaveral in the 1960s. When asked what he was doing, he replied "I am helping put a man on the moon."

Draining the swamp

"When you are up to your neck in crocodiles, it is hard to remember that the first priority is to drain the swamp."

Building a cathedral

Three workers were working on a wall. When asked, the first one said they were laying bricks; the second one said they were building a wall; the third one said they were building a cathedral.

COMPONENTS OF A PERSONAL VISION STATEMENT

What is the purpose of a personal vision statement? Well, on a simple level it helps you decide and remind yourself of what you want to be, what your ultimate goal is. It is very much "big picture" thinking. It should be something you can aspire to, regardless of where you are now, and the distance between the present and your vision. By putting your vision into a written statement, you initiate a process that will eventually enable you to achieve your hopes, dreams, and expectations. A vision statement can open your eyes to your possibilities and provides the first ideas of how to get there.

Professor Butler of Harvard Business School, who has spent the last 18 years researching the relationship between personality structures and finding meaning in one's work, stresses the importance of finding a career that brings out people's passion, as this will keep them engaged and content. When asked about the key ingredients of building a good and sustainable career, he answered in an interview with *Bloomberg Business Review (2010)*:

"When I work with students, they learn about the research that has been done on the relationships between three types of personality variables: deeply embedded life interests, work-reward values, and business skills, and how these three variables relate to the satisfaction between one type of career path versus another. We place a lot of emphasis on deeply embedded life interests, because my research has shown that this is the strongest predictor of career satisfaction, over a long period of time. We work on developing where you want to be 5–7 years after graduation. I do not just mean industry and function, but I also mean organizational culture, geographical location, and setting of your life. You can then begin to work the job question backward. If you are able to develop a vision for 5–7 years out, then you can say: "what job, what experience, and what knowledge do I need to be hired into my vision, 5 years from now?"

Based on our experience and integrating the state of the art thinking from people in the field, we conclude that a personal vision should include the following elements and features:

1. Your vision should look 5–7 years ahead.
2. It is about where you want to be—not where you are!
3. The best visions give you something to grow into—so do not be too modest. Make it big!
4. It describes the essence of the new life you seek, not every detail. (Details come later as you establish goals and activities to move toward your vision.)
5. It is based on your life interests, on your passions and considers your life as a whole, which consists of different circles (See Chapter 5).
6. It is fully aligned with the core values that you hold dear in life.

7. It should be written in the present, not future tense. It describes what you would feel, hear, think, say, and do if you were to reach your vision now.

Try to give yourself permission to let it flow from your heart. Your vision is about what you want from your life, and not what you think you should be wanting. It is about imagining the biggest, the most glorious vision of yourself: the best possible you in about 5–7 years from now.

It is also advisable to use lively language that motivates you to action. Your vision will be a guiding compass that leads you to better decision-making for your sake and, eventually, to more success, if it is made well. And with success we mean success in life, not just in business. As mentioned in the chapter on self-leadership (Chapter 5), this life is not a rehearsal; you just have one shot at living a good and fulfilling life.

CASE STUDY 2

Interview with Uwe Nepiersky, on How to Use Your Personal Vision to Create Your Future Success

Dr Uwe Napiersky, German (51), German, Business Psychologist and Expert on Executive Development, located in Birmingham, UK

In your work at Aston Business School, where you teach Master of Business Administration (MBA) and Executive Education programs, you support managers from around the world, in their career and personal development. Can you describe in what context you work, with personal vision as a tool to foster development?

Visions and ideas about a possible positive future have always been the driving forces in motivating the self and others. I use the technique of "personal vision" in various frameworks. Firstly, for understanding or discovering a personal vision, and secondly, as a transformational leadership and communication skill or competence, with regard to inspiring and motivating others.

The personal vision exercise is not a stand-alone activity. It is always imbedded as a tool or exercise in a coherent learning architecture, and a process for a specific development goal.

Let me give one example of when people work on a personal matter: You are asked to work on your vision that consists of your dreams and goals. In which direction is your career developing, and how would you like it to develop? Where do you ideally want to be in five

(Continued)

CASE STUDY 2 (*Continued*)

or ten years? These are very simple but meaningful and motivating questions when reflecting on your career's future direction.

To articulate or write your personal vision for your life, inside and outside work, is an insightful starting point at the beginning of a learning and development journey, for example, at the start of an MBA program, a leadership or high-potential program, or even a coaching process. It is a personal grounding and reflection step, which sets the foundation to start working on setting one's goals and objectives, for personal development plan/steps.

The inspirational and inspiring power of this exercise lies in the "what might be" mental scenarios. These mental pictures of the ideal self can trigger lots of positive emotions, and boost commitment for a sometimes tough, exhausting, long learning and developmental journey.

Secondly, I use the personal vision exercise as a starter skill development exercise for leaders, when working on the competence: Managing vision and purpose. Ideally, managers should be able to communicate a compelling and inspired vision, and sense of core purpose in a way that imbues enthusiasm and commitment in others. Some managers are uncomfortable speculating on the unknown future, and this exercise helps them to stretch themselves, as they become more transformational and visionary.

Can you share examples from your coaching practice on how people have formulated their personal vision, and how it has altered their lives and careers, please?

In the majority of cases, the vision exercise does not lead to dramatic life changes. It rather confirms people's decisions to follow the specific professional direction they have already chosen. For example, during a leadership development program, people normally start on the vision statement, and then work on a six-step process to create their personal development path and plan.

However, in some cases, the task and coaching support make people realize that they have a different idea about their ideal future. For some individuals, their values and their visions have subconsciously developed in the opposite direction, without their realization.

I worked with one person—let us call him John—during an 8 months leadership development program. We met either virtually or face-to-face, every 4 weeks during the leadership development workshop.

(Continued)

CASE STUDY 2 (*Continued*)

John was an accountant in a global company and was leading around 20 people. The vision exercise made him think and reflect that, ideally, he wanted to do something completely different. During the coaching sessions, John emphasized that he wanted to do something more meaningful, creative, and where he could apply his positive "can do" attitude, instead of following Standard operational processes (SOPs).

He felt odd among his accountancy colleagues, and the organizational structure was not giving him the opportunity to make use of his entrepreneurial and creative skills, which were evident due to the results of other assessment instruments.

The vision exercise was the catalyst for a couple of dramatic changes that John initiated.

Today—2 years later—John is at a different organization, is the head of the finance department of a medium-sized company, and he is writing children's books.

What do you do after the personal vision exercise?

Creating a personal and tailor-made learning journey and development path, which is a facilitator of such a process, is needed to synchronize the head and heart. Normally, I guide the person or the group on how to identify or confirm the selected direction, and to explore the fit between the individual's vision, values, capability, and knowledge. Besides the creation of a personal vision, people should have clarity about themselves, as well as about their critical core values. For example: which values would you not give up under any circumstances in the future? Ethical questions become increasingly relevant too.

The reflections on these issues occur via individual coaching and "reflective team sessions" during which people give feedback, comment and/or reflect on, for example, support and resource, possible obstacles, or how to monitor the planned activities.

In the framework of creating an inspiring personal development plan, the integration of the vision's implications can be quite challenging. But working on your personal vision makes the action steps meaningful and the plan personal.

Any final recommendations on how to work best with a vision to boost one's happiness and success?

This button does not exist. This would be an unrealistic vision. Epicurus, a Greek philosopher, wrote the guide to happiness more than

(*Continued*)

CASE STUDY 2 (*Continued*)

2,300 years ago with lessons on the art of leading a happy life, and it is still an open, philosophical question.

In general, it is an attitude and mindset, and to mature and grow in this field is a process. Reflection, reflection, reflection—and communicate your thoughts first with people you trust. Get feedback, maybe adjust, and start again. Watch out, it is only partly a cognitive exercise. Most of the power comes from the emotional side—being very honest with ourselves.

So, reflect on and act upon your vision!

A personal vision statement, combined with a well-thought out personal mission statement can provide a great deal of support, to create a somewhat new and better life. It can leverage you into a new job or make your current job more exciting. The closer a personal vision and mission statements are to you, your strengths, your personality, your life interest, and your values, the better they can guide your career and your life.

"Creating a Personal Mission Statement will be, without question, one of the most powerful and significant things you will ever do, to take control of your life. In it, you will identify the most important roles, relationships, and things in your life,—who you want to be, what you want to do, to whom, and what you want to give of your life, the principles you want to anchor your life to, and the legacy you want to leave. All the goals and decisions you will make in the future will be based upon it. It is like deciding first which wall you want to lean your ladder of life against, and then begin to climb. It will be a compass—a strong source of guidance amid the stormy seas, and pressing, pulling currents of your life." (Covey, 2004).

As stated before, your vision is the over-arching direction and ultimate goal to which you are heading. Your personal mission statement is about how you will integrate your personal vision into your daily life. It may be a few words, a few paragraphs or several pages. It reflects your uniqueness, and must have a powerful appeal for you. It is about the person you are, and the person you are becoming.

Just having a personal vision does not mean your life changes overnight or that you will achieve all your dreams and live happily ever after. But if you do craft a powerful vision, it will give you clarity, which is the first step in personal change. Your personal mission statement then provides you with the steps to get you there. In this sense, it is an excellent tool for orientating yourself, and starting the process of change.

In essence, your personal mission statement should answer three questions:

1. What is my vision about (purpose)?
2. What does my vision stand for (values)?
3. What actions do I take to manifest my vision and my values?

In practice, there are many people who combine their personal vision and mission statements, and create a hybrid version of a personal vision and mission statement. But there are no rules set in stone here. It is really up to you to decide what works the best. Just be clear about who will be reading this vision statement. If it is only you, it should be written in a way that speaks to you and to you only.

CASE STUDY 3

The Case of an Indian Information Technology (IT) Consultant

Baahir, (36), Indian, IT Consultant, Calcutta, India

The 36-year-old Indian IT consultant had achieved substantial business and personal success, during his 10 years in the IT industry, but was feeling relatively unfulfilled and seemed to have lost his way. He resigned from his post and enrolled in a 1 year full-time MBA program in the UK. He knew that the integration of various business subjects would help develop his capabilities, but he also knew that the personal development component of the program was critical for finding his way in life.

And this was true. Through a series of one-to-one sessions with an experienced coach, he explored his personality, his knowledge and his understanding. And, most importantly, he started working on developing a vision, in line with his values.

Although very entrepreneurial, he came to realize that his values regarding meaning, contribution and the environment had been ignored over the previous decade. With these values in mind, he began to develop a vision for setting up a business, which would be based on sourcing and selling organic farm produce in Asia. He projected himself forward 5 years to describe a business which had gone from strength to strength, and which delivered organic produce at affordable prices to two large regions in India. He then translated this vision into concrete terms, using his newly found business knowledge, sketching out

(Continued)

CASE STUDY 3 (*Continued*)

the strategy, the structure, the skills, and the staff required. Importantly, he placed his set of values at the heart of the new enterprise.

Returning to terra firma, he then developed a detailed business plan to undertake when his MBA had been awarded, and which combined his business knowledge, his developing network and his personal vision as the first step into his new life.

COMMUNICATE YOUR VISION

Once you have formulated your vision, and possibly also your mission statement, it is important to let the world know about it. Thus, you need to communicate it creatively. Only then will you be able to translate it into reality. You may have a life changing vision of a possible future, but if others do not see and know about it too, that vision will not actually unfold. The questions you should pose for yourself are:

- Who do you want to communicate your vision to?
- Who are the stakeholders who can support you in achieving your vision?
- Who can help you? And what can you do to help?

This latter question is also of great importance in this context. As we explicitly explained in the networking chapter (Chapter 11), and at various other points in this book, we firmly believe that the most beneficial relationships are those in which both parties gain. Another recommendation is that you identify the key players and supporters inside and outside the organization who, in one way or the other, will motivate others, to reflect on, and be engaged with your vision.

Once you have identified your stakeholders, think about how to communicate your vision. For example, ask yourself how you can describe your vision in the amount of time you have, during a typical elevator ride (called the elevator pitch). This is usually the time span that people actively listen to you. If you need more time to describe your vision, it means that you still have some work to do, to bring your message to the point and shed more clarity on the subject.

If appropriate, reinforce the vision in the cafeteria, in your circles of friends, as well as in an accidental meeting with potential business partners. If you tell a good story about your vision, people will remember it more easily. The telling of stories captures hearts and minds. The more the channels of communication you use, the better your chance of creating a network in which your vision comes to life. Our visions usually unfold themselves in a social setting; therefore connecting with people is crucial

However, the main message is to always think win–win and to proactively be on the look-out for potential and genuine benefits for other people, otherwise some people might feel overburdened by too much information and requests from you.

CONCLUSIONS

We are all without a doubt, busy people and all have to manage a multiplicity of work challenges, as well as juggle a work-life balance. Developing an over-arching longer-term vision of the future can be an immensely motivating force, an extremely useful tool for prioritizing time, effort, and resources in the decision-making process. Furthermore, such a vision gives one, a sense of personal meaning. Developing a vision can be life - altering and life - enhancing exercise which, done once, can and should be revisited very often, to ensure that you are on your life's course and are maximizing your potential and your time on this planet.

Your Activities for Creating a Personal Vision

Activity 1: Creating a vision by building on your circles of life.

While working on the following activities, bear in mind the words of von Goethe: "Whatever you can do, or dream you can do, begin it. Boldness has genius, power, and magic in it!" At the heart of being clear is your life vision, describing your intentions and ambitions. The very process of developing your vision helps you gain clarity about what you want. And by putting it in writing, you take a big step closer to achieving it. Once your dreams are codified, they become more concrete, and you become more committed to achieving them. You can use any format to write your vision. There is no set length, but if you aim for a page, or possibly a bit more, you will be able to capture the important elements of your vision, without getting lost in tiny details.

Coming up with the right vision can take days, weeks, or even months. This is fine, as this is probably one of the most important activities that you will undertake, regarding your personal development. We highly recommend that you work through part 1 of this book first, and then finish reading and reflecting on Chapter 5: Self-leadership: Circles of Life. That will give you a very good basis to create a vision that is closely connected, to who you are as a human being. Be patient. Start with brainstorming: Jot down random thoughts in no particular order. Do not feel that your vision has to emerge from you just like that! Capture your thoughts, dreams, and desires first. Afterward, you can evaluate them and structure them into the right sentences and words.

My personal vision statement:

_____

_____

_____

_____

_____

_____

_____

Activity 2: Developing a vision using creativity.

This activity uses the right brain for its spatial and creative elements rather than the logical, linear left brain. The task is for you to literally picture a positive fulfilling vision of the future and to draw or paint it, or even create a collage or a treasure map by cutting out particularly evocative pictures of things, which captivate and motivate you. Thinking of the different aspects of your life and the goals that you have in each area, try and encapsulate them in pictorial form. The resulting picture or collage can then be placed in a special place for you to see every day.

My visualized positive future:

Activity 3: The competency star.

If you are interested in a more rational approach to developing a vision, then the competency star that two of the authors developed with Tim Osborne Jones at Henley Business School, and which is based on the work by Carlton Hobbs might be a useful template (see Fig. 7.1).

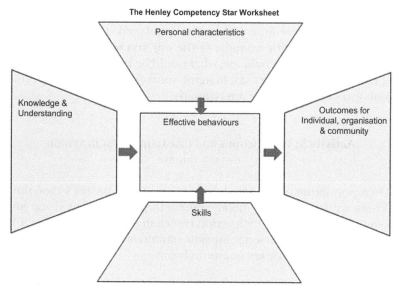

Figure 7.1. Henley Competency Star

By beginning with the end in mind,—what outcomes do you want?,— You can then work backward regarding what the behaviors are that you will need to display. Effective behaviors are the product of your knowledge and understanding, and the practical skills that you have, which are all underpinned by your personal characteristics (personality type, values, and so forth).

You can map your current competency star based on self-assessments from the many exercises in this book. You can also map your future ideal scenario where you can imagine achieving all the outcomes you would wish for yourself, your organization, and your community.

The next step is to see how you can bridge the gap between your current knowledge and practical skills, and this future state. One's personal characteristics are slightly more immovable, but you can nonetheless practise stepping into different, perhaps more challenging personality types and you can also develop enough emotional intelligence to know when you are capable of achieving the vision, and when you may need to temper that vision.

Activity 4: Strengthen the power of your vision.

Visualizations are a focus on a positive, present mental image. Effective visualizations require you to enter a relaxed state, within which you imagine a specific example of the way you want to be. Imagine what you and others would see, what would be heard and what would be felt. Using all your senses, imagine yourself achieving the specific goal. You need to practise this regularly.

Activity 5: What actions do I take to manifest my vision
and my values?

When pondering action steps, bear in mind Joel Barker's thoughts: "Vision without action is merely a dream. Action without vision just passes the time. Vision with action can change the world." Now it is time to write your personal mission statement. To do this, start by reflecting on the three key questions below:

1. What is my vision about (purpose)?

2. What does my vision stand for (values)?

_____

3. What actions do I take to manifest my vision and my values?

_____

And now specify what objectives you are going to set for yourself, in order to start turning your vision into reality.

1. One objective to achieve within the next week.

_____

2. One objective to achieve within the next month.

_____

3. One objective to achieve within the next 3 months.

_____

Now decide carefully on what actions you are going to allocate to these objectives, and write them down.

1. Actions to be taken within the next week.

_____

_____

2. Actions to be taken within the next month.

_____

_____

3. Actions to be taken within the next three months.

If you perform this exercise carefully and implement these actions consciously, you are indeed already on your way to achieving that vision of yourself. Return as often as you like, to your vision and mission statement, refine the objectives, cross off the completed actions, create new actions that you can do in the week, the next month and the next 3 months, and your future success is almost guaranteed.

REFERENCES AND FURTHER READING

Allan, D. (2002). *Getting things done.* London: Piatkus Books.
Butler (2010). *Interview in Bloomberg Business Review.*
Covey, S. (2004). *Seven habits of highly effective people.* New York: Simon & Schuster.
Cameron, E., & Green, M. (2008). *Making sense of leadership.* London: Kogan Page.
Friedman, S. (2008) *Total leadership: Be a better leader, have a richer life.* Boston: HBS Press.
Senge, P. (2006) *The fifth discipline.* New York: Random House Business.

PART III

COMMUNICATING MORE CREATIVELY

CHAPTER 8

COMMUNICATING MORE EFFECTIVELY

Franklin De Vrede and Katja Kruckeberg

OBJECTIVE OF THIS CHAPTER

This chapter seeks to help you gain a better understanding of the different levels involved in the communication process and to familiarize you with different communication and influencing styles that will help you to increase your impact on other people. You will learn why some conversations can become difficult, and how to deal more constructively with potential pitfalls.

INTRODUCTION

We have all been there; with the best intentions, for the sake of the company, and to the best of our abilities, we tried to encourage a colleague to explore alternative solutions or behaviors. But before we knew it, the conversation took a wrong turn. Things were misunderstood. The main message was not received well. At times, the conversation closed, with what was perhaps unnecessarily strong statements that burned bridges, leaving both sides more emotional, than required in times of busy schedules and other important battles to worry about. Consequently, certain situations developed

*Leadership and Personal Development: A Toolbox for the
21st Century Professional*, pp. 145–169

their own dynamics, and we needed to waste more time and energy "watching our back" or restoring normality.

After such a situation, some never learn to re-connect and give others the "silent treatment" for an overly long period of time. While it may be necessary to cut ties to maintain a level of hygiene in one's social networks and to create distance from those who exude acidity in the figurative sense, or deprive us of our energy, we will certainly be better off if we have more choice in doing so or in avoiding unintended consequences. Even if you have to fire someone or cease to focus on a relationship, this could be managed in better ways if you hone your communication skills. Certain conversations can of course, have a positive impact. Everybody feels respected, energized and leaves the room with the impression of "having grown". Great leaders and managers should be aware of these success patterns, and should have the ability of coaching their successors and peers with regard to individual or general recipes for successful conversations.

We shall therefore review different levels, dynamics, and styles within conversations. We will first introduce the Volcano model to demonstrate that communication is much more than just words. Building on this, we will then introduce you to the concept of mental model that is vital when polishing one's communication style as they shape each of our interactions with others. Next, we discuss different communication styles and approaches. To help you deal more smoothly with difficult conversations in future, we will finally present the FIBAR tool that will illustrate the different ways of dealing with these "difficult conversations". To emphasize our crystal clear position: We are firmly convinced that we have hardly seen any *good* leaders without communication skills, but we have seen managers, who do not have the relevant communication skills, put in charge! Having communication skills constantly on your radar is highly recommended, and the following chapter shares our key pointers with you.

DYNAMICS OF CONVERSATIONS—THE VOLCANO

People do not purely exchange words (opinions) while they communicate, but also other messages at a subconscious level. To reveal these other messages and to examine them more systematically, we use the metaphor, *volcanoes of communication,* and invite you to mentally play along with this image. If you imagine two parties engaged in communication, they could be regarded as two sleeping volcanoes facing each other. As we know, a volcano has several levels of activity. The words and the explicit information exchanged could be regarded as the smoke that comes from the two sleeping volcanoes at the surface level. The landscape surrounding the volcanoes could be regarded as a conversation or communication process's situational factors.

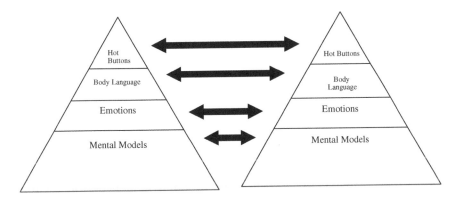

Figure 8.1. Different viewpoints in conversations

A volcano generally seems calm and stable. But this is not the whole picture. Geologists will tell you that if you look deeper into a volcano, you can often see several levels, each with its own degree of dynamic activity, which could be volatile gases, hot mud or boiling lava. As a metaphor, this is quite useful because, in conversations, the lower levels of the "human volcano" are often triggered, by what the other person communicates explicitly or implicitly. The conversation can get out of hand very easily or can generate an unexpected "volcanic" reaction from the other person. Something is said that turns out to be the other person's "hot button" or that sparks someone's frustration, and this person suddenly lashes out with an exaggerated emotional reaction. The different levels active during a conversation are personal mental models, as well as underlying emotions, that influence how a conversation partner regards the other person's behavior. Our body language also conveys many messages. This is why we often hear communication experts say: We can not **not** communicate! In Chapter 4 of this book, you are introduced to the idea of managing your emotional capabilities, which we therefore do not discuss here. However, we would like to introduce you to the idea of mental models and show (in Fig. 8.1) how they influence our communication processes.

MENTAL MODELS

If the volcanoes are kept in mind, it is easy to follow the dynamics of a conversation. The way a conversation develops, is strongly influenced by what is happening below the surface. When we are having conversations, we are not just comparing points of view; we are also confronting mental models.

The term mental models was originally introduced by Peter M. Senge in 2001 and defined as follows:

> *"Mental models are deeply held internal images of how the world works, images that limit us to familiar ways of thinking and acting. Very often, we are not consciously aware of our mental models or the effects they have on our behavior"* (Senge, 2001, p. 8).

Mental models are subtle but very powerful, as they drive our behavior, and influence our thinking and perception strongly. Even more challenging is that we are often not aware of our mental models: Many of them are part of our subconscious mind, or they come so naturally to us that we do not even notice them. Mental models include, for example, influences from the following areas:

- Our national cultural background.
- Our family culture.
- Our industry and vocational culture.
- Our personality preferences and traits.
- Our values and behaviors.
- Our past (career and life) experiences.
- Our language capabilities.
- The values of our circle of friends.
- Our needs and expectations from relationships.
- Our knowledge.
- Our cognitive thinking skills.
- Circumstances and situational factors on which these factors and their impacts depend.

Mental Models Such as Personal Preferences Influence our Behavior in Conversations

As explicitly described in Chapter 2, people differ greatly with regard to the information on which they usually focus. Different people perceive the same situation differently, and extract different information from the same situation. Besides this, people also differ in the way they process and evaluate this information.

Thus, the reasons why we have a different point of view are often because we include different information in our reasoning. Instead of focussing on the details of an issue (detailed thinking), someone may want to put the issue in a broader context (big-picture thinking). Or it may be that while one person just wants to discuss the logical steps of a situation (rational approach to decision making), the other is concerned about how the ultimate decision will relate to the team's values and principles (value/people oriented approach to decision making). MBTI and the Personality 5 tool teach us that, essentially, people are not wired similarly. People act differently, because they absorb information and process information differently. The problem is that many professionals fail to accept this reality. They continue to think there is something called "common sense" that we all share, while we all see the world through different lenses.

CASE STUDY 1 of a Large Oil Company

Organizational mental filters and decision making

Consider the case of a large oil company that needed to take a decision concerning what to do with a drilling platform near the coast of Norway. The platform had reached the end of its life cycle. After a great deal of logical analysis of the facts, a decision was taken to sink it. This would not be done at the place where it was, but it would be towed to the Atlantic ocean and sunk in one of the deeper parts of the ocean. A European environmental activist group discovered this plan and while the platform was being towed, they tried to board it to hang up protest banners, and prevent the sinking.

The oil company's first reaction was to blast the activists off the platform, with strong water hoses. It was, after all, their property and why did they have to take these activists seriously? However, when the BBC got involved and started broadcasting images of what was happening on this platform, people in many countries started boycotting the oil company. At first, the company was not concerned with this and continued towing the platform. But as the public disapproval grew and the company's share price fell, the executive leaders realized that they had to stop the process. Subsequently, discussions started with the activists about the platform's fate. The ultimate decision was that the platform would no longer be sunk; it was towed back to Norway where it now lies in a fjord. The latest news is that there are plans to turn it into an amusement park.

Reality can be perceived in many ways. There is no "common sense" and there is no ultimate truth. We all see matters differently and should therefore keep the words of the famous Porgy and Bess song in mind: "It is not necessarily so". An excellent recommendation is that decision making should always cover the details of a situation, as well as placing this situation in a broader concept in order to consider all the logical implications, and to check how potential decisions impact on other people and the broader community. Every business decision made should also be defendable from an organization's value point of view. In MBTI terms, this is sometimes referred to as the Z-model, as it covers the four functions: sensing, intuition, thinking, and feeling. It is also an excellent tool to prepare for a speech or a business presentation, as it ensures that you reach most of the people in the audience by referring to their differing preferences, regarding the way they process and evaluate information.

The following case study builds on this last point. We interviewed a female accountant with a detail orientation regarding information processing, and a fact orientation when it comes to evaluating information. The case illustrates how knowing about some of her mental filters' psychological factors helped this lady to become more aware of her communication patterns, her strengths and weaknesses, and to challenge her points of view.

CASE STUDY 2

Personality Preferences and Communication Patterns

Tanja (51), German, accountant, Global Communications Company, Chicago, USA.

With the support of my executive coach, I have worked with the MBTI, and thereafter with the P5 tool for a year now. Apart from using the MBTI and the P5 for my personal development, I have found it very useful to see how my personal preferences influence my communication with other people. It was particularly relevant for me to use this tool not only in a professional context, but also in a family setting. My husband is a "big picture" and value-oriented person, while I always go deep into the details of things and have a tendency to choose a fact-oriented, logical approach. I guess, this is why I chose to become an accountant and not a big marketer like my husband.

Patterns in our communication that were hidden from me for decades emerged suddenly, and I found it amazing to realize that these differences in the way we talk and communicate with each other are clearly linked to our personality types. Yes, it is so true, we always filter everything we hear, and we tend to hear only what we are interested in. And, what might be even more important, we also assess the information according to our personal preferences. I have so often thought my husband indulges too much in "blue sky" thinking, and that he is too value and people oriented. And, since I am German and my husband is American, I thought that our national cultures were the main reasons for this difference. Nowadays I realize that our differences are not mainly due to differences in our culture, but in personal preferences, which hugely helped to facilitate our difficulties. Also,

(Continued)

CASE STUDY 2 (*Continued*)

these days I appreciate that his personal preferences, the way he sees things and the way he constantly focuses on future options and speaks about emotions and so forth, is exactly why he is so good at his job. These are the qualities needed in his environment.

Examining the personal differences in the way people differ with regards to how they process information and make decisions was particularly relevant for me to better customize my communication with my husband, my children, and also with people at work. I have also made a conscious effort to further expand my "big picture" thinking skills, as I have found out that these can be trained and I so much admire them in other people,—mainly in those, of course, who also take the necessary level of details and reality into consideration.

HOW OUR NEEDS IN RELATIONSHIPS DETERMINE OUR BEHAVIOR IN CONVERSATIONS?

In trying to further explore, how mental models drive our interactions with others, it is useful to think of the three fundamental needs people have regarding interpersonal work relationships, which are explored in the FIRO-B® (Fundamental Interpersonal Relations Orientation—Behavior) model. The model was created by Will Schutz and was first described in his book "*FIRO—a Three Dimensional Theory of Interpersonal Behavior*" some 50 years ago. However, as this concept is as relevant today as it was back then, we would like to briefly introduce you to the three main dimensions of the model.

- Need *(expressed)* and receptiveness for *(wanted)* inclusion
- Need *(expressed)* and receptiveness for *(wanted)* control
- Need *(expressed)* and receptiveness for *(wanted)* affection

Inclusion refers to the extent to which people want to be included in others activities or has the need to include others in their work. In other words: Do you like working out things together or do you wish to work individually? This could also concern sharing and comparing ideas, or just distilling your own ideas. This is not linked to introversion as explained in Chapter 2, but has more to do with how important the idea of working collaboratively is for you. Someone who is high on inclusion may have the mantra: "We are all together in this, let us help each other." The person who is low on inclusion may often say: "At the end of the day, I have to do it all myself."

Control refers to the extent to which people want to be in charge or want things to be driven by others. People with a high need for control will have a tendency to impose their point of view on others, instead of waiting for them to express what they want. They may have a tendency to take a leading position in an activity, and naturally start organizing roles and tasks. If they are also open to control from others, they will be curious to find out who is in charge and what the plan is. Those, who have a lower need for control, either from themselves or from others, are not so interested in all of this. Questions related to control do not appear on their radar and does not seem important at all.

Affection refers to how personal and intimate a person likes work relations to be, which might have an impact on opening up about motives (what drives you?), showing and discussing emotions, sharing success, and failure experiences, or opening up about your private life. The level of desired intimacy also determines whether trust relationships are built, and whether people give each other the benefit of the doubt (as shown in Fig. 8.2).

Now imagine a conversation between two people with different needs on these three dimensions: Someone, for example, with a high need for control starting a discussion about changing a business approach with a colleague, who first needs to experience a rather high level of affection before he can trust anyone enough to take advice from them. The conversation will probably not flow as easily, as the first person expects it to.

Or, imagine someone who is low on inclusion being questioned by another person, about his ideas regarding a business issue on which he is working. While it seems like a normal thing to do, the person who is low on inclusion will not welcome the questions, and may give very brief answers. This may cause the other to assume that there is something wrong in the relationship.

Not knowing where the other person comes from, or why he or she react in a certain way has caused confusion in many team relationships. It is, of course, not possible to determine with certainty how your colleagues score in these three dimensions, but it helps to develop an active awareness, that

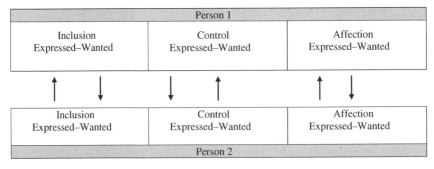

Figure 8.2. Patterns of communication

some or all three of these dimensions play a role in a difficult conversation. Secondly finding ways to invite your counterpart to communicate about why he or she does not respond as expected, is also becoming better at having challenging conversations.

DIFFERENT STYLES OF COMMUNICATION: ADVOCACY AND INQUIRY

Owing to the nature of our education systems, especially those in the western countries, many professionals have learned that one who wins in a discussion is the person who has superior arguments, and who is capable of defending his or her point of view strongly. But as the organizations become more complex, and people have to work in multi-disciplinary teams with people from other cultures or with different levels of authority, this style of assertiveness is no longer adequate. Successful professionals discover that they need to balance the traditional debating style with something else, for an open and constructive dialogue with people from a diverse cultural background.

Advocacy

Our mental models influence the style we use to discuss a difference in opinion. Some people strongly believe that it is important to be assertive. Which we can define as: having a strong point of view and making a conscious effort to express it. In many situations this is effective behavior, especially if used with respect for the other person. But if this style is overused, it results in a communication style that is quite competitive, and therefore not productive. We refer to this style as advocacy, which comes from being an advocate for something. It relates to either defending or attacking a statement. People with an advocacy style quickly adopt a debating manner. Their aim is to find the flaw in other persons' reasoning, or to bombard them with an arsenal of clever arguments. There is no deep listening to others and they will often interrupt others, not allowing them to finish their sentences. The assumption of those predominantly using an advocacy style is that there is a right or wrong in any situation, and that he who sees it the best will win. Accepting anything from others is essentially considered losing.

Inquiry

This style of communicating starts with the assumption that although you see matters differently than another persons, your goal is not necessarily to beat them with your clever arguments.

On the contrary, your aim is to have the conversation as a fair process, in which both the parties feel heard and the different points of view are truly understood. Even more importantly: By truly gaining an understanding of the underlying reasons for other people's viewpoints, you may also find that their "reality" is as valid as yours. This can then help you to have a conversation about reconciling the two realities, without making it a win or lose outcome (see Table 8.1).

The message here is not that inquiry is necessarily better than advocacy. It depends on the circumstances. In certain crisis situations, for example, when lives are at stake or in situations where you operate as the undisputed expert, advocacy may be the right attitude. In addition, when you have to communicate as a clear figure of authority (based on agreed rules, the law, or compliance), inquiry may not be useful. However, in many situations it is best to balance advocacy (expressing your point of view) with inquiry (seeking to understand the other), in order to create a meaningful dialogue leading to an outcome, that all the parties involved can respect.

Inquiry and Bonding

In his 2007 book, *"Hostage at the table"*, leadership consultant and former negotiator of hostages, George Kohlrieser uses the lessons learned from 35 years of experience as a negotiator of hostages, and shows how leaders can use this knowledge to influence people more effectively, and increase performance.

Table 8.1.   Communication Styles

Advocacy	*Inquiry*
• Goal is win or lose	• Goal is win-win or a fair compromise
• Competitive attitude, face, and posture	• Open attitude, de-escalating emotions
• Using strong statements	• Open attitude, de-escalating emotions
• Always proving the contrary	• Truly seeking to understand
• Long sentences, speech style	• Explaining your thinking steps
• Referring to scientific proof	• Helping the other person to clarify his or her thinking.
• "Yes, but ..."	• "That is an interesting point of view"
• "I disagree"	• "Help me understand ..."
• "You are wrong, let me tell you why"	• "So, what you mean is ..."
• Weakening the other party's arguments	• Looking for commonalities
	• Testing scenarios and consistencies

Source: Adapted from Senge (2006), p. 8.

Negotiators of hostages are successful 95% of the time, although they usually have little to offer, and the hostage takers know that they will go to prison. Kohlrieser argues that leaders in organizations–never come anywhere near this level of effectiveness.

What are the communication techniques and methods used in negotiation of hostages? Following Kohlrieser's reasoning; the key to success is to start any communication process by first trying to build a relationship with people. Only when this bond has been established, can one start influencing people's minds.

The main tool for bonding is—as we know, from other chapters in this book—by asking questions, and using an inquiry communication style. As in a coaching situation, you need to develop an interest in the other person. This interest has to be genuine interest; otherwise there will be no bonding. Bonding is created by using the inquiry communication style described above. It is about asking questions to find what motivates the other person. In a hostage situation, it is key not only to ask questions about facts, but also about the underlying beliefs of the takers of the hostages, emotions, and historical events affecting them to make them feel that they are taken seriously. To a lesser extent, the same applies to other communi-cation situations, as well. Once a relationship has been established, you can start focussing on common goals, and can consider talking about a way forward—a way that should consider self-interest of both parties and offers mutual gains to both sides.

COMMUNICATE LIKE A LEADER: TALK LESS, LISTEN MORE!

One of the most overlooked and under-used component of communication is listening. Listening was most recently named one of the most important fac-tors in negotiation (Stewart, Diamond, 2010). People who listen more, collect more information, which will then give them a competitive edge and allow them to connect to the people they are aiming to convince. Listening is also a central leadership skill, as it is the key to gaining followers. Everyone likes being listened to. When you show interest in what the other person expresses, that person will be much more open to the idea of, in turn, listening to what you have to say. It helps to build empathy, and is also important when you want to start changing people's minds on certain issues. First you need to con-nect with the person's inner world, only then will you actually start to chal-lenge his or her perceptions. Leaders need to learn to talk less and listen more. Deep listening leads to new ideas, opens up new horizons and new solutions for one's own self and for others. Deep listening requires an attitude of intellectual openness to listen to ideas that might be contrary to your ideas.

The skill of listening differentiates you from most of the other people who are cut off simply because they talk too much, and do not listen. As Nathan Hobbs, Organizational Psychologist rightly pointed out in

Chapter 4 there is listening and there is hearing. Make sure you know the difference between these two!

These messages are also reinforced by Ita Dureke, a Leadership Development Specialist who has worked with leaders for the last decade. In the following, you can read an interview conducted with her about different ways of communicating with people, and influencing them in a sustainable way.

CASE STUDY 3

Interview with Ita Dureke on Different Communication and Influencing Styles

Ita Dureke (43), Irish, specialist on leadership development, London, UK

As we know, a leader needs to influence and persuade others at different levels inside and outside the organization. Do you think the art of influencing is a trait that people are born with, or can people actually become better at it through training?

People might have different strengths and talents in the field of communication, and there is no doubt that some are naturally better at it than others. This has been clearly proved by research. Nevertheless, everybody can improve vastly in this field. Of course, you need to polish your influencing skills. The key ingredients for success are focus and dedication of energy to your goal. And that applies to most of the goals in the area of leadership and personal development.

But as a manager you have formal power that you can use to influence people. Is that not enough?

In some cases, we influence people simply as a result of our formal power in the business. That is true. In other cases, we rely on our personal authority. We might be able to get others to trust us, or to get them to consider us to be competent and reliable. Either way, we are well advised to make use of alternative communication approaches which, if applied well, can be used to increase our impact, especially if our powerbase is not sufficient. Also, we do not just need to influence people downward in the organization. It goes sideward, upward, and so forth whenever we speak to our stakeholders there might be a need to make an impact.

(Continued)

CASE STUDY 3 (*Continued*)

How can one improve one's ability to influence others? What communication approaches do you have in mind?

Personally, I find the push-and-pull approach an effective way of thinking about influencing. The push-and-pull concepts originate from judo: When one opponent pushes, the other pulls and vice versa. This concept was used in marketing in the 1990s, and I still find it very valid and very easy to apply this concept to illustrate different ways of communicating with other people. In interpersonal terms, push and pull are the two modes of dealing with other people.

Push	Pull
• Declare your agenda	• Explore their agenda
• Focus on your needs	• Focus on their wants and needs
• Indicate your reasoning, ideas, and motivations	• Discover their reasoning
• Suggest ideas	• Ask for ideas and suggestions
• Declare your feelings	• Learn about their feelings

For individuals who wish to polish their influencing ability or those who are looking to refresh their influencing skills, it would be worthwhile building an awareness of these two particular styles of influencing and communicating.

Can you explore the push communication style a bit further?

Push is more about directing someone to a change, rather than inspiring someone to want to make the change. Push styles tend to involve reasoning, logic, threats, punishment and rewards. They aim to convince by delivering a rationale for the change requested. However, although they are effective at producing results and compliance, they do not often lead to commitment.

And how does the push approach differ from the pull approach?

Most effective influencing methods build on the pull style or, as described in your communication chapter, the inquiry style. The aim

(Continued)

CASE STUDY 3 (*Continued*)

of a pull style is to create desire within the person you want to have an impact upon. It is about making the other person want what you have to offer. It is very subtly changing how they perceive the world so that they realize they would be better off if they go for the offered alternative. If you are successful in creating desire in the other person, then the internal emotional set-up in the other person will do the rest, and people will, most likely, move in the right directions. Examples of this approach are visioning, using language that inspires, painting an attractive picture of the future, identifying a common purpose and sense of shared goals, bridging, listening to, involving others, and finding connections, or working together to define the goals and the best solution, or personal charm, personal attractiveness.

Which style is most effective?

There is no right or wrong style because both styles have their merits. They will be appropriate depending on the circumstances and what you are trying to achieve. However, it is fair to say that pull approaches are most effective in developing commitment and a positive attitude towards change. The skill is to identify which style to use, and in what situation.

For example, in turn-around situations, where there are no alternative options, when people are in danger or at risk, or when you are in a specialist's role, a push approach is the way to go. In general, one can say that the push approach is effective but short-lived, as it might result in a lack of commitment or people becoming dependent on the leader, without developing new skills themselves. In summary, one could probably say that pushing is a management method, while pulling is used more by leaders.

Pulling, however, is certainly more difficult than pushing, but it is ultimately more effective in creating sustainable commitment. Also, pull approaches usually result in learning and growth for others, because they are encouraged to use their skills and to work creatively toward a solution.

We agree with Ita Dureke that talking about push-and-pull approaches in communication is not brand new and, like her, we thoroughly believe that it is still a highly relevant concept. Furthermore, if you compare the push-and-pull concept to the newer advocacy and inquiry concept, you will find many similarities between the push and the advocacy approaches, and the pull and inquiry approaches.

As emphasized by Kohlrieser, we also agree that most of the managers have to make more use of the latter category for many reasons. One important reason is our knowledge of how people learn the best and recall information most effectively. You can find a great deal of research—conducted, for example, by companies like IBM—that shows that the most successful approaches to make people remember information fall in the pull category of communication. If you, for example, ask an employee to produce a solution himself, and if he then successfully does so, he will not only feel more committed to the solution, but is also more likely to remember the specifics of the solution.

Thus, we are not talking about old-school leadership methods that might have worked effectively in the last century, but about more creative ways of engaging people, showing people, letting people teach each other, and allowing people to make their own mistakes in order to learn and progress most effectively. By pushing information using an advocacy communication style, the only person training his cognitive skills, is often, just the manager.

CHANGING PEOPLE'S MINDSETS: ASK THE RIGHT QUESTIONS!

If you want to challenge people's opinion and ultimately change their minds on certain topics, you need to ask the right questions that will make them think, that will make them take new information into consideration, and that will make them look at certain issues from a fresh perspective. This is very rarely achieved by merely pushing information through, as these concerns the way our brain works. We need to connect new pieces of information with the already existing pool of information, beliefs, principles, and so forth, which only we can do.

Consequently, the quickest way into another person's information processing and evaluating activities is by asking clever questions. One communication method that actually uses this insight is coaching, which is why we have dedicated a whole chapter to coaching in this book. A good coach should master the art of posing the right questions. However, it should be stressed that coaching is not an influencing method as such, as the coachee should be the one deciding the coaching conversation's outcome. In the following expert corner, Stefanie Demann, a German expert in rhetoric describes alternatives ways of communicating that do not use words.

CASE STUDY 4

Interview with Stefanie Demann on Communication Beyond Words

Stefanie Demann (37), German, communication expert, Nürnberg, Germany

Stefanie, based on your experience, can you tell us about alternative ways of communicating beyond using words?

We know that most people mainly refer to talking, writing and reading when they think of communication. However, there are other ways of communicating. One of the most powerful weapon in a leader's change armory is, for example, *walk the talk*. This means that you actually do as you say. "Actions speak louder than words" is an old saying found in one form or the other in many, many languages around the world. And scientific evidence actually broadly supports this saying's core message. You can talk as elaborately as you wish, you can use as many communication channels as you like, but if your words are not supported by your actions and demonstrated behavior, you are not getting your message across. For this reason, the most efficient way to communicate your vision or your message is through your actions. Leaders shape organizational culture by actions and demonstrated behavior. Role model behavior is the strongest form of direct communication.

Do not just aim to become the most sophisticated speaker, or impressive and charismatic presenter. When you think of improving your communication and persuasion skills, also think about how powerful your actions are. Consequently, if you, for example, want to communicate certain values, you need to act on them. If you want your employees to be positive and solution-focused, you need to show these attitudes as well.

Another of my recommendations is to give people the space to think for themselves and draw their own conclusion. There is nothing more powerful than having people coming up with a conclusion themselves—this is the real art of influencing and communicating. Show people why they should buy into an idea, let them experience it, challenge their thinking skills; and people will use and expand their skills, take pride in producing a solution and the chances are that their followership and commitment will be sustainable.

FOCUS YOUR MIND: WHY DO I WANT TO SPEAK ABOUT THIS?

Many conversations happen "on the go". You meet a colleague at the coffee machine or at the elevator, and you remember to mention an issue that needs to be discussed. Similarly, in team meetings, we can find ourselves raising a point that suddenly comes to mind—an issue that we feel requires a good conversation with one or more colleagues. It is not on the agenda, you have not prepared it, but you still need to mention it.

We often risk sliding into conversations that could potentially deliver different results than we wish, because we do not exactly know where we want to drive these conversations. Many of us recall situations where you walk out of a conversation saying to yourself: "Why did I have to bring that up? Was this really the right timing?" Whenever you feel a strong need to discuss something with a colleague, it pays first to pause, and quickly check a few points.

- **What is your goal?** Why do I need to have this potentially difficult conversation? Often we do not know why we want to discuss something. Many things happen that can trigger an emotional reaction, especially in teams where people collaborate intensively. Someone might not have prepared a meeting well, someone might take too much ownership of activities, or someone might be late for a meeting. It merely seems professional to raise these issues, but what exactly is your goal? Is your aim to educate the other person? Or to clarify what works for you? Is it to explore possibilities and find a better solution? Is it to express dissatisfaction, anger or concern, or is it to understand their point of view? Not knowing what you want to achieve could lead to you emphasizing the wrong point, and consequently not reaching your real goal.
- **Do I need to bring it up at all?** Many issues are not important enough or can be solved in a different way. Did you feel that your colleague claimed too much of the limelight at a board room presentation, making you look like the sidekick? What is reacting here? Is it your professional mindset, or rather your sensitive ego that was hurt? Perhaps your colleague is just good at a certain topic, and becomes passionate whenever he starts talking about it. Sometimes you may come to the conclusion that there is no need to raise an issue at all—it is not a big issue, too vague, or not important enough for what you are trying to accomplish. Besides, if it were that obvious, others who have observed your colleague (and who may be more objective), will give him the feedback he needs. Therefore, also consider whether you are the right person to mention this.

- **How should I best address this?** By having a clear goal for the conversation, you will know how to best address an issue. What style will you use? Will it be a confronting or a friendly conversation? How will you build it up? Will you use a series of experiences to clarify your point, or concentrate on the here and now? Will you make it part of a broader evaluation, or will it be a single-topic talk? Is it the first thing you want to mention, or one of the final points in the conversation? Thinking about how to address the issue helps to convey the right emotion, to stay focused and not combine matters. It also prevents you from becoming involved in topics that are equally important, but not relevant for this conversation.

- **What do I know about the other person?** We all have assumptions about others, some of which are based on experience, while others are based on our imagination. People are complex entities. We need to check our assumptions and be sure that we have a realistic picture of the person we need to talk to.

- **What is the right time and place?** Ask yourself: "Why do I need to have the conversation now and in this setting?" Sometimes it is simply not the right time and the right place for certain topics. Bringing up an issue when someone is racing to get out of the building is just not going to work. Expressing criticism to a colleague about someone in his or her team during a management team meeting may cause loss of face for that person, especially if you have not informed this team leader of your criticism before. Producing suggestions for improvement just before someone has to deliver a presentation might not be a clever move. Let us return to conversations at the elevator or at the coffee machine: Some people require even very simple, practical topics to be discussed in a concentrated, formal setting. It may not be an important topic for you, but perhaps it is for them. Also consider the distraction and noise. Giving someone important messages at a cocktail party, while several other people are passing by and greeting him or her, does not come across as considerate.

THE FIBAR TOOL

It is possible to improve your skills in dealing with challenging conversations. Some people tell us that they believe it is a personality thing: Some people are by nature better with these conversations than others. Our view is that these people are either finding an easy excuse not to change their behavior, or have not found the right way to deal with difficult conversations. Those who are good at challenging conversations, have usually invested a lot of time in understanding their thoughts and behaviors during conversations, and apply a specific method. We next present a tool that has proven itself in practice. We have used it with many executives whom we have coached, and each time they have testified how simple and effective it was.

In daily life, our mental models create "if–then" rules in our brains. For example, IF someone questions the effectiveness of my team, THEN this person should be immediately attacked and convinced of the contrary. This if–then rule is obviously there to protect the team, but it could simultaneously limit your effectiveness as a leader because you are missing on opportunities to hear justified criticism, which can help to improve your team's effectiveness. Whenever we enter a conversation, our mechanisms start working and we often focus on proving our mental model. We do this either with the aim of sharing what we regard as true, or with the aim to make the other person understand that he or she is wrong. A conversation could be very different if:

a.   We became more aware of what mental model we are putting at work in a conversation.
b.   We were to focus on comparing mental models, instead of convincing the other party that our conclusion is better.

The FIBAR tool helps us to do this in a structured way. As soon as you notice that a conversation is moving in the wrong direction, it makes sense to invite your counterpart to look at the topic again, but following the FIBAR steps. These are the elements that determine the mental model we put to work in a conversation:

1.   Facts
2.   Interpretations
3.   Belief systems
4.   Actions
5.   Results

Consider an IT consultant who, as part of a sales team, in an initial conversation rejects a potential client's request to implement a certain system: "F.A.P. is a great logistical system, but I am not going to implement it for you. You need something else." The client shows slight irritation and there is considerable tension in the room. The consultant's colleagues hurry to correct the situation, and promise to return with a proposal that complies with the client's wish. The sales team's post-meeting discussion is not surprisingly a "difficult" conversation. Accusations fly through the room and emotions run high. How can the team leader move them beyond the tangle of this conversation?

Facts: What Happened?

Firstly, it is important to agree on the facts that concern both the parties. We often assume we are talking about the same issue, especially if it is an experience that both the parties shared. But each person is probably concerned with a different selection of facts, one person in the team may answer the question: "What happened?" by saying: "You suddenly made a remark that irritated the client." The other person might look back and see something else: "This was about being a critical adviser to the client." Each party has a completely different set of facts they identified in the situation.

Therefore, it is important to collectively review the facts—free of judgement or interpretations. This will provide a sufficient level of agreement about what the neutral actions in the situation were. In doing so, one has to remember the situation as if someone had taken photos of it. Review the key interactions and events in the situation very precisely. Just reviewing the facts already serves as an eye-opener for the parties involved. An overlooked gesture or comment that was not heard and brought to the parties attention can change someone's entire view of what had happened. The difficulty with this stage is that it requires all parties to calm their emotions and show willingness to recall their thinking. Sometimes this means allowing a long break in a meeting because emotions are running too high.

Interpretations

After you have collectively generated the facts of the situation and have a satisfactory level of agreement about "what happened", it is time to move on. At this stage, it may even be that you agree to disagree on the facts, but you can still take the next step. Now the key point is to know how each party interpreted the facts they recorded.

- Person A. "The fact that the client became a bit irritated is great, because it shows him that we are not afraid to take risks to defend our professional approach."
- Person B. "I think that irritating the client means closing doors instead of opening them, which is not healthy in a client relationship."

If each party explains its interpretation, this helps all of them understand why the other conversation dynamics occurred.

Belief Systems

After people have established the facts and interpreted them, they will filter these through their belief systems. This is an essential part of their mental model related to situations like these—the previously mentioned if–then rule. The obvious belief systems at work here are about how to best serve a client. Not so obvious, but still relevant, types of beliefs could be related to professional pride, freedom to operate, or the level of control. In trying to untangle a difficult conversation, to invite the parties to say what led them to judge the situation in a certain way is the key—to be explicit about their if–then rules. Both the parties could then be challenged regarding the validity and relevance of their rules in this situation.

Action

On the basis of their if–then rules, people come to conclusions and actions. Since matters move very fast in a conversation, people almost react reflexively. Conclusions are instantly drawn. The post-meeting discussion could focus on the concrete actions that an individual took; how these made sense not only in relation to his or her belief system, but also what else he or she could have done. Even though our assumptions may be correct, this does not give us the authority to do whatever we like. In the above situation, the colleagues could have made remarks that decreased the tension, without disqualifying the suggestions of the person challenging the client.

Result

This step is about identifying what the outcome of an experience is; how parties feel about what happened; especially now they know what led the others to behave as they did. The parties may have learned something, or may now regret not having checked with each other that there was a plan for the meeting. The conversation could finish with recommendation on what to do next time for a different result. The FIBAR model can thus be used for evaluation, as it can help you to analyze where a conversation went off track. It can also be very useful during a meeting as a guiding framework.

CONCLUSION

It is a given that there will be differences of opinion, especially in a work environment. People are wired differently, and therefore there is no one right answer to something. When we expect a conversation to become difficult, it makes sense to briefly reflect on how to handle it, and to focus on what we want to achieve. In dealing with our colleagues' reactions, we have to take into account that our emotions and mental models constantly react to each other. Becoming better at identifying these reactions prevents unnecessary escalations. Ultimately, we can send difficult conversations in a positive direction if we use a deliberate approach as indicated by the FIBAR tool. We thus send the message to you, the reader, that communicating well is both an art and a science, and brushing up on the science and practising the success patterns will help you evolve even further. Whatever someone's skill profile is, there is always room for improvement and further development. It is not a definitive state.

Your Activities for Enhanced Communication Skills

Activity 1: Reflection on difficult conversations.

Think back to a recent difficult conversation and list the following:

1. At which point did the conversation derail?

_____

2. What were the reasons? Was it because of what was explicitly said, or was it because of how you or others interpreted it?

_____

3. Were you clear about what you wanted to achieve, or did you just want to bring your point of view across?

_____

4. Was there a point in the conversation when you knew that going further would cause trouble? (But you still pressed on?)

_____

Activity 2: Your preference in interpersonal behavior.

In this activity, we invite you to obtain a first indication of your preferences in relationships with regards to the three dimensions referred to in the FIRO-B®, namely control, inclusion, and affection. Start reflecting on these areas by looking at the behaviors associated with the three needs as presented in the table below, and mark how often you display such behaviors. The author of this chapter designed this Table 8.2 in order to precisely identify your preferences in the control, inclusion, and affection dimensions, use the FIRO-B® questionnaire available from Oxford Psychology Press in the UK (OPP) in several languages.

Table 8.2.   Preferences in Relationships: Self-Assessment

	Inclusion	*Control*	*Affection*
Expressed	Talking and joking with others Never------------------ Always	Taking positions of authority Never------------------ Always	Comforting and supporting colleagues Never------------------ Always
	Taking a personal interest in others Never------------------ Always	Proposing your idea within the group Never------------------ Always	Bringing gifts to show appreciation Never------------------ Always
	Involving others in projects and meetings Never------------------ Always	Making winning a priority Never------------------ Always	Showing concern for the personal lives of others Never------------------ Always
	Recognizing achievements of others. Never------------------ Always	Facilitating the conversation Never------------------ Always	Being trustworthy and loyal Never------------------ Always
	Including ideas and suggestions of all Never------------------ Always	Influencing the opinion of others Never------------------ Always	Sharing personal opinions or private feelings Never------------------Always
	Offering helpful tips to new colleagues Never------------------ Always	Establishing structures and procedures Never------------------ Always Dividing Tasks and roles Never------------------ Always	Coaching & Developing others Never------------------ Always

(Continued)

Table 8.2. (Continued)

	Inclusion	*Control*	*Affection*
Wanted	Being at social office areas (coffee corner, canteen) Never------------------ Always	Asking for help on the job Never------------------ Always	Being flexible and easy going Never------------------ Always
	Wearing elegant clothing Never------------------ Always	Involving others in decision making Never------------------ Always	Listening carefully to others Never------------------ Always
	Decorating your office with personal memorabilia Never------------------ Always	Requesting precise instructions and clarification Never------------------ Always	Displaying a friendly body posture Never------------------ Always
	Seeking recognition or visibility Never------------------ Always	Giving priority to the wishes and needs of others Never------------------ Always	Asking others about their feelings, fears and anxieties. Never------------------ Always
	Getting involved in high profile projects/ activities Never------------------ Always	Asking for permission and provide progress updates Never------------------ Always	Trying to please others Never------------------ Always
	Going along with what the majority wants Never------------------ Always	Raising issues for others to consider. Never------------------ Always	Giving others more than they want or need. Never------------------ Always

Source: Adapted from Schnell and Hammer (1997), p. 5

Activity 3: Your communication habits.

1. Take a look at advocacy and inquiry's characteristic behavior. Which style do you mostly use when people confront you with a different point of view?

2. Identify someone you know who often uses advocacy and write down what you admire in this person, and also what reactions this person triggers in you.

---

3. Think of a recent dispute you had with a colleague. What would have happened if you had used more inquiry? What sort of questions could you ask the next time you return to that dispute?

REFERENCES AND RECOMMENDED READING

Diamond, S. (2010). Getting more. *How to negotiate to achieve your goals in the real world*. New York: Crown Business Books.

Kohlrieser, G. (2007). *Hostage at the table*. San Francisco: Wiley & Sons.

Schnell, E., & Hammer, A. (1997). *Introduction to the FIRO-B in organizations*. Palo Alto: CPP Inc.

Senge, P., & Scharmer O. (2001). Community Action Research: Learning as a Community of Practitioners, Consultants, and Researchers. *Handbook of Action Research: Participative Inquiry and Practice*. P. R. a. H. Bradbury (Ed.). Los Angeles: Sage.

Senge, P. (2006). *The fifth discipline: The art and practice of the learning organization*. New York: Doubleday.

CHAPTER 9

ADVANCED FACILITATION SKILLS

Claire Collins

OBJECTIVE OF THIS CHAPTER

The aim of this chapter is to offer you some insight into the usefulness of facilitation in managing and leading groups and practical tools and techniques, for the teams to reach the optimum outcome.

INTRODUCTION

As mentioned many times in this book, change is a constant feature of life in these modern times and, as a result, our ability to harness change and be successful influences the well-being of the individuals, organizations, and societies that we connect with. Companies often fail to get their business strategies implemented and often spend huge sums of money employing external consultants to help them. However, the talent and energy to drive innovation and progress often already exists in the teams of people within the organization. Generating positive results may simply be a matter of releasing those teams' creativity, and harnessing their energy for the correct focus.

Leadership and Personal Development: A Toolbox for the 21st Century Professional, pp. 171–183
Copyright © 2011 by Information Age Publishing
All rights of reproduction in any form reserved.

Facilitation is a process which can help you to unlock this box of talent and creativity and is a skill which you can use formally and informally, for one-off meetings or for groups that meet on a regular basis. It is an alternative to the more directive forms of organizational change for managers and leaders. In this chapter, we will explore the meaning of facilitation, its application, its benefits, a facilitator's necessary skill sets, and different ways of applying these in different settings. Last but not the least, you will be invited to practice some of the relevant facilitation skills yourself.

WHAT IS FACILITATION?

Facilitation simply means to "enable" or "make easy" and usually involves someone acting as a group facilitator, helping the group or team to achieve one or more agreed objectives. Weaver and Farrell (1999) define facilitation as "… a process through which a person helps others complete their work and improve the way they work together" (p. xiv). It is a way for you to work with a group or team towards a common goal. The scope of this goal may vary from covering the agenda of a normal team meeting, to supporting a board of directors to create and agree upon a company strategy. It is a way of managing effective discussions and delivering outputs for major projects or visions.

WHEN IS FACILITATION APPROPRIATE (AND NOT APPROPRIATE)?

When groups or teams meet to discuss ideas, generate plans, develop strategies, explore projects, and so forth, facilitation is an appropriate process to use. It requires all the participants to approach the discussion with equal (if different) input. There are times when other approaches might work better, for example, if the manager wants to communicate a particular message or decision, and then a more appropriate way to do this might be a presentation or direct communication. It is important for the facilitator to guard against being used as a mouth-piece for senior management for them to get what they want, only with the appearance of consultation. This has been termed "facipulation" by Robson and Beary (1995), combining the words "facilitation" and "manipulation".

THE BENEFITS OF FACILITATION

It is often difficult when working in organizations to develop well-formed, agreed-upon strategies for managing complex issues. Certain management styles favor an authoritative approach where teams are told what to do and how to do it. However, by adopting a facilitative style, either as a manager or by working with an independent facilitator, you can change the work culture in a team or group, and improve outcomes for business performance. Some of the benefits you might gain from using facilitation are:

- The bringing together of varied expertise–groups may consist of members of a regular team or may be specially formed. In either case, each member will have knowledge, skills and experience to offer, which will build the competency of the group as a whole.

- Better decision-making-well-structured and managed processes-will ensure, that all relevant issues will be discussed, obstacles identified, and opportunities explored. This results in higher quality, more feasible, lower risk solutions which carry greater ownership and a higher chance of success.

- Team building-especially in teams that work together regularly, the opportunity for collaboration, equal discussion, and sharing of ideas helps to build the team's strength, engagement, and effectiveness.

- Process improvement-facilitation is very effectively used to scrutinize and improve processes where members of the group may represent stages in a process and can use their expertise to critically examine the existing practice and promote improvements in efficiency and effectiveness.

- Clearer communication-as familiarity between group members develops, the quality of communication can improve. While the dynamics between the members can occasionally be problematic (see dealing with conflict), an understanding of how they communicate, and gaining clarity of message can still be developed.

THE FACILITATOR

Sometimes you may merely choose to use a facilitative style in leading a meeting of your team. However, if you wish to take a full part in a particular meeting, or even be absent from a discussion in order to enable the team to be more independent, you might decide to use an external or independent facilitator. In the definition of facilitation offered by Schwarz (1994), he mentions the facilitator as a person who is

> *"... acceptable to all members of the group, substantially neutral, intervenes to help a group improve the way it identifies, and solves problems and makes decisions, in order to increase the group's effectiveness."* Schwarz (1994, p. 4).

While facilitators will usually be entirely "content free,", concentrating only on the process, they may sometimes be asked to contribute knowledge or expertise to the discussion. In this situation, Jones and Bearley (2001) recommend stepping out of facilitation for a moment to enter the discussion, and then revert to the facilitation role when this has been concluded. The group's prior consent should be sought for this and the contribution should be limited to facts rather than opinions. You run the risk here that a dependence on the facilitator can be created (Higgs & Rowland, 2000), therefore the frequency of such contributions should be minimized.

The facilitator cannot be neutral when tending the group process. Schwartz (1994) splits group facilitation into two types: "basic facilitation," in which the facilitator guides the group towards a process for effectiveness, and "group developmental facilitation," in which the group members expect to play a part in monitoring and guiding the process and look to the facilitator to enable and teach them this role. The role of the facilitator is that of an expert when related to the process and the group's developmental stage.

FACILITATOR SKILLS

As a skilled facilitator, you hope to possess a range of competencies to enable you to oversee successful group outcomes. In her research, Stewart (2006) suggests a comprehensive array of competencies which might develop from basic (threshold)-level facilitation, through to expert (high-performing) levels. A diagrammatic representation of these competencies is given below (Fig. 9.1). As a developing facilitator, you may wish to undertake some self-reflection and self-assessment of your skill levels against these parameters, and perhaps create a development plan to strengthen some of your key skills.

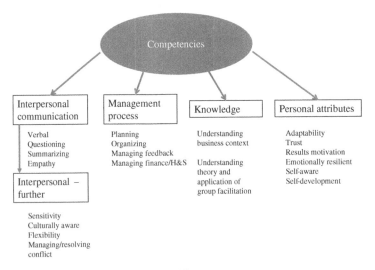

Figure 9.1. Competencies of skilled facilitators

HOW DO YOU KNOW WHEN FACILITATION HAS BEEN SUCCESSFUL?

In the above mentioned research there was full consensus that facilitation succeeded when the workshop owner and the participants met their objectives in the time available. Success was still merited, the research showed, when the objectives were partially met because the objective had changed to something more relevant, or where a constructive discussion had led to new ideas, decisions, or the resolution of related problems. The effects of a successful workshop are generally very positive. Group members leave feeling energized, focussed, enthused, and motivated, having a clear vision and direction for future action. The following was quoted:

"At the end of the workshop, the group feels a sense of satisfaction and achievement:

- that the workshop was a valuable use of their time
- that they achieved the right result
- that they have met the objectives and produced the deliverables, although these are not necessarily what they aimed for, at the beginning"

THE GROUP

There is no doubt that one of the key variables in the process of facilitation is the group itself. A group or team is made up of a number of members, each with their own unique characteristics, and experiences. They may also have different views on the facilitation workshop in which they are participating.

During the planning of the workshop it is important for you to gather as much information on these views as possible, and test the likely tools and techniques to be used. As far as possible, you should aim for "process congruence" (McFadzean, 1999) as one or more members' reluctance to use a particular technique can reduce the overall effectiveness. Besides the members' individual characteristics, the group as a whole will have a certain profile of maturity and experience which the facilitator can tap into to improve effectiveness. McFadzean (1998) developed a useful model called the Attention Pyramid (Fig. 9.2), which represents a group's increasing maturity and expertise, and indicates the level of creative work that the group can undertake to achieve its goals.

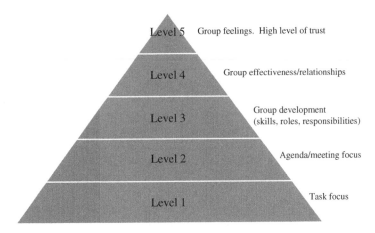

Figure 9.2. The attention pyramid adapted from McFadzean 1998

At the most basic level (Level 1), the group is only focused on their task. With that in mind, the intervention you use should only relate to the achievement of this task. Level 2 groups are able to attend to their task and the meeting structure, and therefore, the facilitator may include a discussion of the structure as well as the task. Further levels add the ability to pay attention to skills, roles and responsibilities, relationships and finally, at Level 5, to team feelings and the level of trust. In the preparation for the session, you should, as facilitator, assess the level of the group's ability, and include interventions aimed at the appropriate level.

CREATING THE PROCESS OF FACILITATION

McFadzean and Nelson (1998) suggest that the process of facilitation consists of three stages:

- Pre-session planning
- Running the group session
- Producing a post-session report

A more detailed model is suggested by Stewart (2006) and is summarized below (Fig. 9.3).

It might be argued that the most important stage in the process is planning. Without sufficient attention to detail at this stage, the project's risk is increased and the overall chance of success is diminished. In order to create the right environment for a successful facilitation, you should consider the following steps:

The Facilitation Process

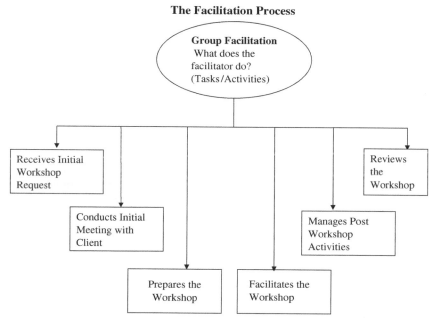

Figure 9.3. The facilitation process
Source: Based on Stewart, 2006.

- Contracting with the client (perhaps an external client or internal stakeholder). In the contracting process, as much detail as possible should be agreed on, in advance. For example, if the client is to be present, what role will they take? What outputs (report, and so forth) are expected? What time is available for the session (and is this realistic)? Where and when should it take place? In addition, the facilitator should speak to as many group members as possible, to gain an understanding of their perspective on the workshop, their lens on the issue at hand, and their vision and expectations of the process and outcomes. (Tip: Sometimes it is better if the main client/senior leader simply provides support by introducing the workshop and then leaving it to the team, to work independently. This can be helpful in ensuring all the group members' full and open participation).

- Diagnose and understand the problem-examine the background and underlying issues.

- Identify behaviors that might enhance or diminish group interaction-uncover any underlying conflicts or difficulties

- Develop the meeting structure and process, and organize the appropriate environment and resources for the meeting to run smoothly. This may include: venue, materials, catering, lighting, temperature, seating, and so forth. Leave as little to chance, as you possibly can!

CASE STUDY 1

A Real-life Facilitation Scenario in the UK in 2010

A senior manager engaged two internally trained facilitators to run a workshop on agreeing how the organization's value set could be communicated to clients, and be incorporated into the design of its programs.

The facilitators thoroughly contracted with the client and planned the session. Some negotiation was carried out on the length of the time available to achieve the agreed objectives. The group members were contacted and their views sought. The senior manager agreed that he wished to play a part in the session as an equal member of the group.

Very early in the session, it became clear that the senior manager could not take on a team member role and repeatedly took over the session to control and shape the outcome; at one point he admonished a team member for his behavior. The session was becoming unproductive and unstructured.

The two facilitators called a "time-out" and suggested that the other group members took a coffee break. After a discussion with the senior manager, during which he was reminded of his agreement during contracting, he decided that he would absent himself for the remainder of the meeting.

The session re-commenced, followed the agreed structure and outcomes that the group members deemed successful, and were agreed upon.

In the review meeting, the senior manager acknowledged his behavior, was impressed by the final outputs, and praised the facilitators' clear intervention.

RUNNING THE SESSION

Having planned the workshop thoroughly, you should now be well prepared to run the session. However, there are some areas that will help to enhance the smooth running of the process:

- Timing – try to work out your timing as accurately as possible and adhere closely to this. If you have planned well, you should have sufficient time to reach the desired goal. This is particularly true when running activities. Use a timer if it helps.

- Be flexible – sometimes you do have to move the items around, if the unexpected occurs. Flexibility and agility within a workshop are high-performance skills. Do not be afraid to stop and think for a moment about their effect on the overall outcome.
- Roles – you should have agreed on the roles and responsibilities beforehand. However, sometimes individuals feel the need to step outside the agreed boundaries. Use your structure to help you facilitate inclusive discussions, and try to maintain a balance where possible.
- Managing conflict – it is not always possible to have an entirely calm and peaceful facilitation session. Conflict can arise if a group member becomes uncooperative, or two or more members start disagreeing. It is not the facilitator's role to referee such situations. If roles have been agreed on beforehand, there are some parameters around which one can work. However, if everything else fails, take a break, and deal with the issues "off-line" with the hope of returning in a more constructive mode.
- Ground rules – it is a good idea to discuss and agree on some ground rules at the beginning of any session. If the group members can suggest these rules themselves, perhaps as an early exercise, there is likely to be better ownership of the parameters. Have the rules up somewhere where they are clearly visible throughout the session and can be returned to as required. You can include any element in the ground rules, that the group (and you) feel appropriate. This could include:
  - Use of mobile telephones
  - Only one person speaking at a time
  - Time-keeping (being on time for sessions, observing break times strictly, and so forth)
  - Mutual respect
  - Confidentiality
  - Giving feedback

CASE STUDY 2

A Real-life Facilitation Scenario in the UK in 2010

A group of professional associates engaged an independent facilitator to run a session aimed at to creating a strategy for the future. During the contracting process, the chairman of the group died suddenly. The group decided that they would continue with the meeting, as they believed that this was what their colleague would have wanted.

(Continued)

CASE STUDY 2 (*Continued*)

The session was planned in detail in advance with the facilitator able to speak to all, but two of the group participants. The detailed agenda and activities were agreed on with the acting chairman and his deputy.

At the session it quickly became apparent that all the participants (themselves trained facilitators) actually wanted to run the session, and each had an idea of how it should be conducted. The facilitator stayed calm and spent the first 30 minutes deciding with them as a group, on how the session would be run. The group demonstrated high-level attributes on the Attention Pyramid, and were flexible regarding the time and structure in order to achieve the best outcome. By staying calm and being agile, the facilitator could steer the session to an outcome, which everyone regarded as successful.

ADDITIONAL CREATIVE FACILITATION TOOLS AND TECHNIQUES

At the Beginning of a Workshop

- Icebreaker or energizing exercises—such exercises can be used to introduce the group members to each other if they have not met before or do not know each other well. They could also be used to get the team members, who do know each other to get into the facilitation mindset, to mentally leave other distractions behind, and to encourage early interaction. An example of an easy icebreaker is simply to get everyone to introduce themselves and say one thing about themselves that the others cannot guess. An energizing exercise might be to run a short general knowledge quiz in teams at the start; this should generate much chatter and laughter.

Exercises to Generate Data

- There are many exercises that you can use to generate data within a session. The type of intervention should be considered beside the group level on the Attention Pyramid (McFadzean, 1998).
- A simple example is brainstorming with the participants simply adding as many ideas as possible on the given subject to a flipchart

or to post-it notes. In the first stage, the ideas are not discussed or judged, but as many ideas as possible are captured in a given time. Once this process has been completed, the group may choose to group the items into themes, or go through a prioritization process, to home in on the most probable winners.

- Another idea would be to assign a different theme to each team. Each team brainstorms its theme and after the agreed time, the teams rotate and group or prioritize another team's output.

- Reversal-for a given scenario, the group reverses the question and generates as many answers as possible. For example, the question could be: How can we please our customers and obtain repeat business? The reversal might be: How can we drive our customers away and ensure they never work with us again? This technique usually generates plenty of data which, when reversed, turns into the recipe for success!

- Mind-mapping-with the main theme in the center of the page, the teams generate ideas for sub-themes radiating outwards. This technique generates many ideas, but also demonstrates that the teams have already identified the linkages and associations between issues.

There are many different creative exercises that you can use in group facilitation. Please see the recommended reading section below, for more sources of ideas.

FINAL KEY TIPS!

- Prepare, prepare, prepare-reduce the risk.
- Be clear about facilitator's role and responsibility for the process.
- Is it a facilitation or facipulation?
- Get the right people in the room-ask them what they BRING to the process.
- Client/owner presentations (what and why)-agree on them beforehand.
- Confirm the scope and objectives (how).
- Be flexible (use alternative techniques/designs).
- Say NO! If you are asked to undertake facilitation without proper preparation, it is better to say no than have a failed workshop, the ramifications of which may be widespread and long-lasting.

CONCLUSION

Facilitation is a very useful and powerful process which, used well, will help you to generate creativity, engagement, focus, and energy in groups and teams; in turn, it can deliver key business outputs and performance success. The process should seem almost effortless in its execution if the right amount of planning and preparation has taken place. As a facilitator you can build expertise in the competencies that make the process and outcomes successful. By following well-researched structures, the likelihood of a workshop's success can be greatly enhanced, and the potential outputs for you, the team, or the organization will undoubtedly improve.

Your Activities for Strengthening Your Facilitation Skills

Activity 1: Contracting for a facilitation workshop.

- Agree on a facilitation topic with your client(s).
- In a discussion with them, agree on all the matters you need to plan the session. These may include:
  - o Who is in the group (roles, responsibilities, background)?
  - o What is the purpose of the workshop?
  - o What are the desired outcomes (overall goals, not answers)?
  - o Get permission to speak to the other group members.
  - o Discuss the background of the project, and the accomplished work.
  - o Agree on the venue and timing of the session (Do you think it is feasible? Make recommendations).
  - o Discuss any underlying cultural/personality issues, or perceived obstacles to a successful outcome.
  - o Agree on what the final output will be. What will it look like (a report, a presentation)? When is it required?

Activity 2: Design and prepare for a 30 minute facilitation workshop.

Based on the above, design and prepare a 30 minute facilitation workshop:

- Develop an appropriate structure for the session (30 minutes may only cover part of the client brief)!

- What interventions will you use? Why?
- What materials do you need?
- What environment will you work in and does this present any issues?
- What will your outputs tell you? What will they look like?
- How will you capture the data and report it?

REFERENCES AND FURTHER READING

Higgs, M., & Rowland, D. (2000). Building change leadership capability: The quest for change competency. *Journal of Change Management, 1*(2), 116–130.

Hogan, C. (2003). *Practical facilitation: A toolkit of techniques.* London: Kogan Page

Jones, J., & Bearley, W. (2001). Facilitating team development: A view from the field. *Group Facilitation: A Research and Applications Journal, 3*, 56–65.

McFadzean, E. (1998). Using adaptive structuration theory to explain group creativity, *Working Paper No. 9918*, Henley-on-Thames: Henley Management College.

McFadzean E. (1999). A framework for facilitating group processes. *Strategic Change* (Vol. 8, Issue 7, pp. 421–431), November 1999.

Nelson, T., & McFadzean, E. (1998). Facilitating problem solving groups: Facilitator competencies. *Leadership and Organizational Development Journal, 19*(2), 72–82.

Robson, M., & Beary, C. (1995). *Facilitating.* Farnham: Gower.

Schwarz, R. (1994). *The skilled facilitator: Practical wisdom for developing effective groups.* San Francisco: Jossey-Bass.

Schwarz, R. (2002). *The skilled facilitator: Practical wisdom for developing effective groups* (new and Rev. ed.). San Francisco: Jossey-Bass.

Stewart, J. (2006). High-performing (and threshold) competencies for group facilitators. *Journal of Change Management, 6*(4), 417–439.

Weaver, R., & Farrell, J. (1999). *Managers as facilitators.* San Francisco: Berrett-Koehler.

CHAPTER 10

POLISH YOUR COACHING SKILLS

Patricia Bossons and Denis Sartain

OBJECTIVES OF THIS CHAPTER

The aim of this chapter is to enable those who work as managers to choose the type of conversation they have with one of their team members. We furthermore aim to clarify the following questions: What is the difference between using a coaching style and a management style? How do you judge which is the most appropriate style in any given situation? And then, of course: What does a coaching conversation look like and how do you have one with a staff member?

INTRODUCTION

How do you coach someone when you are also their boss? Is it appropriate to even try? What happens if it gets mixed up half way through? How clear is your understanding of what you are doing when you are coaching?

Sometimes, these questions are brought up by practicing managers when we run coaching supervision sessions for in-house coaches. Managing

---

Leadership and Personal Development: A Toolbox for the
21st Century Professional, pp. 185–201
Copyright © 2011 by Information Age Publishing

the boundaries between what can be discussed in a coaching conversation as opposed to a management conversation's focus is an important issue to consider, if you are thinking of developing your coaching skills in order to use them with people who also report to you. It is also important even if you are planning on working in this way with people, with whom you have different work relationships—you can use a coaching approach to a conversation with your colleagues, your boss, even your suppliers and clients at times. The key point is your judgment regarding whether it is the right choice for the situation, and to be clear about your understanding and approach to coaching.

In this chapter, we will try to explain what coaching is and why it is a useful part of a manager's toolkit. We will take you through the GROW coaching model, which is the fundamental coaching process which can keep you on track as you progress through a coaching conversation, and help you mark it out as different from a usual management conversation. Finally, we will look at the key issues to be prepared for, as you use coaching skills as part of your management role.

SIMILARITIES AND DIFFERENCES

In our roles as tutors of the Henley Business School Certificate in Coaching program, we have asked over 600 participants to think about the ways in which coaching is similar to, and different from some of the other activities it can be confused with. A high proportion of these people are managers using coaching skills, as part of the way they do their job. Some of the groups participate in the program as an in-house training. They are, therefore, all managers from the same company. There is plenty of experience to draw upon. In the Table 10.1, we show the similarities and differences which are commonly mentioned when we ask the participants to reflect on coaching versus (performance) management.

One of the basic rules in coaching is that there are no right and wrong answers. A manager could have a coaching conversation or a management conversation with an individual for most of the given situations that arise at work, and either could be useful. However, they would be useful in different ways, and it is likely that in some situations one approach will achieve a better result than the other.

WHY SHOULD MANAGERS BE ABLE TO COACH?

When a director of learning and development (L&D) from a large organization was talking to us before subjecting more than 100 of his

Table 10.1.   Coaching Versus (Performance) Management

Similarities	*Differences*
• Aim to improve a situation	• Coaching focuses on the individual, not the organization
• Time spent talking about an individual's problem	• Manager focuses on solving the problem for the person
• One-to-one and confidential	• Manager tells the person what to do
• Support	• Coaching helps people find their own answer
• Trying to get someone to be more effective	• Performance management linked to specific outcomes
	• Management conversation has consequences
	• Coaching conversation is non-judgmental

middle and senior managers to a coaching skills development program at Henley, the key reason he gave for wanting to do this was simply that he needed his managers to be able to "do more". By this he meant that due to reorganizations, redundancies, and acquisitions and so on, his managers had to achieve much higher levels of output, than had previously been experienced. He was concerned that for one person to do three people's jobs seemed pretty impossible—even though at that time, this was pretty much what many of his managers had to do.

The answer to "Why should managers be able to coach?" could well be, "So that the organization can achieve its business results even in tough times." Some of the benefits this L&D director wanted from the coaching program included better motivation and retention of the key staff, more empowerment at all levels, and, especially, the freeing up of senior management time, by enabling others to take more responsibility.

THIS IS WHAT IT LOOKS LIKE IN REAL LIFE

In the following, you will find a description of a typical management situation, emotions running high and a solution needed quickly. We will show the two potential approaches that are available to a manager at this point.

Communication Approach A—the management side of the conversation might go something like this:

Manager: "What's up?"

Julie: "I want you to have a word with Mark. I have asked him to up-date the Web site five times since May—that is 3 months ago—and still nothing has happened. I tried to talk to him about it, but he just says there are other priorities and he will get back to me as soon as he can. I find him really rude, and I cannot be bothered talking to him any more…"

Manager: "Okay, Julie, what exactly have you asked him to do, and why is it so important?"

Manager: "Right, so you need this information on the Web site before the conference on the 9th and Mark is not getting on with it. Have you asked him what else he has to do?"

Manager: "Why do you not go back to Mark and explain exactly why this is so important? From what you are telling me, I do not think you have made it completely clear, why he needs to get on with this over and above the marketing page update."

Manager: "While you are talking to him, can you ask him to get that report he wrote last week over to Tom, please? Tom needs it next Tuesday."

Manager: "He's not really rude—I know what you mean, but it is just his way. Stand up to him."

Manager: "I want this sorted out today, please! Let me know how you get on, and I will talk to Mark if there is still a problem."

Manager: "I really think it might be an idea for you to go on the Assertiveness Skills course that Linda runs. Why do you not book for it?"

Manager: "Let me know how you get on and if you want me to have a talk with him, but you need to try first."

Communication Approach B—a coaching conversation might look like this:

Manager as coach: "Okay, Julie, you have asked me to coach you on the issue you are having getting the Web site updated. We have got an hour right now. If this is not enough, we can schedule another session, so

	let us see how far we get. This is a coaching session, not me talking to you as a boss or a colleague. And before we start, I would just like to say that everything we discuss will be completely confidential. If anything comes up that seems to be more like a management issue, we will note it and keep it to one side, and afterward we can decide what to do about it. Is this okay?"
Manager as coach:	"So, Julie, tell me what you would like to get from this session?"
Julie:	"I need to get the Web site updated before the conference on the 9th. If it is not done really soon, the whole conference will be at risk. We are mainly publicizing the conference through the Web site and it is the only way we are taking bookings! At the moment we only have about 30% of the attendance we are looking for—and they are the only people who have heard about it and are expressing interest. They have not been able to book yet. I am getting phone calls asking me how they can do this and so are the other administrators. We are all getting really fed-up. I just do not know what to do ..."

(Julie is getting increasingly worked up at this point and the coach intervenes.)

Manager as coach:	"I have the impression that you are pretty fed-up with the situation! And that the Web site's update is really important for you."
Julie:	"It is important! Organizing the conference is one of my most important jobs of the year, and my reputation is really suffering."
Manager as coach:	"In sum, you want to find a way to get the Web site updated as soon as possible, and it is your responsibility to ensure this. Right?"
Julie:	"Yes!"
Manager as coach:	"Okay! Now, what have you done so far?"
Julie:	"It is Mark! It is his job to do the Web updates. I told him to do this 3 months ago, and I have reminded him at least four times, but he still has not got round to it—and now he is being really rude whenever I speak to him."

Manager as coach:	"Is Mark the only person who can help you with this?"
Julie:	"Yes! Although he does have a couple of people working for him who can do things once he has prioritized them. I tried to talk to them directly, but they told Mark and he got really angry with me."
Manager as coach:	"What other ways are there to make Mark pay attention to your job and its urgency?"
Julie:	"I suppose I could arrange to talk to Mark again and apologize for not going through the official system."
Manager as coach:	"How do you think you could make sure that Mark gives your job the priority it needs?"
Julie:	"I could make sure he understands that there is a really tight time-frame and show him the request history so that he knows I did start the process with a good lead-in time. He only got back to me after his team-members told him I had approached them directly. Perhaps he did not get the original request."
Manager as coach:	"Do you think he was deliberately ignoring you?"
Julie:	"No, I guess not. He has always been pretty quick before."
Manager as coach:	"What do you think would be the best way to have the conversation with Mark? Is there any other information you could gather before you talk to him?"
Julie:	"I could actually have a chat with marketing and get them to show where the conference fits in with the other things they need Mark to change or add to the Web site. I know they will be able to show that the conference is the next big event coming up, and needs to be the top priority even though some of the other issues might be bigger in the long run."
Manager as coach:	"That sounds like a promising plan. What are you going to do first?"
Julie:	"I will go and see marketing this afternoon and get the details, and then I will make an appointment to

see Mark as soon as possible. I will not do it by e-mail this time."

Manager as coach: "What are you going to ask him for?"

Julie: "I am going to show him the prioritizations from marketing, show him what I need on the Web site, and ask him to get the information up by the end of this week. That will give us 6 weeks to make bookings for the conference."

DE-BRIEF OF THE ALTERNATIVE COMMUNICATION APPROACHES

In the following, we want to highlight the differences between the two different ways of tackling the same conversation. Obviously, these are rather stylized conversations cut short to make the point. The main differences are:

In the **management conversation,** the manager wants to solve the problem himself, and as soon as possible. He is taking Julie's account at the face value—starting with Mark being the problem, and accepting the responsibility to solve the problem. He is making suggestions and giving Julie advice, and then talking about other tasks in the same conversation.

In the **coaching conversation,** the manager has completely taken himself out of the equation and made it clear to Julie that this is a different type of conversation. He has put a time limitation on the session, contracted for confidentiality, and how any issues which might not be best dealt with through coaching, will be handled.

The conversation itself is focused on allowing Julie to explore the situation in her own words, and to come up with her own solutions. The coach is asking questions to enable Julie to think about the issue in a more structured way—after he allowed her to vent out her frustration! While she was getting her frustration off her chest, he was listening and acknowledging, but was not getting drawn in. This is one of the key differences in the two conversations. He clarifies with Julie what she actually wants to happen—note it is about getting the job done, not about dealing with Mark!

He helps her explore different aspects of the current problem, then to look at possible ways forward, and finally to put together a plan of action. He is also most specific about making sure that Julie commits to a time to complete her actions. All of this is decided by Julie, not by the coach. The coach, however, does repeat some of the things Julie is saying, to make sure that she is clear as to what she is committing to.

WHAT THE MANAGER IS DOING WHEN HE OR SHE IS COACHING

There is actually a structure in this coaching conversation, and it is the most well-known and fundamentally useful structure to ensure that a coaching conversation stays on track. Many other coaching tools and techniques can be learnt and used, but this underpinning structure can be used as the basic framework for a conversation, regardless of whatever else is done. This structure is known as the GROW model, and is worth practicing and remembering. If you find yourself getting lost in a coaching conversation, getting distracted, wondering if you are still coaching or have started doing something else, scanning the stages of the GROW model will soon have you re-grouped and back on track.

THE GROW MODEL

The GROW model (Figure 10.1.) was first described by John Whitmore in his well-known book *"Coaching for Peak Performance"* (2007). It is now widely known and was modeled on best practice, rather than theory. This is the structure used by people who were excellent at helping others come up with their own solutions to their problems—often without even knowing, that

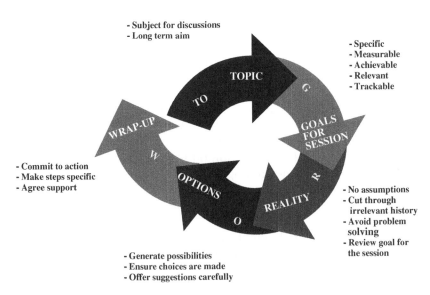

Figure 10.1. The GROW model
Source: Adapted from Whitmore (2007).

this is what they were doing. Whitmore noticed this and transcribed the structure. It is now the "industry standard" coaching model.

There are four stages to an effective coaching conversation. These stages have been named after the specific focus of the conversation at each stage. Thus, G is for goal—"What does the person being coached actually want to achieve?", R is for reality—What is happening right now?", O is for options— "What could you do?", and, finally, W is for will—"What will you do? When?"

It is convenient that these four letters also spell the word that a coach is hoping to help his or her coachee to do—GROW! This is easy to remember. The following details of the GROW model are explained in the way we use them as a part of the material for the Henley Certificate in Coaching.

The Table 10.2 further clarifies the role of the coach in facilitating the coaching conversation. It also highlights the most common hurdles a coach can be faced with, during the four different phases of a GROW conversation. When first practicing the GROW Model, it is recommended that you follow the sequences quite linearly. The more astute and skilled you become as a coach, the more you will probably adapt the model to the conversation, and to your coaching style. However, for the model to enfold its full potential, it should still actively apply to you as the coach during a conversation.

In the following you will find helpful questions to guide you when using the GROW Model. These questions have been proved to be extremely helpful in our coaching practice. You can, of course, supplement this list by adding your own sets of questions, while you continue to polish your coaching skills. Just remember: Asking intelligent and useful questions and listening attentively to your coachee's answers is at the heart of every good coaching conversation that produces real outcomes for the coach.

Table 10.2.   Phases of the GROW Model

Phases of the GROW Model	What is the work of the coach?	Most common coaching pitfalls
Goal	• to enable the coachee to be clear about what he or she wants • to elicit a mandate	• rushing • assuming the topic is the mandate
Reality	• to draw the coachee's attention to new things	• interviewing the coachee
Options	• to elicit a choice and a feeling of efficacy in the coachee	• supplying the options • "selling" a specific option
Way forward/will	• to enable the coachee to recognize and manage his or her motivation	• motivating the coachee • "managing" the coachee

Source: Based on Whitmore (2007).

Goal: *What do you want?*

- What is the goal of this discussion?
- What do you want to achieve (short and long term)?
- How much personal control do you have over your goal?
- When do you want to achieve it by?
- Is this challenging, attainable, and measurable?
- How much time do we have?
- What are you looking for from me?

Reality: *What is happening now?*

- (WHAT, WHEN, WHERE, HOW MUCH, HOW OFTEN)
- Who is involved?
- What have you done about this so far?
- What results did this produce?
- What is happening (both internally and externally)?
- What are the major constraints to finding a way forward?

Options: *What could you do?*

- What options do you have?
- What if....?
- Would you like another suggestion?
- What are the benefits and costs of each?
- What would you do differently now?
- How do you feel about this?

Way forward/Will: *What will you do?*

- What are you going to do?
- Will this meet your goal?
- When are you going to do it?
- What obstacles could you face?
- How do you set about overcoming them?
- Who needs to know?
- What support do you need?
- How will you get that support?

- On a scale of 1–10, what is the likelihood of your success in carrying out this task?
- Do it!

The following case study describes how coaching was used as a central tool for an organizational development activity in a global construction organization at Henley Business School.

CASE STUDY 1

A Coaching Intervention at Henley Business School

An organizational development intervention introducing coaching skills.

Henley Business School was approached by a leading international construction organization to help with the issues it was experiencing managing senior talent in the company. The global HR director was particularly concerned about succession planning for the most senior, director-level jobs in its various companies. Each managing director had a "little black book" with the names of individuals of the various companies in the organization, and the overall executive board also had its own ideas concerning suitable individuals. However, through acquisition the company had expanded into a number of new countries over the last 3 years, and had changed its strategy quite significantly.

The main concern was that many of the senior managers in line to take over the top jobs, once the current incumbents retired in 3–5 years' time, had not been consulted about their views on their future careers. There were many assumptions and the list of names was somewhat unchecked, and out of date.

A development intervention was devized by Henley Business School, which would work at two levels. At one level, it would be run for groups of 12 senior managers at a time, and give them a chance to review where they were in the organization, receive an up-date on the organization's strategy, and take part in a leadership development workshop and network, with each other and the executive. At another level, they would have the opportunity to receive completely confidential one-to-one coaching to help them reflect on anything that the workshop process highlighted, and any personal outcomes and goals following from this.

(Continued)

CASE STUDY 1 (*Continued*)

The overall process occurred in several stages. Firstly, each participating manager gathered the data. This included 360-degree feedback data, performance reviews, psychometric test results, career history, and statements of career aspirations–whatever would help create a full picture of where the individual was at this point in time. Next 2 days workshop was held at Henley. This workshop was jointly facilitated by Henley and the HR director, and was focused on leadership and personal development. Each afternoon, each participant undertook a one-and-a-half hour coaching session. The first session tended to focus on how the specific participant had got to where he or she was at that time, using all the data collected before the workshop. The second session tended to focus on what the workshop had highlighted, and how the participants wanted to make sense of this for them in the future.

Resulting from the workshop and the coaching sessions, a specific personal development plan was being aimed at, discussing this with the participants' line-manager (usually a member of the Board) within 6 weeks of the workshop. Development had also been undertaken with the line managers so that a truly "adult" conversation, or dialogue, would be possible at these meetings. This would include conversations about whether the individual wanted to be considered for the general manager position, or wanted to stay in a technical post, or even eventually leave the organization. Additional coaching sessions were available to support each manager, at intervals throughout the process.

The overall point of this case-study is to illustrate how important it was to allow each individual manager the chance, to reflect on what he or she wanted to do in a confidential coaching session, as well as, to experience the workshop and the dialogue with his or her boss. This intervention, which has now been running in this organization for more than 3 years, is a powerful example of how using coaching in an organization can bring real, and very strategic, results.

CONCLUSIONS

As with all new skills, a coaching approach will take some practice if you have not used it before. This is true of both a formal session and a general conversation, but also for you to use the GROW model's structure in a more general conversation if you decide that a coaching approach might be helpful in a given situation.

One very useful way to develop competence through this model is to experience some coaching yourself. This is a really powerful way of understanding the effect of the different stages of the model, in terms of how it facilitates thinking. Probably, the most important point to make about using coaching skills as a manager is that it is a specific, and a different way of having a conversation and that, as a manager, you need to be able to have a range of conversations—not just to coach people! The skill is to judge what is appropriate when, to be flexible about using what seems to be working, and knowing when to change an approach, if it is not. It is usually best to signal to someone that you think a coaching conversation might be a useful thing to do; if you do not and you have a different role in that person's life as well, he or she might well be confused by your sudden change in style!

Your Activities for Practicing Your Coaching Skills

Activity 1: GROW Model Exercise.

We would like to suggest you have a go with the GROW Model. Even if you have been coaching for a long time, it is always useful to practice the discipline of using a process such as GROW, and seeing if this differs from your normal coaching conversations. This then gives you something extra to reflect on, to develop your practice. If it is all new to you, then running through this exercise will help you experience the difference between a coaching conversation and any other kind of conversation. Notice where you get tempted to side-track, or get sucked into the content. Resist this! And notice what strategies you can use to resist these temptations.

The exercise is straight-forward. Also feel free to have the GROW model and the questions at hand, if you find this useful. You can make this activity less awkward in the way in which you introduce the session to your coachee, therefore:

Find someone who is willing to have a coaching conversation with you, perhaps to achieve a personal development goal. Allow about 45 minutes for this first session, and see how far you get. The contracting piece could be more or less as in:

Step One—Contracting

"Thank you for making the time for this coaching session. I am developing the idea of using coaching as a part of the way I exercise my management role. In this session I would like to try out a particular process with you to see if it is more effective for you, than a general management conversation. Is that okay with you? I have got my notes with me—just in case—to help me stick to the process."

Then acknowledge the confidentiality, time-frame for the session and any other points you need to make.

_____

_____

Step Two—Using the GROW Model

This is where you help the coachee state what it is he or she wants from the session. Using some of the questions from the list can be useful. Remember, you might need to revisit this stage several times to check whether the goal changes as the coachee becomes clearer during the session. Once you have established his or her goal, work through the GROW model, noticing what happens at each stage. Feel free to go back-and-forth between the different stages, depending on what seems most useful for the coachee.

_____

_____

_____

Step Three—Ending the Session

Bring the session to a conclusion at the time outlined at the beginning (you might want to flag these 10 minutes or so before the end, for example, "We have about 10 minutes left, would you like to summarize where you are with your goal now?", or some such prompt. You will most probably not have run through the whole model, but you will have experienced how the process works. If this seems appropriate at this time, contract for a follow-up session (or more!) by all means.

_____

_____

_____

Step Four—De-brief

Since you set this up with your coachee as a practice session for you, he or she will not be surprised if you ask him or her for feedback. It can be a good idea to mention that you will be doing this in the initial contracting conversation. Spend about 20 minutes asking the coachee for his or her reflections on the session. The following areas can be useful prompts:

- How was the relationship and the rapport between us?
- Did you feel listened to?
- What was the most useful thing about the session for you?
- Was there anything that was unhelpful?
- Is there anything you would have liked me to do differently?
- How did this conversation differ from other conversations we have had?
- What challenged you the most?

And, of course, any other questions that fit the context.

_____

_____

_____

Using a process such as the GROW model is useful in itself, of course, but also useful to outlining the differences between a coaching conversation and other kinds of interaction in the workplace. This is particularly helpful when you are thinking about coaching as a manager, and need a way of delineating this as a specific activity which only happens sometimes.

Activity 2: Start using the GROW Model in management conversations.

Once you feel more comfortable with this approach, you can start using it in a working context as well. You are recommended to prepare a Din A4 sheet that you can use to make notes while you are having the conversation. This will help you to stay focused on the purpose of the conversation, and ask good questions to help your employees to produce relevant and practical solutions that they feel committed to.

REALITY	OPTIONS
GOAL	**WAY FORWARD / WILL**

REFERENCES

Bossons, P., Kourdi, J., & Sartain, D. (2009). *Coaching Essentials*. London: A & C Black.

Clutterbuck, D., & Megginson, D. (2005). *Making Coaching Work*. London: CIPD.

Clutterbuck, D., & Megginson, D. (2005). *Techniques for Coaching and Mentoring*. London: Elsevier Butterworth-Heinemann.

Hardingham, A. (2004). *The Coach's Coach*. London: CIPD.

Skiffington, S., & Zeus, P. (2000). *Coaching at Work*. Australia: McGraw-Hill Book Co.

Whitmore, J. (2007). *Coaching for Performance*, Boston, USA: Nicholas Brealey Publishing.

PART IV

REFINING YOUR RELATIONSHIP SKILLS

CHAPTER 11

HOW TO BUILD A NETWORK THAT WORKS

Didier Gonin

OBJECTIVES OF THE CHAPTER

The main objective of this chapter is to motivate you to network more, and to use your network to enhance your life and career opportunities. We will discuss how to build, map, enlarge, and maintain your network, and explore some critical networking skills and attitudes.

INTRODUCTION

In his book on social capital and networking, Wayne Baker (2000) from the University of Michigan suggests that "success depends on two factors: what a person knows (human capital), and the network of relationships he or she has developed (social capital)." He adds that the world has changed in such a way that no-one can know enough about his or her profession anymore, so he or she has to draw upon professional knowledge and resources that exist in other people's heads. One of the biggest lessons that people need to unlearn when they enter the world of business is that success is an individual matter.

Leadership and Personal Development: A Toolbox for the
21ˢᵗ Century Professional pp. 205–222
Copyright © 2011 by Information Age Publishing

Networking can be described as the cultivation of our social capital; a process of building, and maintaining valuable relationships with others; a way of broadening our own perspectives by tapping into different ideas and approaches. Currently, networking is becoming an increasingly essential professional endeavor, based on mutually beneficial relationships, as it is one of the most powerful ways to become an effective influencer and to develop a smarter type of capital. Last, but not the least, it can provide each of us with vital support in times of change, difficulty, trouble or stress!

In this chapter, the reader is invited to explore the benefits of networking, and learn how to build and grow a network. We will introduce the idea of mapping your network and familiarize you with networking skills and attitudes.

BENEFITS OF NETWORKING

There are many benefits in networking—personal, career related, business, and organization benefits. They are often interrelated and networkers know that there is no border between personal and professional life. Executives and managers understand the benefits of networking, even though they may not always dedicate enough time and energy to doing it! Good networkers naturally ask for help when they need it, and they then know who to turn to. They ask themselves: *"In what area may I need support? Who can I turn to if/when I need help?"*

If we have a good network, it is easy to obtain advice and different perspectives, because most people like to share their expertise with people they know and trust. It is a very natural and human need to wish to be connected with friends, and/or like-minded individuals, people we want to spend time with, learn from, share thoughts, and feelings. As communication is a two-way street, we can also find much satisfaction in networking by helping others, by sharing our experience or expertise.

The more we network, the more we communicate, thereby increasingly clearly explaining the objectives that we pursue, and gaining confidence in ourselves and in our capability to achieve our goals. One therefore needs to ask oneself: *"How, and with whom, can I get an opportunity to explain what I want to achieve, my objectives?"*

A large number of managers adopt a "low profile" and tend to consider the act of "marketing" or "selling" themselves negatively. By networking and expanding our contacts, we can simply make ourselves better known without being self-centered or egoistic, and raise our profile in such a way, that others will naturally think about us when an opportunity arises (job, project, new product, or service). Networkers, therefore, need to consider approaches to ensure that they themselves and their work are better known.

Last, but not the least, networking has an impact on the bottom line, on the generation of referrals and on increased business, as most new business is gained through word-of-mouth, and positive recommendation. People like to pass business to people they know, like and trust. It is imperative to develop one's contacts, and build positive relationships with a large variety of people.

CASE STUDY 1

Unforeseen Ripple Effects of Networking

Franco Iacometti (50), Italian, partner at Org Value Consulting, Milan, Italy.

Franco recalls the time when he was with General Electric Information Services (GEIS), working as the Human Resources director for EMEA at the beginning of the 2000s. His responsibilities entailed a great deal of international travel as he was based in Paris for 3 years, while his family lived in Milan. He says: "*I felt I was under a great deal of pressure, with a lot of commuting between Paris and Milan during the weekends on top of all my business trips!*"

Then the part of the GEIS business for which Franco worked, was sold, and he managed the transition to a new company inside GEIS. In 2003, he decided to leave GEIS, to go back to Italy and set up his own company with a partner.

Reflecting on his experience over these years, Franco adds: "*When I was at GEIS, I did not dedicate enough time to building and maintaining my network because of the situation. I then realized how important it was.*"

When he left GEIS, Franco reconnected with his former GEIS Training and Learning manager, who had also gone independent, and had created his own company not long before: "*He put me in touch with a major player in the leadership development field in Europe. I contacted them and, not long after, I got involved in delivering leadership seminars for Fujitsu with them. I have been associated with them since then, working on several projects in Europe.*"

Franco's story illustrates how, by reconnecting with a former colleague, he was then connected to a whole network of associates working for another leadership development provider, a beautiful example of the ripple effects of effective networking!

BUILDING/GROWING MY NETWORK

Building our network starts with getting to know the persons we meet, or work with better. It can start with simple open-ended questions: *"What is your favorite city (or country)? What are your favorite films? What are your favorite books (or authors)?* And, evolve to deeper questions such as: "What are you passionate about?" "What are your long term goals?" *"What would you like to do that you have not yet done?"*

These questions suggest that we communicate with others at different levels, too often limiting ourselves to "Band 1", that is talking about things and events (*cars, the weather, holidays, politics, a piece of work at hand*), because we may find it difficult to go to "Band 2" where we start sharing concerns, feelings, emotions, personal reactions (*our fears about losing our job or not being up to it; our passion for something; our reactions to a management decision*), or, even more difficult, to talk at a deeper level about our underlying drivers, motivators, and values (*our personal purpose, vision, beliefs, hopes, aspirations, and desires*).

Some of us protect ourselves so much when interacting with others that we cut ourselves off from others, as well as from ourselves. It is when I communicate with others on Band 1, 2, and 3 that I am likely to build authentic relationships and, paradoxically, to get to know myself much better. It is by opening ourselves, receiving from others and responding to others that we start valuing someone. In turn, this can lead us to incorporate someone else's values, and to change due to someone influence, as illustrated in the stages and depth in relationship diagram (Fig. 11.1).

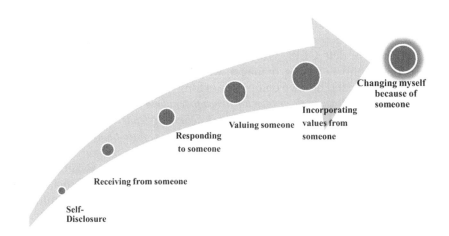

Figure 11.1. Stages and depth in a relationship

As we get to know someone and build new relationships, we have to be careful about the way we truly listen. Stuart Emery (2010) believes that in most of the situations, we do not listen to really discover the other person's reality. He states that we usually listen to assess the rightness or wrongness of the other person's reality, compared to our own. In order to counter this tendency, good networkers listen for, and sense the effects they produce around them, as well as the effects other people have around them; their responses to others. They further seek to identify these people's thoughts and feelings that may have nothing to do with the networker, patterns in what people say and do, the things they keep repeating, their need to be heard, discrepancies between what people are saying, and what they feel is going on, the feelings revealed in people's gestures, faces, and voices, what is not being said, omissions, unfinished sentences, and innuendos.

When we open up to others, listen to them, receive what they share, and choose "three-band" communication, we establish deep communication with others. Here are some unmistakable signs of the moments of "deep communication" that we all aspire to: A sense of physical well-being, being relaxed, a sense of being yourself, being open, breathing freely, not censoring thoughts and feelings, being ready to explore alternatives, being interested and engaged, generating new ideas, building on each other's ideas, looking at ourselves, others and situations with a touch of humor, breaking new grounds, being naturally silent with someone, gaining new insights, and sensing that this exchange and relationship are rich and valuable. Wow! What is it, then, that prevents us from building such rich relationships and becoming great networkers?

MAPPING MY NETWORK

For many of us, our network comprises a larger number of people than we may think. This is because we rarely take the time to identify all the persons we know, and to reflect on the type of relationship that links us to them. As a result, we often only discover how important our network is at critical stages in our lives (stress, divorce, organization changes, new responsibilities, being fired, assignment to a job abroad, decision to leave an organization, promotion, and so forth). Rather than waiting to discover the importance of our network when we are in the midst of stressful situations, it can be very useful to take the time to map our network to prevent stressful situations from happening! Let us take a step back to do this and to review its effectiveness. The Fig. 11.2 can assist us:

Our first task will be to identify and list all the leads and people we know, and who we can add to one of the above four quadrants, differentiating first between the *short-term contacts* (who could help us over the next year) and *long-term contacts* (who could still help us after a year), and then between the

	1. Stakeholders People who can help you to achieve your objectives	2. Allies People who can give you personal advice and support	
Organizational	3. Strategic contacts People who can help you achieve the organization's mission	4. Personal contacts People who can help you develop personally/career wise	Personal

Figure 11.2. Mapping your Network

Source: Adapted from Craig 1997.

organizational contacts (who can help us achieve our goals and the organization's mission) and *personal contacts* (for whom the relationship with us is important).

- In Quadrant 1, **Stakeholders**, you put the names of the people who can help you achieve your short-term goals, or hinder you from achieving them. They include your manager, your team, colleagues from other functions, and contacts in other organizations such as clients, suppliers, and so forth.

- In Quadrant 2, **Allies** are the names of people at work and around you, who can give you advice, information, and honest feedback. Allies are people you like and trust. They provide essential mutual and moral support. Some could become friends over the long term.

- In Quadrant 3, **Strategic contacts**, you put the names of the people who can help you achieve your organization's mission over the long term: executives, human resource (HR) contacts, senior clients, contacts in competitors' organizations, government, local community representatives, unions and work councils, special interest groups, associations, journalists, and academics. If you change the job, you will hand over most of your short-term contacts to your successor, but continue to maintain most of your strategic contacts.

- In Quadrant 4, **Personal contacts** are the people who help you to develop personally and professionally over the long term. They include mentors and coaches who can give you long term advice and counseling, and open doors for you, introducing you to the other useful contacts, particularly people who keep you up-to-date about the current trends in your professional sector.

Some of your contacts will fall into various categories, since relationships change and evolve over time. The purpose of mapping your relationships is to check if you have a reasonable and rich spread of contacts for your different purposes, and to take action to build a larger network when necessary. Ideally, your network should be broad and diverse (people from different cultural background, disciplines, experience, ages, genders, points of view), containing one or two high-status people (executives, "movers and shakers"), including stronger and weaker ties (frequent or less frequent interactions), constantly developing and being nurtured, in order to maintain existing relationships and adding new contacts to the network.

CASE STUDY 2

Victoria Bioux on Networking's Importance for Executives

Victoria Bioux, Belgian, expert in Leadership Development, London, UK.

Victoria, as an expert in leadership development and leading change, why do you think networking is such a hot topic for business people today?

There is no question that networking is essential today because we are living in a world that is moving increasingly faster, where boundaries are erased between people, businesses, and communities. In order to remain in touch with the dynamic pace of today's business climate, it is necessary to stay connected, get involved with others, and show that you contribute to the professional domain that you belong to. Tapping into what is going on outside your own work is a way to stretch your vision, exchange ideas with others, and nourish your personal brand in the professional community.

Networking is also a way to ensure visibility in the job market. Job security is no longer a valid term. Many people tend to forget the importance of staying connected to the outside world once they have landed a good job, and then experience a wake-up call when they one day find themselves in need of a career move. If you want to keep evolving in your career, the best way to look for new opportunities is through your personal network.

How do you define successful networking?

It is important to consider who you would like to become part of your network. This means that selectivity is the key. For example, LinkedIn is a great tool if it is used correctly. Just having a large network is not necessarily going to bring you added value—quality is the key.

(Continued)

CASE STUDY 2 (*Continued*)

By inviting people with whom you have worked with and developed a relationship with through the professional community, you have the basis for building a quality network. The next important step is to keep nourishing your contacts by staying in touch. This may mean contributing value by providing tips and ideas of readings or activities, that you think can be of interest to them and making sure you get the chance to meet once in a while, to maintain a personal connection.

How do you build a well functioning network?

There are a few important steps to keep in mind if you want to build a well functioning network: Consider who is currently a part of your network, and whom you would like to be in future. A good place to start is to draft a networking plan where you include the different kinds of professional associations, bodies, and communities that you are a part of, or are interested in becoming a member of. Think about how these may be complementary in terms of the value that you can bring to them, and what they can bring to you.

Cultivate your existing contacts by making sure you have some form of exchange on a regular basis. You can do this easily by using social networking platforms such as LinkedIn. Dropping your contacts a personal line once in a while, is an easy way to stay connected. Develop a "what can I do for you?" attitude. Whatever you put into, it will always come back to you in positive returns. By being helpful to others, they will be there for you when you are in need of information or a contact.

Make sure you always have your business cards with you when you go to events, conferences, and networking meetings and do not forget to exchange them with new people you meet. When you get a new business card, a rule of thumb is to always make a note on it, in terms of where and how you met so that you can keep a track of your contacts over a period of time. Following up with a personal note and a wish to stay in touch, usually works well as a way to start building a new relationship.

How do you make other people remember you?

One way is to share anecdotes that convey your character, and say something about your competence. Another important aspect is to show your personality by simply being yourself, and always demonstrating your

(Continued)

CASE STUDY 2 (*Continued*)

readiness to support others. If you meet at an event, make sure to get enough one-to-one face time, in order to know the other person a little. Take an interest in who people are and what they do. In the dialogue, try to identify common interests that you can build on, as you continue to develop the relationship. Use this interest as an anchor and follow up with a personal note after your initial meeting.

Have you had any experience yourself with the so-called unforeseen ripple effects of networking?

Absolutely! In my case, my personal network has contributed both to my private and professional life, in both unexpected and wonderful ways. I strongly doubt that the career opportunities I have had in the past would ever have emerged, had I not had the benefit of my network. The "six degrees of separation rule" that refers to the idea that everyone is on an average, approximately six steps away from any other person on the earth carries an important message: Whatever you put into your network will spread and come back to you. Cultivate your contacts and they will remember you, recommend yourself to others, and create a positive ripple effect.

Do you think that everybody can become a networker—also the less extroverted people who do not find it easy to get into contact with people?

Anyone can be a networker. Those who are less extroverted and do not like to attend social events can likewise create new contacts and stay connected on-line. The important point is to find professional communities that work for you: While some of us prefer to meet people face-to-face, others connect equally well through blogs, chat rooms, or Facebook. The opportunities are out there for everyone— all you need to do is to choose the best networking forum for you!

MAINTAINING/ENLARGING MY NETWORK

Once we have established a map of our network, we can reflect on how we keep these relationships alive, and how to enlarge our network. Let us look at some meaningful options:

- Rather than focusing on ourselves, our needs, and aspirations, we can start by thinking about the various members of our network and ask ourselves: What can I do for him/her? Do I know his/her interests? Can I help him/her with key priorities, or interests?

- We can connect people: Can I help people connect with others, whom they may be interested to meet?
- We can share with others: Are there any interesting articles or references I could circulate, once and a while, among members of my network?
- We can thank people for their advice and support, or for pieces of information that they have given us.
- We can give positive feedback, recognize other persons' successes, congratulate and encourage them, and find original ways to celebrate their accomplishments.
- We can consider involving some of them in projects that we are initiating.
- We can participate in annual conferences, meetings, or specific workshops.
- We can ask people in our network to introduce us to people they appreciate, and know better than we do.
- We can use our business trips more wisely, planning to meet people we otherwise would not meet. This is obviously particularly important for people who manage people remotely.
- We can have lunch, dinner, or share a glass of wine, a cup of coffee or tea with people, or plan for informal meetings with persons in our network.
- We can give little or significant gifts to members of our network.
- We can create a networking file or use the mind mapping technique to create new network maps by associating different names with different areas of interest.

Whatever we decide to do with and for the members of our network, we should be very careful to respect confidentiality at all times, to avoid talking behind others' backs and gossiping, and to over-rely on e-mails, when we have the opportunity to talk to people face-to-face! By doing this, we will make sure that our network is alive and vibrant. We will also discover that it will, very naturally, grow, as new members join!

USING THE NETWORK TO NETWORK!

Using our network to network requires personal discipline: Organizing our contact details so that we can access information easily, planning to regularly keep in touch with people in our network, managing our time well—stepping back, and spending sufficient time networking without over-indulging in this activity, dedicating significant portions of our time to the persons we love and appreciate, giving others contacts, asking colleagues, friends, and relatives to help us connect with new people. The more we do this, the more we will realize that "it is a small world!" since, as in any profession, if we network well, we will soon be connected with a core of international experts.

In my experience, lots of nice things start to happen as soon as you spend enough time networking: The joy of reconnecting with friends you have not seen for months or years, sharing news, discovering new aspects of others as they engage in new activities or interests, being invited to participate in a new initiative project, and so forth. If I think of my career, for example, I realize how naturally I was offered certain jobs because I had been involved, a few years earlier, in group work or an organization task force.

Beside this, using the network to network literally means using the Web to accelerate and optimize the way we network. E-mail can, of course, help us to stay in touch with colleagues, friends, and relatives, like never before. We can share ideas, news and thoughts, ask or give advice or feedback, but also point out useful blogs, documents, Web-based resources, and useful Web sites. Without spending hours creating another blog, each of us can connect quickly with hundreds of people, and it increasingly becomes our responsibility to ensure that this is for appropriate, ethical, and value-adding purposes.

NETWORKING ATTITUDES AND SKILLS

As with many other leadership attitudes and competencies, people acknowledge them when they see them being lived by others. What do people mean, when thinking of someone they know, they say: "He/she is a born networker"? The N.E.T.W.O.R.K. acronym list below is an attempt to highlight some of these characteristics. The reader, keeping his/her experience in mind, is invited to complement it:

- **No Judgment:** Let us start by addressing the major blocker and inhibitor to networking! When asked about what characterizes of good networkers, people invariably mention a non-judgmental view of people and situations. In other words—and if we reframe this statement more positively—people who are good at networking have a strong ability to suspend judgment, to explore issues with others rather than on their own, to look for solutions that will be advantageous for all the parties involved, to encourage, and respect the expression of different/diverging opinions, to give others a chance to propose their ideas. Let us ask ourselves how often we say: *"Let us not fight and judge!"*, *"Let us not conclude too quickly."*, *"Let me try to understand what you are saying."*, *"What could be a solution?"*

- **Empathy:** A born networker is a person who has a great capacity to put him or herself in another's shoes, "to walk in another's moccasins for 2 weeks" as the old American Indian saying suggests, to accept that the world could be seen from another perspective, to change or abandon his or her way of thinking, or feeling about something. How often do I ask: *"What do you think about this?"*, *"What is your feeling about this?"*, *"Can you tell me more?"* Empathy is obviously linked to two fundamental leadership skills: our capacity to ask open questions and our capacity to listen actively, with great attention, to the answers we are given.

- **Trust in Self, Others, and Life Processes:** Networking starts with the self, that is with being "grown up," autonomous, self-confident, responsible, and with freeing ourselves from what blocks us, and prevents our development. Because I trust myself, I can trust others and develop a growing, living network of friends, associates, colleagues, and relatives that leads me to discover more about myself, about others, and about the richness of the world, because, at a deeper level, networking is not only about being connected to people, but even more importantly, about being connected to life and the world, I am part and parcel of. My networking ability is linked to my level of trust in life and life processes (Capra, 1996). One therefore needs to consider the following: *"Do I trust myself enough?"*, *"Am I fully aware of what I am capable of?"*, *"Do I trust others enough?"*, *"Can I heal breeches of trust?"*, *"Do I love life?"*, *"Do I fully value the life I have been given?"*

- **World Citizenship:** Today there is simply no professional network that is not international, and many organizations continue entering the global stage. Rather than talking about "cultural differences" through the distorted and very limiting lens of "nationality"—and continuing to behave as if the only subject is the different ways Germans, French, English, Chinese, and others think and act-let us be more open to the world! Let us hone our networking skills by traveling, and discovering the rich aspects of so many diverse cultures. On top of this, because of e-mail and the Internet, we are increasingly connected, and a lot of great things are just at our fingertips! This formidable evolution is inviting us to become—as Socrates used to say during his many "walk and talk" wanderings in the forum in Athens—"citizens of the world".

- **Open Mindedness and Curiosity:** Being curious about others, about the immense diversity of human interests and pursuits seems to be a key pre-requisite for effective networking. Each of us has our own interests and passions. Occasionally, these can isolate us from others, and from understanding that there are other interests and passions than ours. Being curious about what others are interested in, inviting them to speak about what they are passionate about creates the connection that can lead to other connections. Being open-minded starts with a desire to communicate, to create rapport, to share experience, and personal stories with others. It starts with self-disclosure that, in turn, often creates in others the desire to self-disclose and to share meaningfully. We just have to be curious and open to develop fully.

- **Risk Taking, Experimenting, and Innovating:** Good networkers take risks by opening up, self-disclosing, and daring to say things other persons would not say. It is by being authentic when we communicate with others that we invite others to self-disclose and share. We have to open ourselves to the great ideas that others have. Strangely enough, it is by making ourselves vulnerable that we become, together with others, great communicators, networkers, and leaders! Good networkers build bridges, not walls. They create an environment where others are encouraged to take risks, to experiment with their ideas, to try new things, including new behaviors. In other words, good networkers know that preserving the status quo is often a dangerous illusion. They challenge the process. They keep asking themselves, and others: *"How could we do this better, differently, in a smarter way?"* Since errors are made, and if and when a mistake is made, they do not inflict blame or guilt, but ask: *"What can we learn from this?"* Good networkers seek innovation. They know that networks are the best incubators for innovative solutions. They trust the process of life that leads to breakthrough products and services.

- **Kiss and Embrace Complexity:** The accelerated rate of change, the levels of ambiguity, change, and complexity in our world are such, that they make many people take refuge in simplistic, simplified opinions, and world views (economists, financial people, politicians, and many journalists nurture this simplification tendency). Change and complexity are parts of the very fabric of our world. Born networkers understand this. They respect and value complexity. Which does not means that they strive for complicated ideas or solutions— on the contrary! It is because we respect life's complexity that we can seek simplicity: By being in touch with our true self, by clarifying our values, and what we desire and aspire to. We can seek simplicity in tackling complexity without resorting to one-dimensional thinking or, worse, caricaturing or reducing ourselves, others, or the world. Networking is one of the most natural ways to find ways— individually and with others-to live a happy life in a sustainable world (Craig, 1997).

The reader is most welcome to add his/her own contributions to this list of traits. Looking at these characteristics, it could be said that a good networker is an avid learner, a person capable of learning, everyday, from everything that happens to him or her, and, particularly, is capable of learning from all the persons, whom he or she meets.

CASE STUDY 3

Thoughts on Networking in Organizations

Observations of an international leadership and management development coach and facilitator:

When facilitating leadership development seminars for groups of executives or middle managers, I regularly observe the impressive extent to which the participants can learn from each other. Since one of my roles is to create an environment where people can share experiences and develop, I rejoice when the participants declare, at the end of a seminar, that they have appreciated the opportunity to "network with colleagues" from other cultures or functions. However, this happens so often, that it makes me wonder whether this is a confirmation of what recent studies on trends in leadership development suggest, namely that executives and managers are showing a growing desire not to learn from theoretical models, but from an in-depth exploration of their real work challenges, to learn from, and with their colleagues, to learn from real experience, to learn about leadership from leaders, and so forth (Mannaz, 2009). I also worry. If they appreciate the opportunity so much to meet with colleagues during a workshop, to share experiences and learn from one another in this context, could it also be because they truly lack such an experience in their actual work environment? And the more I think about this, the more I conclude that for many of them the answer is: 'Yes!'"

Why? Is it because many of them actually live in functional, national, or regional "silos," isolated from colleagues they should know and understand? Because they are under short-term pressures? Because they are too operational and not strategic enough? Because they are measured on sub-system targets that do not take the bigger picture into account? Because they very rarely look up from their work? Because they simply do not step back and take the time to think about their network, and its importance? Do we talk about "being Zen" because of our incapacity to be balanced and

(Continued)

CASE STUDY 3 (*Continued*)

Zen-like? Do organizations stress the importance of coaching so much because their managers do not coach? And do organizations today increasingly talk about the importance of networking, because of their incapacity to create authentic networking cultures and environments?

What worries me most in this observation is that networking is, *par excellence*, something that starts with each of us. It starts with the way we look at ourselves and understand where we are in the world or-to use Fritjof Capra's wonderful expression-with the way we understand our position in the "*Web of Life*" (1996). Capra uses a poem by Ted Perry, inspired by Chief Seattle, as an epigraph to his book:

"All things are connected like the blood which unites one family. Whatever befalls the earth befalls the sons and daughters of the earth. Man did not weave the web of life; he is merely a strand in it. Whatever he does for the web, he does to himself."

What a refreshing source of inspiration for all networkers!

An increasing number of executives and managers acknowledge the importance of networking. Some are very good at it. Others maintain they feel unskilled. Let us map our network, and think about how we could become better gardeners of our own network by cultivating some of the skills and attitudes evoked in this chapter!

CONCLUSIONS

Networking is about establishing long-term relationships for mutual gain, and creating a lasting, positive impression with people, and for them to think of you when an opportunity arrives. Networking is a life-skill and not easy to acquire for some. But once developed, it will take you almost everywhere. Think of networking inside and outside the organization. Raise your profile through networking, source new project opportunities, strengthen relationships with important stakeholders. Also increase your knowledge, exchange best practices, and benchmark performances. And, most importantly, enjoy the networking process itself while you are busy.

Again, networking is about building high-quality relationships where you first think of what to give and then of what to take. Networking is NOT about rapidly increasing the quantity of people you meet and become acquainted with. The number of business cards you have on your table after attending an event might say nothing about your achievements in terms of having networked well or not. Networking is about mutual gain and long term. It takes time to develop a two-way relationship and you need to understand the needs of others, come from a "pull" approach (see Chapter 8) rather than a "push" approach, to truly engage and include them into your network and vice versa. If this is your attitude towards networking, new opportunities, and a bunch of good and beneficial relationships will come your way in no time.

Your Activities for Practicing Your Networking Skills

Activity 1: Reflect on the chapter you have just read.

What did you learn about networking?

_____

_____

_____

What key insights did you obtain?

_____

_____

_____

Activity 2: My personal network mapping.

Take a piece of paper and draw your personal network according to the mapping model presented in this chapter. What can you see when mapping your personal network?

Do you need to pay attention to a specific area?

_____

_____

_____

Do you need to pay attention to specific persons?

_____

_____

_____

Activity 3: Develop your networking attitudes and skills.

Looking at the list of attitudes and skills that characterize "born net-workers" (see the N.E.T.W.O.R.K. Section above), is there one in par-ticular that you would like to develop?

_____

_____

_____

Activity 4: What actions will you take to become a better networker?

_____

_____

_____

REFERENCES

Baker, W. (2000). *Achieving Success Through Social Capital: Tapping Hidden Resources in Your Personal & Professional Network*. CA: Jossey-Bass.

Capra, F. (1996). *The Web of Life: A New Scientific Understanding of Living Systems*. NY: Anchor Books, Doubleday.

Capra, F. (2002). *The Hidden Connections: Integrating the biological, cognitive and social dimensions of life into a science of sustainability*. NY: Doubleday.

Craig, S. (1997). *Make your Mark!* NY: McGrawHill.

Emery, S. http://www.stewartemery.com/ retrieved November 30, 2010.

Mannaz (2009). Innovation in Leadership Development. *White Paper*, http://www.mannaz.com/

CHAPTER 12

BUILDING RELATIONSHIPS AND WORKING IN TEAMS ACROSS CULTURES

Erich Barthel

OBJECTIVE OF THIS CHAPTER

In this chapter you will learn more about how to achieve cross cultural competence, by using your strengths outside your comfort zone.

INTRODUCTION

Imagine you were offered two opportunities for a job during the coming year. Both are challenging, and you will have to work hard to keep up with the demands.

- Opportunity 1 is a position in a project team in your home country's capital. The team members are graduates from the country's best schools who have been selected for their professionalism and performance orientation. Some of them have already been members of the team that won the company's "Most Efficient Team" award last year.

- Opportunity 2 is a position in a project team to be formed in an emerging country's capital, some 10,000 miles away from your home. The other team members are excellent graduates from top universities in Paris, Shanghai, Istanbul, and Bangalore. Some of them have already worked successfully in other teams in their home country.

Which opportunity would you choose? You could start your decision process by asking yourself questions you have learned from your courses, or from books on strategy:

- What strengths do I possess? Which position will help me to improve my competencies?
- What weaknesses are bothering me? Which position will help me to eliminate these barriers to my career?
- What opportunities can be derived from the offered positions? What opportunities will I have at the end of the project?
- What threats do I have to keep in mind? Will both projects end with a positive outcome for me?

The chapter focuses on the opportunities you will find working in diverse teams across cultures, and how you can achieve the best results if you decide to choose the second opportunity.

DOES CULTURE MATTER?

The Dutch cross-cultural management guru Hofstede (1997) uses a computer analogy to clarify the difference between what all human beings have in common (the operating system), and what makes them differ from each other (the software). He describes culture as a collective programing of the mind that distinguishes the members of one category from people in another.

This programing is deeply manifested in our value system. Values are our tendencies to see elements of the environment as good or evil, beautiful or ugly, natural or unnatural, normal or abnormal. They are taught in early childhood, mostly implicitly, and remain in our subconscious, unless we explicitly try to reflect on them. Values strongly determine our behavior, as they are directly connected to our emotions. We feel good if actions fit into our value system; we feel bad if we regard actions as evil, unnatural, or abnormal.

Nancy Adler describes the connection between culture, values, attitudes, and behavior as a self-stabilizing circle. Values implicitly or explicitly determine what a person finds desirable. They determine people's attitudes and disposition to act in a certain way under given circumstances. Behavior is learned in accordance with the existing value system, and can be regarded as culture, since all the members of a group share it. In this circle, portrayed below in Figure 12.1, it is almost impossible to change one item (for example, behavior) without influencing the other elements.

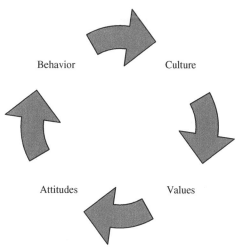

Behavior   Culture

Attitudes   Values

Figure 12.1. Influence of culture on behavior and behavior on culture
Source: Adapted from Adler, 2008, p. 19.

THE CULTURE SHOCK PHENOMENON

Others' unexpected behavior may lead to culture shock. You may start with highly positive feelings towards a new project, but after a few meetings you may feel misunderstood, or you do not understand why the other members do not act as they indicated they would.

British people, for example, often try to be very polite, if a suggestion is made that they are not interested in and will therefore not directly say what they think of this. While a German or US team member might actually state what they think about an idea, British team members will call it an "interesting idea," and will continue their discussion without returning to the suggestion. The team member who made the suggestion might then be confused, and his emotions will switch to anger or frustration. There is a difference between what he has heard and the actions he observed. It will

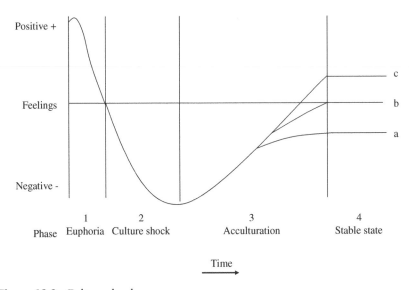

Figure 12.2. Culture shock
Source: Adapted from Hofstede, 1997, p. 210.

take some time of acculturation to overcome this shock, which is depicted in the Fig. 12.2.

CULTURAL DIFFERENCES

Hofstede (1997) described cultural differences on four dimensions which have become known as:

- **Individualism—Collectivism**
  - o Individualism: People primarily define themselves as separate individuals, and their main commitment is to themselves. Competition is highly valued.
  - o Collectivism: Tight social networks in which people clearly distinguish between their own groups (in-groups, such as relatives, clans, and organizations) and other groups.
  - o Not only does the behavior of those in collectivist cultures differ from the behavior of the people in individualist cultures, the perception of this behavior also differs.
  - o Team members from individualistic cultures might emphasize individual decisions and individual responsibility, while members

from collectivist cultures can be expected to focus on the relationships being established within the group.
  - Only a minority of the world's people live in individualistic cultures.
- **Power Distance**
  - Reflects the extent to which less powerful members of the organizations accept an unequal distribution of power.
  - Team members from high power distance cultures will interpret the actions of the team leader differently, from those who are used to low power distance. In teams of high power distance cultures, the team leader has to show more authority, than we might expect from a traditional western point of view.
- **Uncertainty Avoidance**
  - Reflects the extent to which people in a society feel threatened by ambiguity, and therefore try to avoid ambiguous situations by providing greater certainty and predictability. Germany, for example, is rated higher on uncertainty avoidance compared to the UK.
- **Career Success and Quality of Life**
  - Career success societies emphasize assertiveness and the acquisition of money and goods (materialism).
  - Quality-of-life societies emphasize relationships between people, concern for others, and the overall quality of life.

Hofstede later added the idea of Confucian Dynamism, which is a strong devotion to work ethics and respect for tradition. Building on Hofstede's work, Wharton professor Robert House then started a project for which the data collection took almost 4 years and which constitutes the rock-solid starting point of the Global Leadership and Organizational Behavior Effectiveness Research Program (GLOBE). The study was based on Hofstede's original four dimensions of culture, supplemented by three new ones: Performance Orientation, Future Orientation, and Humane Orientation.

- **Performance Orientation:** The degree to which a collective encourages and rewards group members for performance improvement.
- **Future Orientation:** The extent to which individuals engage in future-oriented behaviors such as delaying gratification, planning, and investing in the future.
- **Human Orientation:** The degree to which individuals are encouraged and rewarded for being fair, altruistic, friendly, generous, caring, and kind to others.

We can see that the development of culture and cultural differences continues. Rather than simply relying on cultural differences, it is important to make use of these differences and diversity, and to build cultural competencies as part of your leadership and personal development. In the following interview, we spoke to Lena Lauridsen, a global expert on Intercultural Management, who provides very practical insights into how to continuously work towards improving your intercultural competencies, which will help you to succeed in today's business world.

CASE STUDY 1

Building up Cultural Competencies as Part of Your Leadership Development

Lena Lauridsen, Danish, 35, global expert on Intercultural Management.

Lena, from our experience, we know that having intercultural competencies is important for professionals today. How do you define intercultural competence?

Intercultural competence is the ability to interact successfully with people from other cultures. It includes competencies like cultural sensitivity, how you manage uncertainty, intercultural communication, and your abilities to build commitment. It all boils down to whether you are able to create trust and, thus, motivate the people whom you are working with.

An interculturally competent manager uses different ways to motivate, communicate, and manage people, according to their cultural background. He not only knows about cultural differences, but also accepts, respects, and understands the meaning behind the behavior. An example: You have been told that Indians prefer never to answer "no" and consequently answer "yes" to everything, but this still frustrates you. You have knowledge, but what are you supposed to do with it to overcome your frustration?

Interculturally competent people decode and react to the Indian "yes" before it becomes a frustration. They know how much, for example, honor means for an Indian. Saving face is a well known expression, but you can also "give face," for example, honoring others by preventing them from losing face. This explains the Indian "yes". No is a negative answer, which disrupts harmony and makes others lose face. Furthermore, what does "yes" really mean? In the Anglo-Saxon part of the world, "yes" is a positive answer which obliges you to

(Continued)

CASE STUDY 1 (*Continued*)

do something. However, an Indian "yes" is not an answer, but an acknowledgment that people are listening to you: I hear what you say.

As an interculturally competent person, you have already traveled to India and have developed strategies to overcome the polite "yes." You are also aware of your cultural background, and how other people perceive you. You understand and master the structural patterns of culture, cultural dimensions, and you know that there is no right or wrong, good or bad. We just have different ways of doing things.

When we refer to intercultural competencies, are we talking about transferrable skill sets or is not it necessary to build specific competencies and knowledge regarding every culture we deal with?

International business life has long realized that cultural differences are a key factor in getting things done in business. Working in Germany, China, or the USA, for example, requires totally different styles of managing and co-operating. It is, of course, of great benefit to study American culture, when you work exclusively with the USA, or are planning to move there. But this is seldom the case in today's business life.

Most people today do not have to travel outside their office to work globally. We have colleagues, partners, customers, and suppliers spread around the globe; we work in virtual teams and need to handle a team consisting of several nationalities. We communicate with Bangalore today, Boston tomorrow, and Barcelona on Friday. It is not enough to know just about one culture.

This is why we use tools in the form of cultural dimensions which enable us to work globally, helping us to recognize certain structural cultural patterns, and relate our experiences to them. The does and does not of one culture is nice to have, but if you do not understand the meaning behind the behavior, they potentially do more harm than good.

Can you expand on these cultural dimensions?

Let me give you an example: You are a project leader, and in your team you have three different nationalities. You need to deliver results for your management and, simultaneously, need to inspire your team to work and deliver on time. You can use four different cultural dimensions as a starting point. First, power distance: Do your team members want you to be a visible project leader who has control,

(Continued)

CASE STUDY 1 (*Continued*)

and supervises? Or are they more motivated by a project leader, whose role is that of a coach, and interferes only if asked to? Here we already see that there are different ways to motivate team members.

Then we go a bit further with the help of the second dimension: Do your team members focus only on their tasks, or do they need to build trust, and a relation between them? And how is the communication undertaken? Is it okay to start an e-mail without addressing the receiver properly?

We also look into the personal motivation factors such as decision making with these dimensions. Who takes a decision within the team? Does the most capable team member do this, or do you need to listen to all the team members and reach a consensus? Finally, we look at the need for structure, which is also expressed in a dimension: Some team members are fine with not receiving an agenda before a tele-conference, and the minutes afterwards. But others prefer to be well prepared for a meeting.

As a project leader, you need to navigate these very different needs, and make sure that all the team members are working towards a common goal. These few examples using the dimensions demonstrate clearly that you cannot treat everybody alike. This is where you need to use your intercultural competence.

How do people actually build intercultural competence?

It takes knowledge, experience, and personal commitment. I have seen a few natural talents, but most people need hands-on experience, need to learn from mistakes, and need training in intercultural management to master cultural dimensions correctly. During this kind of training, people also start reflecting on their weaknesses and strengths, and thus realize what they need to work on. The most difficult task for most of the people is to start reflecting on their cultural behavior and to control their first reactions.

Many managers consider working abroad for a few years to extend their working experience, and in some cases to speed up their career. Do you have any generic advice for these people on how to prepare themselves for these stays?

(Continued)

CASE STUDY 1 (*Continued*)

I have lived in five different countries on three different continents, and if there is one thing I have learned then it is: *You really need to want it*. If you go abroad just to speed up your career or because everyone else does so ... forget it! You need to be open-minded, curious, willing to do things in new ways, and to accept that your way is not necessarily the best way. It is not uncommon for someone who has done a fantastic job in the Netherlands, not to get anything right in Russia. I, of course also recommend cultural training to develop cultural competencies further.

What kind of recommendations do you have for professionals who are not interested in living abroad, but still wish to enhance their intercultural competence? How can they integrate this into their leadership and personal development journey?

I know people who have never lived abroad, but are very competent interculturally and the choice of location does not play a role when it comes to building intercultural competence. Ask your company for cultural training and seek out positions that involve global activity. Today, many workplaces are multi-cultural, and culturally competent people are greatly needed to increase effectiveness and help their company get the most from a diverse workforce. Having insight into your department and colleagues' cultural backgrounds puts you a step ahead.

DIVERSITY IN TEAMS

You will find different types of diversity in teams. Teams may be diverse in different aspects such as age, gender, education, and ethnicity. All aspects of diversity may lead to a certain culture. Whether one culture dominates may depend on the proportion of people belonging to the different cultures.

- In **homogeneous teams,** all team members share the values relevant to the task they have to fulfil. There will hardly be any cultural conflict.
- In **token teams,** all but one member share the same culture. It will be more difficult for the token member to convince the rest of the team of his or her diverging opinions.

- In **bicultural teams**, there will be arguments between the sub-groups. If there are an unequal number of team members one culture may have a tendency to dominate the other.
- In **multi-cultural teams,** a minimum of three cultures are represented. To be successful, these teams must find ways of forming their shared interpretation of the world.

HOW CAN YOU DEAL WITH DIFFERENT CULTURES IN TEAMS?

Depending on the team's composition, different strategies may be appropriate (Figure 12.3). If you are the token member in the team, the most promising strategy would be to adapt to "their culture." At first glance this might make you feel like a loser in a competition, but in the long run it will give you the competencies necessary in a fast-changing environment.

Conversely, as a member of the majority, you could stick to your culture's way, forcing the minority to change their attitudes and behavior. Again, the coin has two sides: You may feel like a winner as you do not have to leave your comfort zone, but you miss an opportunity to learn.

Creating cultural synergy is perhaps the most promising strategy. Not only does it create positive emotions of a win-win situation within the team, but it is also the most important argument for the organizations to invest in diverse teams.

Figure 12.3. Strategic option to deal with different cultures

Source: Adapted from Adler, 2008, p. 118.

You need to be aware of the situation to create cultural synergy. You should be able to describe the situation from your cultural perspective and from others' cultural perspectives. Try to explain the differences by reflecting on the values behind the perspectives. Do you also see cultural overlaps and similarities between the perspectives? We should start thinking of alternatives that comprise even more of the involved cultures' elements. Make sure that the other team members can accept your solution.

HOW TO MAKE THE MOST OF DIVERSITY IN TEAMS

When asking managers about diversity, you often hear that they do not like to work with a diverse workforce. Whenever there is a well-described process and things just have to be done in a way that the past experience has shown to be the best, there seems to be no argument for working with a diverse workforce. Diversity obviously increases ambiguity, creating higher complexity, disturbing the clarity of the processes.

However, there are advantages and the more experienced you are with diversity, the better you can make use of these advantages. Cultural diversity expands the field of potential solutions by providing different perspectives and multiple interpretations of the aspect addressed. Diversity will increase the number of ideas and (it is hoped) quality. More concentration is needed to understand each other. If there is a climate of trust and mutual respect, even misunderstanding can create new ideas when you start to talk about the issue. Teams can become more effective and productive in traditional processes, when a stage of shared understanding and commitment is reached.

Nancy Adler states that a team's success depends less on the presence or absence of diversity, but on how diversity is managed. If well managed, diversity can become a team and an organizational asset. Highly developed teams will use their diversity, and not regard it as a hindrance.

ARE YOU PREPARED FOR WORKING IN A DIVERSE TEAM?

Working successfully in a diverse team requires cultural competence. But how do you gain this competence and how can you develop it further?

Cultural competence can be defined as an individual's efficient use of appropriate knowledge, skills, and personal attributes when working with people from different cultural backgrounds. To develop cultural competence, you have to work on your knowledge, your behavior, and your attitudes.

- Relevant **cultural knowledge** can be general and specific. **General knowledge** refers to all the components of culture, the differences between cultures, and the mechanisms that make cultures unique. **Specific knowledge** includes all the information of a certain type of culture. If you are going to work together with people from China and India, it might be appropriate to learn about these countries' political and economic systems, the history, the religion, and their customs. If you delve a bit deeper, you will find that there are different cultures in one country, and this knowledge can be used when you start communicating with these people. It is important to learn about your own culture if you want to examine how it differs from others. Knowledge can be trained in seminars and workshops. You might find it helpful to read books or to watch videos.

- **Skills** can be seen as the *behavioral component* of cultural competence, including the ability to communicate in the language appropriate for the task, and adapting properly to other cultures' norms. Skills are learned by executing the behavior associated with these cultures. Consequently, simulating real-life situations and on-the-job training are more appropriate, than any kind of classroom situation.

- **Personal attributes** are probably the most difficult part to develop. Developing personal attributes is not just adding something new to your person. Personal attributes can best be described as your personality. Developing these attributes is as challenging as changing your personality, your attitudes, your traits, and your values. Neither everybody is willing to make this change, nor is everybody able to do it. There are some personal attributes that make starting easier. Being able to step outside your mental framework is often linked to a strong, but sensitive personality. If you are experienced in conflicts, able to give and accept positive and negative feedback, you will see a challenge and not a threat when misunderstandings occur. Be prepared to commit yourself to the team's success, feel responsible for the results without losing control if the results do not appear in the time you expected. If you are motivated by curiosity and able to look at your mistakes with some humor, you certainly have the relevant prerequisites to get the journey started.

TEAM BUILDING IN AN INTERCULTURAL CONTEXT

Team building is often described in four steps as illustrated in Figure 12.4: Forming, storming, norming, and performing. In a diverse team, forming

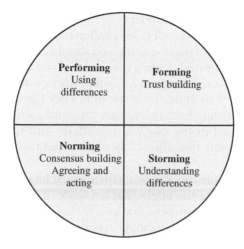

Figure 12.4. Four phases in team building
Source: Adapted from Tuckman (1965).

and storming specifically take more time, and require all the group members to be especially cautious and patient. In the norming phase, the members and leaders have to be careful not to go too far. If the team is unified by high efficiency due to its commonly accepted norms, it might lose its ability to create new ideas derived from different assumptions.

- **Forming:** When team members meet for the first time, they try to find out how they can best contribute to the team and how they can ensure that they become an accepted team member. Productivity is relatively low, as much of the energy is spent on learning about relations and the task.

  As a *team member*, you might find it helpful to ask yourself what you already know about the other members and what you still need to know. In order to become an accepted group member, find out how your arguments are interpreted, and be careful when interpreting the arguments of others. The overall aim of this stage should be trust building. Therefore, make sure that everything you do is regarded as a sign of respect and tolerance.

  As a *leader*, you have to ensure that nobody is left out due to cultural misinterpretation at this early stage. Some members might be in danger of this, if more individualistic and competitive members regard their reticence as low interest and weakness. You should look for ways to encourage trust within the team.

- **Storming:** As a result of cultural shock, team members may start challenging the purpose of the team, its goals, and its ability to achieve a satisfactory result. Conflicts appear and emotions run high.

People feel they are misunderstood and wonder whether it is worth staying in the team. Leaders are challenged to give clear guidance.

As a *member* of a diverse team, you should carefully check why you might feel depressed. Even if you feel that you did everything right, this might be a sign that you lack empathy or sensitivity to the situation. You have to understand the difference between intention and impact, regarding both the signals you send—which will not always be understood in the way you intended—and the arguments you hear. Find a way that allows you to give and take feedback on how you act.

The *leader* role can also be challenged. If he or she is from a western culture, he or she might find it a waste of time to allow a discussion on the team's purpose and goals. They have been clearly set out earlier and every team member has signed a contract and committed himself/herself, to these goals. In a diverse team, you need this discussion. Allow everybody to express his/her expectations and develop commonly accepted standards. Discuss the criteria that you will use to assess each team member's contribution. Make clear that you may have different expectations from different members. Install rules for conflict management. Last but not the least, make sure that your leadership style is accepted and understood. Team members from a culture with a high power distance, might need some explanation regarding why you allow people to give you feedback on your performance.

- **Norming:** Productivity starts to increase and norms are becoming accepted. Some have to be improved, but this can be built on agreements that have been made. With any luck, conflict management works, and the members feel encouraged to follow the norms.

   As a *member*, you need to ask yourself how close and personal you want your relationships to be. Norms will improve communication and performance. Motivation can best be gained from progress in efficiency, and the improvement of relations.

   As a *leader*, you see the progress and you reward members who show their commitment to the team. Tasks seem easier now. You can impress your superior with higher productivity and even better prospects. Perhaps you now feel that working with different cultures is less challenging than you thought.

- **Performing:** Productivity is at its peak. The team members are highly committed to the team and to their tasks. They enjoy following the rules and norms that help them to work highly efficiently, and are looking forward to keeping relationships stable.

As a *member*, you contribute to the group's success and communication has become a routine. Different opinions are now interpreted as a sign of individuality and personality. You may start asking yourself whether this is a team in which you want to remain—everything is so normal now even the pressure of productivity is the same as it is in any high-performing group. However, although the output has increased, your opportunities for learning seem to decrease. This could be the time to leave the team to increase your learning.

As a *leader*, you can now define your role very similar to that of leading a homogenous group. One of your major tasks is to keep the productivity and quality on the level you have reached. From an intercultural perspective, there is another element that should be kept in mind: How can a balance be found between the team's efficiency in the sense of routine and productivity, and opportunities for change and innovation that can be found in a diverse team?

CONCLUSIONS

Working with diverse teams across cultures requires certain prerequisites, but it is a great opportunity to increase cultural competence. Like any competence, it consists of obvious parts, like language skills, and knowledge about other countries, that can be directly presented to those who are interested, and subconscious elements embedded in your personality and value system. Cultural competence will become a part of your personality, and it will allow you to see the world in different ways. You can test your team's ability. And, since you are used to coping with unforeseen perspectives, you can use your abilities as an asset in the fast-changing world.

Your Activities to Practice Your Coaching Skills

Activity 1: Test your intercultural knowledge and apply it to a real life example.

Please read the following case of Helmut, human resource (HR) consultant who started working for a firm in London after having left his German consultancy firm.

Helmut (45), German, HR consultant, Frankfurt, Germany.
   It was only 3 months ago that he joined the company, an international consultancy based in London. He was full of enthusiasm

when he arrived at his first meeting in London. Ken, Donald, Mary, and Linda, the head of the department, gave him a warm welcome. They were very polite, remarking that they were proud that they had won him over to their team, and were looking forward to a great and successful future.

After a short introduction, the project meeting started. They had met to prepare a proposal for an important English client, who wanted to buy a company in Germany. Owing to the topic Helmut felt himself encouraged to contribute by mentioning specific characteristics about business in Germany. He got the feeling that the others appreciated his comments. More than once he heard them say: "Thanks Helmut that is an interesting idea. We should take that into consideration when we come to our final conclusions."

In the end, the proposal did not contain any of his ideas.

The next day Helmut dropped an e-mail to Ken, whom he found the most sympathetic of his new colleagues. He asked him directly whether he had done something wrong. Ken answered that the incident should not upset him, as the ideas did sound very interesting, but the proposal had to fit to the customer's demands. "And we know this customer very well!" he continued, finishing the e-mail with an invitation to Helmut to come to London whenever he wanted, to learn more about the way business is done in the company.

Helmut felt that he had to be active, and decided to ask Linda for an opportunity to visit some clients in London. "A great idea!" Linda answered. "We will try to find a good opportunity."

During the next weeks, Helmut contacted potential clients in Germany and it was difficult to fix a time for his visit. The consultancy was much less known in Germany than in Britain, and he started getting frustrated. When he met Linda during a short visit she paid to Berlin, she seemed to be dissatisfied with the progress he had made. "Let me know how I can help you," was her last comment before she left.

At that moment Helmut knew that he wanted to resign from the company, and started writing his resignation.

Now think about the following questions and try to apply some of the knowledge and insight gained in this chapter:

In what cultural shock stage was Helmut?

_____

_____

How did he get there?

_____

_____

What could Linda have done at an earlier stage to avoid severe problems?

_____

_____

Activity 2: Can your team raise its cultural diversity potential?

This test was designed to help you to determine your team's intercultural readiness.

1. Our team loves to try new techniques to improve work processes.
2. Our team helps to develop its members' competencies.
3. Our team is able to use its members' diverse experience and knowledge to solve problems.
4. Our team is effective in ensuring its members' motivation.
5. Our team is able to use its members' different strengths.
6. Our team often uses creative techniques to develop new solutions for given problems.
7. In our team, we collaborate very collegially.
8. In our team, we discuss problems in regular meetings.
9. In our team, we regularly reflect on the demands placed on us.
10. Overall, our team is very good at learning from a critical review of our experience.
11. Within our team, we feel free to talk about mistakes.
12. We actively provide each other with feedback.

13. Our team's skills are above average.

14. Our team has a high potential for innovation.

15. In our team, we trust each other.

16. We learn from each other.

17. In our team, we appreciate different points of view.

18. In our team, we respect our members' different values.

_____

_____

_____

If your answer is "yes" more than 15 times, you are certainly doing well. If your answer is "no" more than six times, you still have a way to go. Perhaps you should try to improve collaboration within your team or to improve the acceptance of different points of view. Some team-building exercises might help you increase the trust and understanding. There is no one exercise that fits all. Good ideas for such activities can be found in the recommended readings.

REFERENCES AND RECOMMENDED READING

Adler, N. (2008). *International Dimensions of Organizational Behavior* (5th ed.). South-Western, MA.

Brodbeck, F. C., Frese, M., & Javidan, M. (2002). *"Leadership made in Germany: Low on compassion, high on performance,"* Academy of Management Executive, (Vol.16).

Halverson, C. B. (2008). Team Development. *Effective Multicultural Teams: Theory and Practice.* Berlin: Springer Science + Business Media.

Hampden-Turner, C., & Trompenaars, F. (2000). *Building Cross-Cultural Competence: How to create wealth from conflicting values.* New York: Wiley.

Hofstede, G. (1997). *Cultures and Organizations: Software of the Mind.* New York: McGraw-Hill.

Hofstede, G. J., Pedersen, P. B., & Hofstede, G. (2002). *Exploring Culture: Exercises, Stories and Synthetic Cultures.* Yarmouth: Intercultural Press.

House, R., Hanges, P., Javidan, Dorfman, P., & Gupta, V. (Eds.) (2004). *Leadership, Cultures, and Organizations: The GLOBE Study.* CA: Sage.

Johnson, J. P., Lenartowicz, T., & Apud, S. (2006). "Cross-Cultural Competence in International Business: Toward a Definition and a Model," *Journal of International Business Studies, 37*(4), 525–543.

Thomas, D. A., & Ely, R. J. (1966). *"Making Differences Matter: A New Paradigm for Managing Diversity,"* in Harvard Business Review on Managing Diversity (pp. 33–66). Boston: Harvard Business School Press.

Trompenaars, F., & Hampden-Turner, C. (2005). *Riding the Waves of Culture: Understanding Cultural Diversity in Business* (2nd ed.). London: Nicholas Brealey.

Tuckman, B. (1965). Development sequences in small groups. *Psychological Bulletin, 63*, 384–399.

CHAPTER 13

RELATIONAL ASPECTS OF COACHING AND COMMUNICATION

Claire Collins

OBJECTIVE OF THIS CHAPTER

The main goal of this chapter is to help understand the criticality of the inter-personal relationship between the coach and coachee in developing a strong working alliance and thereby delivering effective coaching interventions.

INTRODUCTION

Whether you wish to apply your coaching skills as an executive one-to-one coach or through the creation of a coaching environment for your team or organization, you will be involved in a relational intervention with your coachee/client. You will be working with individuals who, for whatever pur-pose, want to manifest a level of change in themselves. This change may be for their individual benefit, but it may also be a change which will enable

---

Leadership and Personal Development: A Toolbox for the 21st Century Professional, pp. 243–256

them to perform their role more effectively and, therefore, be for the benefit of the organization.

Many factors are important in creating the best circumstances for successful coaching. These include: The skill, experience, and style of the coach; the readiness of the client to change; and the process that is employed in the coaching sessions. However, one of the most important elements to take into account in striving for the most effective coaching engagement is how good the interaction, between you and your coachee is. The quality of the coaching relationship—that which exists between the coach and the client—is known to be critical in generating the level of awareness, and the motivation to change required for an effective outcome. Stober & Grant (2006) state that:

> "Regardless of preferred theoretical perspective, the foundation of effective coaching is the successful formation of a collaborative relationship."

When considering your development as a coaching manager or leader, your ability to form an effective and fruitful relationship with others will be essential to building a positive coaching culture in your team or business.

THE NATURE OF COACHING RELATIONSHIPS

The coaching relationship is one of many kinds of one-to-one helping relationships, such as mentoring or individual consultancy. In all of these situations, the way that the professional and the client develop the interactions between them, and the more trustworthy and robust these interactions, the more likely it is that the intervention will achieve its aspirations, goals, or objectives. The value that the coach provides for the client or coachee, is vital for the crux of the relationship. This can be termed a person-centred approach as it puts the client at the core of the intervention, and all attention and intention are focused on supporting his/her desired change.

The core skills of this person-centred approach include: Active listening, respect for the client and adopting their internal frame of reference (seeing things from their point of view), all elements that are covered in this chapter.

Chemistry

The complex set of dynamics between the coach and the coachee is often informally described as the "chemistry" of the relationship. Like all human interactions, it has many dimensions, and can vary in positivity from time to time, although this does not need to lead to problems as long as the coach and coachee recognize these dynamics remain open and work together.

First Impressions

The first impression that two people make on each other have a significant impact on the course of their subsequent relationship. First impressions can be strong and persistent, and can reveal a lot about the other person, although they can also be misleading at times. These impressions can affect the coaching relationship, either positively or negatively. The issues that make such an initial impact evolve over a very short space of time. Firstly, you may notice the physical appearance of your opposite number, his/her age, gender, height, ethnicity, and so forth, then perhaps you notice his/her voice tone or mannerisms; later, after some more time, you notice things about his/her characteristics and personality; and, finally, you may learn about his/her values and beliefs. We pick up these clues at a subconscious level, but they can have a profound effect on our decisions, about who we want to work with.

The beginning of a coaching relationship can be loaded with both the parties' needs. In her book, "*The Coach's Coach*" (Hardingham, 2004), Alison Hardingham describes three types of needs: belonging, closeness and control. These types are based on the work by Schutz (1958), and are common forces that exert influence on all types of relationships (de Haan, 2008):

- **Needs Related to Belonging**—The coachee wants to know if the coach is similar to him/her, or how he/she sees him/herself. This is important to know whether this coach fits in with his/her identity. An association with others with whom the coach has worked may also suggest a level of belonging to a particular group or type. Inclusion needs are related to the coachee's view of him/herself and where he/she fits in. As a coach, your part in this is to reassure the coachee that you understand his/her position, and can support his/her needs. However, the most important point is that you are open and honest with your client. This means that if he/she is not comfortable with you as a coach, you should willingly withdraw from the relationship, perhaps helping to find a more compatible replacement.

- **Needs Relating to Controlling**—In any relationship, there are needs centred on controlling, and being controlled by others. Often the need to control is related to the feeling of fear or threat to an individual's competence, or even safety. Control within the coaching relationship may swing back and forth, depending on the issue being discussed and the coachee's level of confidence with that issue. As the coach, negotiation is an important principle to establish; this begins at the very start of the relationship when settling the contracting context. Later on, the coachee may want you to take control, if he/she feels particularly unsure in a situation, or he/she may want to hold the reins of an issue. In this case, careful and active listening is essential, to moving the negotiation forward.

- **Needs Related to Closeness**—People first experience closeness in their early family life and this sets the pattern for later. These needs carry forward into working relationships, and are certainly present in the coaching relationship. Your coachee may want to experience a coaching relationship which is close and personal. On the other hand, some coachees need to maintain a "professional distance" from their coach, and keep things at a more impersonal level. As a coach, it is important for you to try and sense this early through questions and listening. In turn, you should try to have a level of self-awareness to understand your need for closeness and how this may influence your coaching stance, and to know how you should respond to different coachees' needs.

WITHIN THE COACHING RELATIONSHIP

Once the coaching relationship has formed, it may take many forms, each perhaps as an individual, as the coach and coachee themselves;—two unique individuals forming and building a new interaction. A productive coaching relationship may be seen as an example of a "working alliance" (de Haan, 2008). This alliance probably has a basis in other relationships, that either the coach or the coachee have experienced, such as mentor/mentee, doctor/patient, peer review, or sparring partner. During the course of the coaching relationship, you may find that there is evolution from one type of relationship to another, depending on a number of factors, such as the circumstances, which may have changed since the last session, the themes being discussed, or other changes experienced by either party.

In order to build and maintain a healthy and productive relationship with your client, one of your most important responsibilities as a coach is to continuously monitor the current nature of the relationship, to listen to your coachee's world view, and follow his/her levels of need. This may involve you having to adapt the style or approach you take within the coaching sessions. Our experience from many years of psychotherapy research suggests that all known approaches are equally effective, and that what matters most are the personalities of the coach and coachee and how they are matched (Roth & Fonagy, 1996; Wampold, 2001).

Coaching Success

As mentioned before, the "working alliance" is closely related to the success of a therapeutic intervention (Wampold, 2001), and based on many similarities in form, this can also be assumed for the coaching relationship, which may, therefore, be termed the *"coaching alliance"*. The quality of the relationship that you have with your coachee, therefore, seems to directly impact the effectiveness or success of the outcome, in whatever way this is estimated. Let us now examine some of the aspects within this *coaching alliance*.

Good Communication

Communication is the process of sharing information within a shared interpretative framework, that allows information to be meaningful and useful (Haslam, 2004). Competence in communication skills is the key to building any type of interpersonal relationship (Nelson & Cooper, 2007) and is, therefore, also vital in the coaching relationship. Strong communication skills help in a number of areas:

- Interpersonal trust and trustworthiness
- Willingness to respectfully challenge authority
- Your ideas' openness to challenges
- Ability to listen and appreciate others' points of view
- Open dialogue is the norm and is highly valued
- Communication between individuals is balanced
- Polite, appropriate assertiveness is encouraged
- Knowledge and information are readily shared

These aspects of good communication are particularly relevant to coaching relationships. Establishing open, honest and balanced communication, as early as possible will help to initiate rapport, and will establish the trust necessary to create transformational change.

Your ability as a coach to encourage good communication draws on particular attributes, such as mature emotional intelligence and cognitive complexity. This is relevant, as positive communication is more than mere verbal ability, but includes non-verbal signalling and sensitivity to emotional contexts, individual differences and personal integrity. One of the pitfalls of communication is that messages, through any channel, are open to interpretation. This interpretation can be influenced by very many factors, often referred to as "noise". These factors include:

- The person delivering the message
- The environment
- The mood of the giver and the recipient
- Personality factors

- The context—what might have happened immediately before, or some time ago
- The recipient's attitude to the giver

All of these influences result in messages between people being encoded by the giver, passed on, and then decoded by the recipient. Between the encoding and decoding stages, the meaning of the message can be altered, and the recipient may not understand the message in the way the giver intended. This can lead to misunderstanding, and can result in difficulties in the coaching relationship. There are ways in which this misinterpretation can be minimized and communication between the coach and the coachee kept as clear and understandable, as possible. Using "unconditional positive regard" for your client can , for example, enable you to give messages with a positive intent that can be sensed by your coachee; use clean and clear language—do not introduce technical jargon or colloquialisms that may be misinterpreted; give yourself time to think about what you want to say—prepare your sentence mentally to check how it may be received; keep your coachee's personality in mind when you speak—he/she may use particular frames of reference, which can help you give meaning to your communications.

Interpersonal communication also includes responding skills, such as *questioning, paraphrasing, encouragement, clarification, summarizing, reflection,* and even *confrontation, besides active listening, described below.* Another surprising skill in effective communication is *silence.* This can be very powerful, particularly in coaching. Not leaping in with a comment or question, but allowing your coachee to sit with his/her thoughts for a while can be the very time when he/she is able to access deeply held insights or feelings, which can unlock critical change opportunities. Silence can, indeed, be golden.

Active Listening

As a coach, your ability to listen actively to your client will give you a vital skill to respond agilely to his/her individual and often-changing needs. Your understanding of the coachee and his/her worldview may greatly enhance your coaching relationship's productivity. If your coachee feels truly heard, he/she will be able to experience a high level of trust in you, as his/her coach. This in turn, allows you both to access much deeper levels of self, and manifest lasting and significant change.

The term "active listening" has a number of characteristics: It is a positive act, where the coachee is enabled to see things differently as he/she externalizes his/her issues. The coach is clearly actively paying attention to what the coachee is saying, and giving him/her space and support to express important, meaningful matters. This active attention is a part of building a strong coaching relationship. Carl Rogers (1961) used the term "unconditional positive regard" to describe the therapist or coach's stance with regard to his/her client, when engaged in this intense listening activity. He believed that just giving the client this level of attention helped to build self-esteem, and increase his/her confidence to take action towards his/her goals. Active listening, a vital skill in itself, may be instrumental in supporting change for your coachee.

Empathy, Rapport, Openness, and Trust

All of these four elements contribute to forming and building a strong and effective relationship with your coachee. They are all related to each other, and are concerned with the solid foundation, upon which the change process of coaching can take place.

According to Roman Krznaric (2010), empathizing with someone "creates a unique human bond that can spur us to take action on their behalf". He suggests that empathy is one manifestation of kindness, and that it sensitizes us to the lives of others. This, therefore, allows you to see the world through the lens of your coachee, and to support him/her through an understanding of his/her experiences and beliefs.

Rapport is necessarily established at the beginning of any new coaching relationship. Alison Hardingham (2004) defines rapport as "mutual recognition and respect". In this sense, recognition is two people, who may start as strangers, becoming familiar with each other and beginning to "see" each other as partners in the relationship. This begins to build a level of comfort. Respect is necessary for the coachee to feel safe and to have TRUST in you, his/her coach. Without respect and trust, the coachee may fear that you will try to control or change him/her in a way that is unhelpful, or perhaps harmful.

Rapport and trust deepen as the relationship is built. Sometimes, rapport may be broken, perhaps following a misunderstanding or critical incident. However, as said above, clear, open, and honest communication between you will help restore the balance, and re-build the rapport and trust needed to induce lasting and desired change. In establishing rapport, the components of active listening (see above) are essential, so that you can "tune in" to your coachee's communication, whether verbal, behavioral, or emotional.

Nancy Kline's "Time to Think"

In her book, "*Time to Think*" (Kline, 1999), Nancy Kline says that: "Everything we do depends for its quality on the thinking we do first" and "[o]ur thinking depends on the quality of the *attention* for each other". Her philosophy, learned from her mother is that the key to leadership is to listen attentively, and to have (and give) the time and space to think. If these two conditions are met, Nancy believes we can all begin to think clearly and afresh for ourselves.

To complement this thinking and bring it fruition, Nancy also advocates the need for *incisive questions*. In our thinking, we sometimes encounter blocks when we feel we cannot move any further, or we do not know how to move our thinking to a stage of taking action. These blocks usually take the form of assumptions that the thinker cannot overcome, and which prevent ideas from flowing further. The incisive questions that free these blocks took two years to practice, but eventually developed into a system which is clean and logical, replicable and teachable. From these questions, further development brought about the encapsulation of ten behaviors known as "the thinking environment" and which help people think for themselves.

The 'thinking environment" has ten components which can help you have the most powerful coaching conversations you can imagine. It is a technique which I recommend for your coaching practices. Listing these ten components below does not explain the intrinsic power that they hold—you would have to read all of Nancy's books for that. However, you will see some common factors from the other sections above, and even in this form they will give you a checklist to think about for your coaching encounters. The ten components are:

1. Attention—Listening with respect and interest
2. Incisive questions—Removing assumptions that limit ideas
3. Equality—Treating each other as thinking peers
   a. Giving equal turns and attention
   b. Keeping agreements and boundaries
4. Appreciation—Practising a five-to-one ratio of appreciation to criticism
5. Ease—Offering freedom from rush and urgency
6. Encouragement—Moving beyond competition
7. Feelings—Allowing sufficient emotional release to restore thinking
8. Information—Providing a full and accurate picture of reality
9. Place—Creating a physical environment that says to people: "You matter"
10. Diversity—Adding quality because of the differences between us

Ending

The final phase of a relationship may be termed "ending" or "separation". The reasons for the ending may be various but hopefully, you and your coachee reach an agreement, that the objectives of the coaching have been reached. Other reasons may be that you have reached the end of an agreed number of sessions, or that there is a physical separation, such as a job move, which ends the connection. It is important that, wherever possible, you reach a logical and agreeable conclusion in your final session. You may jointly agree that the coachee may contact you in future to check his/her progress, or even return to coaching. Ideally, the coachee's goals have been realized, or a robust action plan is at least in place to achieve them. The final key issue is to ensure that your coachee is prepared and ready for the ending, and that you separate on good terms and with the feeling of a job well done.

SOME SUGGESTIONS TO HELP YOU BUILD GOOD COACHING RELATIONSHIPS

From the wealth of literature and some real-life experiences here are suggestions to support you in building great coaching relationships:

1. Be yourself. It is most important that your coachee works with the "real you". This does not mean that you should not be adaptable in your stance, but you should certainly let your own self shine through; to not do so is disingenuous and very hard to maintain. It is also likely that your coachee will see through this, which will put any trust you have built up in the relationship at risk.

2. If, at the very beginning of a new coaching relationship—whether with a member of your team or with a new individual—you, for whatever reason, do not feel that you have the basis of a good relationship, you may want to suggest that another coach may be more suitable. However, you should handle this situation with extreme caution, as some individuals may see this as a rejection, playing on previous sensitivities. This should never be portrayed as a problem in the relationship, but rather that another person may have different attributes which will help the coachee to achieve the very best.

3. Demonstrate *active listening* (Peltier, 2010). Active listening involves the following skills and behaviors:

    - Stop and pay attention
    - Use physical listening. Use your body language to give a clear impression of listening
    - Ask appropriate questions
    - Restate. Summarize, paraphrase, reflect
    - Listen for feelings. Notice what people seem to be feeling as they speak
    - Share. Reveal important reactions appropriately

- Withhold judgement while listening. Allow the speaker to make his/her point and listen with an open mind
- Acknowledge differences. And use these positively to explore ways forward

4. Offer your coachee "unconditional positive regard". In order to do this, you need to empty yourself of your needs so that you can concentrate on the needs of your coachee. Personal preparation before a coaching session is highly recommended, and may vary from coach to coach. You may need to spend some time reviewing the previous session's notes, or reading through diagnostic tests or biographical materials, to get to know your coachee. This may involve spending a little time on personal reflection, mentally filing any issues which are occupying your thoughts and clearing your mind, to concentrate entirely on your client.

5. Enjoy the learning that every coaching session brings. It is my experience that, although your purpose is to serve your coachee, and support him/her in manifesting the desired change, it builds your learning, each time you undertake a coaching session. This might be in using new tools and techniques, or some insight of self-awareness, of how you work with others in a coaching setting. These opportunities to learn never seem to cease, no matter how experienced you might become, and they are one of the many aspects of coaching that makes it as fulfilling for the coach as it is for his/her client.

CASE STUDY 1

David, Partner in a Law Firm, Reading, England

David was a team leader in a large law firm; he was also a salaried partner. He came to coaching as he had been put on the equity partnership track. However, at his last appraisal he was given a feedback that his management style was somewhat abrasive, and that clients sometimes found him abrupt.

At his first coaching session, he began by telling his coach, that he was sure he did not really needs coaching, and that there was not a problem. His coach let him speak for quite some time as he explained his strengths, experience, client skills, and how highly he was regarded in the firm. His manner was that of a highly confident and competent individual, although he was a bit too willing to sing his own praises. In the first part of the coaching session, his coach spoke very little.

(Continued)

CASE STUDY 1 (*Continued*)

She simply let him speak freely, occasionally nodding and indicating, that she was listening carefully to what he had to say.

After a little while, David really began to warm to his subject, relating a number of stories about his successes in the firm. However, he also talked about his team and the problems that he believed, existed. He noted that a number of the junior staff seemed unmotivated and unwilling to put in the level of work that he believed was necessary. He gave several examples of where he felt his team fell short of his expectations. In his belief, he was the only member of the team who was really pulling his weight, and producing all of the output. He did note though, that a number of his regular clients had moved their business to another team.

By now, David had been speaking uninterrupted for quite some time. Then, unexpectedly, he slumped in his seat and declared that he was absolutely exhausted by his work. Finally, his coach asked him why he thought this was so.

She had wisely allowed David to speak freely and express what he thought the issues were, without interrupting his flow of thoughts and feelings. By doing this, she had created space for David to talk about his situation and bring himself to the realization of how tiring it was for him. Once the coach and David began to explore how the situation was affecting him, she was able to use insightful questions to open up a conversation about David's role in the work situation.

Without making any judgement and by remaining neutral, the coach probed David about his contribution to the position. As he was by now clearly prepared to be open and honest with his coach, he slowly revealed that he felt his stress levels spilled over to the way he treated his staff, and even to his relationship with some of his clients.

From here, the coach was able to work with David to uncover some of the sources of his stress, and to support him in proposing options to deal with them. She asked him how undertaking these actions might help him in his work dilemma. David easily gave her a number of different ways that he felt he would be able to behave differently towards his team, and how that would begin to improve the motivation and willingness of everyone concerned. In turn, this would also have a positive impact on their client relationships.

By using active listening skills and being open and honest with David, the coach enabled him to get a number of difficult issues off his chest. Despite being very defensive at the beginning of the session, the coach's patience and neutral posture allowed David to lower his barriers, and really benefit from his coaching.

CONCLUSIONS

In this chapter, we have offered you insights into the vital importance of a healthy coaching relationship. We have looked at some of the components of the relationship, and how they contribute to delivering effective results for successful change. The stages of the coaching relationship are discussed, from formation to ending, showing what interactions take place.

Much of the process in learning the coaching intervention is the key to the relationship and, conversely, the quality of the relationship that you can create and sustain. This further affects the process and outcomes of your sessions. Elements such as *active listening, incisive questioning, trust, rapport, empathy, and openness* are important. The sections above give you checklists and ideas, for ensuring that your coaching relationships include all the essential ingredients and knowledge. You will also find another couple of recommended books.

Your Activities to Practice your Relationships Skills

Activity 1: Active listening.

Set up a mini coaching session with a partner in a suitable environment, in privacy, free from distraction and interruption.

Make the introductions you need to and begin your coaching session. From the outset, pay attention to your coachee. Try to notice the following:

- His/her body position—is he/she relaxed, alert, upright, slouched, tense?
- His/her tone of voice–is it slow, relaxed and resonant, fast-paced, high-pitched?
- What is he/she saying–note his/her phrases and how he/she is expressing him/herself. Is he/she providing information, expressing problems, describing the situation, asking for something?
- From time to time, when appropriate, you might wish to check your understanding with him/her. You might do this by paraphrasing what you have heard, and repeating this to your coachee to check that you have understood his/her points.
- Notice, whether your coachee changes any of the above as the session progresses. Does he/she become calmer or more animated? Does he/she move from information giving to problem

---

solving? Does he/she seem passive, or does he/she become engaged and motivated?

- Give your coachee time and space to respond in his/her own way

When you have concluded your coaching session, spend 15 minutes writing down your observations from all of the different aspects above, physical, aural, or emotional. What was the quality of your listening compared to one of your previous coaching sessions? What else did you notice about your coachee, and his/her situation? How will this help you develop excellent coaching relationships and effective outcomes in future? How could you develop your skills further?

Activity 2: Rapport

Set up another mini coaching session with a (different) partner in a suitable environment, in privacy, free from distraction and interruption. Make the introductions you need to, and begin your coaching session. Pay attention to building rapport with your coachee from the outset:

- Subtly observe his/her posture and body language. Match his/her positions sympathetically
- Affirm his/her conversation with supportive indications, such as nodding or showing understanding
- Use active listening skills (see Exercise 1) to develop your understanding of your coachee's issues
- Practice "unconditional positive regard" by giving your coachee all your attention; avoid judgement, be open and have compassion
- Share some information with your coachee. This may be on commonalities such as background, interests, experience, and relationships
- Use open questions, evoking in-depth responses from your coachee
- Give your coachee time and space to respond in his/her own way
- If conflict arises, face it openly, and explore the way forward with your coachee. Openness and honesty on both sides will help to rebuild the strength of the relationship

- Keep the conversation on an adult-to-adult level
- Whatever coaching process you use, draw the session to a close in an appreciative way, acknowledging the work done, and what has been achieved

After the session, spend 15 minutes reflecting on the level of rapport you had with your coachee. How did this differ from your previous coaching sessions? How did it make you feel? Which parts worked well, and which worked less well? What would you like to strengthen further–and how?

REFERENCES

De Haan, E. (2008). *Relational Coaching: Journeys Towards Mastering One-To-One Learning*. Chichester, UK: Wiley.

Hardignham, A. (2004). *The Coach's Coach: Personal development for personal developers*. London, UK: CIPD.

Haslam, S. A. (2004). *Psychology in Organizations*. London: Sage.

Kline, N. (1999). *Time to Think: Listening to ignite the human mind*. London: Cassell.

Krznaric, R. (2010). Some of the deepest forms of kindness are based on understanding. *Psychologies magazine*. Hachette Filipacchi

Nelson, D. L., & Cooper, C. (Eds.) (2007). *Positive Organizational Behaviour*. London: Sage.

Peltier, B. (2010). *The Psychology of Executive Coaching: Theory and application*. New York: Routledge.

Rogers, C. (1961). *Client Centred Therapy*. London: Constable.

Roth, A., & Fonagy, P. (1996). *What works for whom? A critical review of psychotherpay research*. London: The Guildford Press.

Schutz, W. (1958). *FIRO: A three-dimensional theory of interpersonal behaviour*. New York: Rinehart and Company.

Stober, D., & Grant, A. (Eds.) (2006). *Towards a Contextual Approach to Coaching Models*. Hoboken, NJ: John Wiley.

Wambold, B. (2001). *The great psychotherapy debate: models, methods and findings*. Mahwah (NJ): Lawrence Erlbaum.

PART V

ELEVATING YOUR LEADERSHIP CAPABILITIES

CHAPTER 14

SYSTEMIC LEADERSHIP

Daniel Pinnow

OBJECTIVE OF THIS CHAPTER

This chapter aims to help you examine and sharpen your leadership potential. The systemic leadership approach provides the conceptual foundations for our analysis.

INTRODUCTION

Leading people is a complex process in a complex system. Being a leader in a system–whether a team or a business–first of all requires being able to lead one person within the system—yourself. Or, as Peter Drucker, one of the most influential and visionary pioneers of management theory, puts it: "A leader can only learn to lead one person—himself" (2001). Only if you can lead yourself, can you be expected to lead others and a business. But only if you understand yourself, can you expect to lead yourself.

The discussion on how to be a good leader is as old as mankind. One theory has superseded the next, and we have acquired broad, scientifically proven knowledge of different management styles' effects. Hence, theoretically, we seem to have enough knowledge about successful leadership, but

Leadership and Personal Development: A Toolbox for the
21ˢᵗ Century Professional, pp. 259–272
Copyright © 2011 by Information Age Publishing
All rights of reproduction in any form reserved.

poor knowledge about how to implement it in our daily life. We are information giants but implementation dwarfs. The systemic leadership approach leads you away from theoretical discussions, management toolboxes, and practical guidelines, on "how to be a good manager". Instead, it focuses on the nerve center of your leadership potential—you.

As a leader, you have had and continue to have many different influences, for example, your history, your family, and the environment in which you work. The principles of systemic leadership allow you to research this playing field, understand the different influences, and develop new ways of dealing with situations. Following the systemic leadership approach means, investigating why you act the way you do in certain situations. Through this, you can improve your emotional intelligence, enhance your self-management, and gain an understanding that your inner attitude to a given person, people or situation has a major influence in programming the outcome.

THE OLD SCHOOL OF MODERN MANAGEMENT: SEE THE WHOLE

Niklas Luhmann, founder of the sociological system theory, defines a company as "a closed system of individual parts, whose boundary sets it apart from its environment" (2000, p. 14). He points out that in order to understand the system you should not only be primarily interested in the business structure, but also in the multiple situations, relationships, attitudes, values, and behavior. Within the system, there is never just one cause of a particular behavior or a particular situation. Its main challenge is best illustrated by the metaphor of the Titanic problem: when looking at an iceberg, what you see above the surface of the water is only a fraction of the whole. The biggest part lies hidden below the surface. Here, powerful currents are at work, which should not be underestimated. They determine the direction of the iceberg. The manager is not only a part of the system, but needs to view the whole system–including what might not be obvious at first glance. If the manager is not aware of these hidden elements, he can easily flounder.

THE NEW SCHOOL OF MODERN MANAGEMENT: AVAIL YOURSELF TO COMPLEXITY

Living up to a systemic leadership role requires leaving traditional management thinking and taking the discussion about leadership to a higher level, that is viewing leadership from a systemic standpoint. The systemic leader no longer discusses "How do I lead an organization?" or "How do we lead an organization?" Rather, he asks "How does the system lead itself?"

Be aware that, in complex systems, it is impossible to predict anything with a hundred percent accuracy. Since the individual parts of the system are interlinked in multiple ways, any intervention will lead to incalculable side effects. Instead of trying to control the system, managers need to observe themselves and the system, and make changes where necessary. In keeping with the motto "inspiration is better than prescription", the manager sets out rules and limits for the system, thus indirectly initiating changes and allowing the organization to develop by itself.

A leader should inspire individuals through optimal conditions and incentives, for achievements of which they would be incapable alone. In these terms, human management means "human management"—inner conviction, communication skills, a sense of value, and resource orientation. The manager needs to encourage the system's learning and development capacity, while also undergoing a constant learning process himself (Van Velsor, 2006).

EXAMINE YOUR PERSONAL LEADERSHIP POTENTIAL

To explore your leadership skills, you need to identify your resources, your beliefs, values, styles, and strengths, but also your alleged weaknesses. This analysis is definitely not something that you will have completed by the end of this chapter. However, if you are open to the activities on the next pages, you will initiate a continuous process, that, once started, will support you throughout your life. Before you begin to analyze your potentials, take a look (in Table 14.1) at the features that build successful leadership (Pinnow, 2011).

Table 14.1.   Components of Systemic Leadership

1. Self-knowledge
2. Communication
3. Being able to let go
4. Withstanding conflicts
5. Dealing with change
6. Conferring meaning
7. Having power
8. Providing guidance and making decisions
9. Inspiring people
10. Loving People

CASE STUDY 1

The Example of a German Branch Manager

Michael, German, a branch manager in the banking industry, Munich, Germany.

When I moved to this little city close to Munich in Germany to assume the position of the branch manager of one of Germany's biggest banking houses, I was the fifth manager within only 6 years in this job. I decided not to let this bother me too much, and started with a bunch of strategic ideas as well as with a lot of faith in my abilities. I started a series of local marketing activities. I soon discovered that none of my ideas worked the way they were supposed to, and that the harder I worked on them, the less our branch benefited. I realized that the tools and strategic approaches that had worked in my former positions, were somehow not applicable to this part of the country. Instead of looking for a new job like my predecessors had done, I worked with a coach and analyzed the branch and its people's dynamics. We found that I had completely ignored the very personal way that the local people did business. Customers would not entrust their money to a bank, unless they knew their bank consultant personally. Once I recognized these hidden patterns, I started all the innovation processes from within instead of top-down, and took special care to consult the established staff members. Today, after 3 years, we are not only able to expand our business, but I feel more satisfied than I ever did, in my previous positions.

---

1. Self-knowledge

Not every thought, action and emotion can be explained by rational and obvious motives. For this very reason, self-knowledge and acceptance of the leader—and that includes your less desirable characteristics–are of great importance. You should be aware of the determining factors of your personality, your individual influences, role models, and limited viewpoints. This "inner narrative" has a decisive impact on a person's leadership style. Another hallmark is authenticity. This does not mean that you have to be liked by everyone, but rather that you have an inner moral compass, which you can rely upon at all times.

2. Communication

Communication fulfils two central functions: the transfer of knowledge and information on the factual level, and the establishment and maintenance of relationships on the emotional level. A good manager is therefore, the interface between networks, collating, and distributing information, and bringing the right people together. It is through communication, that opinions, expectations, or knowledge are exchanged, so that modern companies' most important capital—know-how—can be increased.

3. Being Able to Let Go

A really good manager renders himself redundant, because it is only by distributing tasks and responsibilities, that managers have the necessary time and energy to deal with the things that really matter. You should set priorities and decide what you can delegate to your staff. In so doing, you also give your staff an opportunity for development, and create an atmosphere of trust and partnership.

4. Withstanding Conflicts

A manager's daily duties are characterized by conflicts and opposing interests, all of which it is their job to reconcile. Good managers must allow such conflicts to happen, and be able to withstand them. They decide between alternatives, engineer compromises, and steer a steady course between the need to preserve the necessary structures, to adapt to a changing environment, and envision the future. Managers also have to constantly revise their judgment of when to hold back and let others do the work, and when to intervene. Despite these "management dilemmas", managers have to take decisions, act upon them and ultimately be able to live with their consequences. They must be able to accept, that their decisions will never meet everyone's approval.

5. Dealing with Change

Change management should be a constant feature of corporate governance. This is not what we find in practice, however. Managers fear change, and change in management usually takes place when it is too late, for example, in times of acute market weakness or the imminent threat of a merger. What about you? Do you see changes in a positive light, accepting, institutionalizing, and initiating them, in order to put your own organization at the forefront of change? In practice, such change in processes usually fails due to resistance from the staff. A participatory management style has proved to be the most successful, when handling recalcitrant staff. Managers should attempt to involve all the employees in the process without pressure or coercion. They should make their staff feel that successes along the way are everyone's achievement, and not just that of the boss.

6. Conferring Meaning

In order to encourage achievement, managers should communicate the purpose of their work to their staff. Only when the employees are clear about the reason for their work or the change project, will they be willing to share the responsibility for it. To create the right conditions for "conferring meaning", managers should provide their staff with background information, give them an opportunity to ask questions, and allow communication through all channels. The fish should like the bait, not the fisher. Rituals such as company celebrations give rise to a corporate identity, reinforcing employees' sense of belonging. They are made to feel that they really are the company's most valuable capital, and that the company is prepared to spend a bit on their well-being. This positive team spirit gives overtime a meaningful purpose, and generates a self-fulfilling prophecy.

7. Having Power

Like other systems, systemic leadership, too, is based on power. Power should not only be seen as a negative quantity—it also has very positive dynamic characteristics. Good management arises from power, because it is the basis of decision-making and responsibility. It is important that managerial power is clear and accepted. Power in the traditional, formal sense is no longer center stage in these new, modern management times. Today, good and effective management is based more on power through meaning. This power is person-related, and arises from the manager's personality. Only executives capable of relationship management can achieve this power. It is no longer a case of command and obedience, control, and punishment, but of relational power.

8. Providing Guidance and Making Decisions

A good manager should set an example and maintain a balance between disruption and security. This doesn't mean managers are forbidden to show any sign of uncertainty. Rather, they should be able to recognize, determine and utilize inner feelings such as insecurity, anxiety, and doubt.

Managers should be aware that everyone has their own work rhythm, and that not all the employees are the same. They have to switch between leading and pacing in keeping with the relevant situations and employees.

9. Inspiring People

Good managers must also be able to inspire others. They pass on to others the passion they feel for something, and they also generate enthusiasm and commitment in others, through their words and deeds. Through recognition and praise, managers can also inspire this passion in their subordinates.

10. Loving People

Since management is always about people, managers should also be capable of feelings and sensitivity. Only vulnerable managers who show emotions will be seen as trustworthy by their staff. These emotions do not include intimate emotions, but sincerity, respect, decency, and fairness. It takes self-love, self-knowledge, and self-acceptance by the managers to communicate a sense of value to their staff.

LEARN TO LEAD YOURSELF–LEARN TO LEAD OTHERS!

Being a successful and contented leader is not a fixed state but a continuous process. You may already possess some of the ten mentioned criteria. Some of them will come to you naturally; others may require a long and challenging learning process. In the previous chapters, you have already worked on some of the characteristics of a systemic leader by exploring your strengths and values, envisioning your future, and polishing your communication and relationship skills. Now it is time to take a look at the whole picture (in Fig. 14.1). Leading yourself is not as easy, as it might sound. It is not about arbitrariness, egocentricity, or self-fulfilment at the expense of the company. Leading yourself requires the will and ability to criticize yourself, and the courage to acknowledge your imperfection and mistakes.

There are three wheels that drive the change process: an open, respectful, and fair mindset; clear and transparent values and attitudes; and your

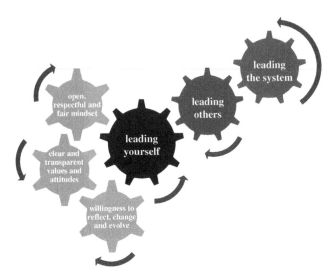

Figure 14.1. The wheels of systemic leadership

willingness to reflect, change and evolve. They do not warrant you any success, but they will provide you with the necessary energy to drive the process of leading yourself, leading others, and leading your system. Therefore, before you start to work on the following activities, make sure you are ready, and feel comfortable about facing the whole picture. Ensure the following:

- You really want to examine your leadership potential.
- You feel ready to take over responsibility for your leadership development.
- You take all the time you need for this process.

CONCLUSION

Your success in the area of systemic leadership is not a status, but an ongoing process. And it takes a lot of energy to change habitual behavior. Make sure you supervise your team every once in a while, and readjust its formation. Perhaps you could ask a close friend to remind you, for example, in 3 months' time, to run through the activities below again. Or you could post a note, a photo you like or a quotation on your desk, to remind you to stay on track. Now–and only now–that you are leading yourself have you set the basis to lead others, or your organization. Moreover, you have increased the probability that, as the next goal, you will not get in the way of your project.

Your Activities to Practise Your Systemic Leadership Skills

Activity 1: Look beyond your titles!

Your leadership energy has nothing to do with your job, or the hierarchical level you have achieved. At this point you should therefore put your titles, position and even your achievements to one side, and concentrate merely on your being. Think about your behavior, using the ten features of a systemic leader mentioned above, and ask yourself how well you comply with each of these requirements. How do you justify your leading position? How do you handle change? What attitudes do you have towards your staff? Look into the mirror, and draw a profile of what you see:

1. My best friend would describe me as ...

_____

_____

2. I am very good at ...

_____

_____

3. I would like to improve ...

_____

_____

4. This person is a role model for me because ...

_____

To take this activity a step further, ask yourself who is your most con-structive critic? What would be his or her answers to the above ques-tions? How would he or she describe you?

Please write down the answers accordingly.

Now that you have a profile of yourself and a picture that you assume a discerning second person might draw, take a look at the two and compare them.

What is your first impression?

How do you feel about what you see?

Activity 2: Reveal your team.

Leading yourself requires you to understand yourself. Why do you do the things the way you do?

Our behavior is determined by our patterns of attitudes and subjective norms that we have built since our earliest childhood. Over the years, we have established an "inner team" of supporting and disrupting characteristics. The good news is that we are not helpless puppets of our behavior patterns. But in order to leave the beaten track, we first need to realize we are on it (Van Velsor, 2006). You have already worked with two aspects of your team–your strengths and values—in the previous chapters. To discover your whole "inner team" comprising of your supporters as well as the disturbers of your behavior as a manager, take a closer look at the single members, and explore their group dynamics.

In the first step, please think about a typical situation in your life as a manager, into which you step again and again. Describe this recurring situation in some detail.

1. I often face the following situation:

_____

_____

2. This is how I behave:

_____

_____

3. These are my supporters and disturbers–my feelings, needs, and values–that steer my behavior within the described situation:

_____

_____

4. This is how the other actors behave:

_____

_____

Now that you have described the situation, your behavior and the feelings that drive you, make sure you do the following activity.

Take a blank sheet of paper and visualize your recurrent situation. You might need more than one try to draw the picture of the situation, and your inner team. Do not stop before you feel you have best described both.

Where on the paper would you locate yourself? Draw yourself at this point.

Which other persons are involved? Place them on the paper with the fitting position and line of sight.

Now position the supporters and disturbers you have described above.

Who else is missing? Add the missing spots.

Activity 3: Rearrange your team.

Take a look at the picture you have created. There may be members of your inner team of whom you have been aware for years, and of whom you are very proud. Others may have been almost invisible, and some of you might have tried to ignore, or even suppressed for a long time.

It is not possible to fire any of your team members, even if you wanted to. They are a part of you. In order to succeed as a leader, it is imperative that you

- become aware of your whole inner team,
- accept your whole inner team,
- work with your whole inner team.

Think about the members of your inner team whom you really like, and who help you to succeed; Supporters who strengthen you not only in the above situation, but all through your life. What do they do to make you feel good? What kind of power do they provide?

_____

_____

Take a look at the team members who continuously disturb your management life. Think about the sources they feed themselves from. What position did they take to date? How did they influence your behavior?

_____

_____

Which of your supporting aspects could take care of the disturbing features? Could, for example, your strengths move your anxiety to lose to where it is no longer a direct obstruction? Start to rearrange your team on your paper. Take your time to discover the answers to these questions, go for a walk, listen to some music, or talk to a close friend. Whenever you have an idea, draw the picture of your rearranged team, and see whether the new placement works for you. Once you have found your ideal team formation, remember it, and try it out in your management life. You will find that accepting your whole inner team will provide you with a lot of energy and self-confidence, to live as a successful and contented leader.

REFERENCES

Drucker, P. (1956). *The Practice of Management*. New York: Harper and Brothers Publishers.

Drucker, P. (2001). *The Essential Drucker*. New York: HarperCollins Publisher.

Fazio, R. (1990). "*Multiple processes by which attitudes guide behavior: The MODE model as an integrative framework.*" In: M.P. Zanna (Ed.). *Advances in Experimental Social Psychology*, *23*, pp. 75–109. New York: Academic Press.

Kouzes, J., & Posner, B. (2007). *The Leadership Challenge* (4th ed.). San Francisco: Jossey-Bass.

Luhmann, N. (1984). *Soziale Systeme*. Frankfurt, Suhrkamp Verlag.

Luhmann, N. (2000). *Organisation und Entscheidung*. Wiesbaden: Vs Verlag.

Pierce, J., & Newstrom, J. (2002). *Leaders and the leadership process: Readings, self assessments and applications* (3rd ed.). New York: Irwin Publishing.

Pinnow, D. (2007). *Elite ohne Ethik?: Die Macht von Werten und Selbstrespekt, F.A.Z.* Frankfurt: Buchverlag.

Pinnow, D. (2009). *Führen–Worauf es wirklich ankommt*, (4th ed.). Wiesbaden: Gabler Verlag.

Pinnow, D. F. (2011). "Leadership—What really matters. *A handbook on systemic leadership*". Heidelberg: Springer- Verlag GmbH.

Satir, V. M. (1978). *Your Many Faces: The first step to being loved*. Berkeley: Celestical Arts.

Van Velsor, E., Taylor, S., & Leslie, J. (2006). "An examination of the relationships among self-perception accuracy, self-awareness, gender, and leadership effectiveness," *Human Resource Management*, *23*, 249–263.

CHAPTER 15

STEPPING INTO YOUR LEADERSHIP ROLES

Mike Green

OBJECTIVE

This chapter has two main objectives. First, it aims to show how we all need to be able to step into different leadership roles if we wish to make a positive impact on our organizations, working lives and community at large. Second, it seeks to show how changes in behavior and attitude can be made, by "stepping into" different ways of leading.

INTRODUCTION

By studying what effective leaders do over a 20 year period–how they think, how they feel, and how they behave—researching the best practice and reading biographies and autobiographies, Cameron and Green (2008) identified five leadership roles which leaders need to step into, if they are to be truly effective. In the majority of situations requiring change, these five roles are essential to a lesser or greater degree, although different change situations will require each of the roles deployed to a different degree.

Leadership and Personal Development: A Toolbox for the
21ˢᵗ Century Professional, pp. 273–285

This model of change leadership clusters leadership behavior around areas of focus, rather than diligently listing "leadership competences" or identifying particular individual behaviors. The five roles are flexible and dynamic, representing modern, commonly understood leadership archetypes. The beauty of each of the roles and the model of leadership in general, is that they can be learned, tried out, experimented with, and generally acted out. This is done through social learning, – for example, imitation and role play (Bandura 1977) – as well as through behavioral routes, such as determining observable behaviors that are needed to achieve the required rewards.

THE FIVE ROLES

From our observations of effective leaders we saw that they focused on the following five areas at different times in the leadership process:

1. **The Discomfort.** What is not working at the moment, and who knows about this? Where is this organization hurting?
2. **The Buy-in.** How can the human resources and talent in the organization be harnessed? How can people be inspired, motivated and engaged?
3. **The Connectivity.** How do we ensure that the organization knows enough about itself, its purpose and competencies, and is well connected enough to self-organize and change in a healthy way when it needs to?
4. **The Project.** What needs to be done to manage the key projects and ensure that all the relevant resources are acquired, and that the projects are delivered on time, within the budget, and with the right quality?
5. **The Design.** What are the structural and process designs for the future?

These areas fitted naturally into five distinct roles. These roles are:

1. The Edgy Catalyzer, who focuses on creating discomfort to catalyze change.
2. The Visionary Motivator, who focuses on engagement and buy-in to energize people.
3. The Measured Connector who focuses on a sense of purpose and connectivity across the organization, to help change to emerge.
4. The Tenacious Implementer, who focuses on project plans, deadlines and progress to achieve results.

5. The Thoughtful Architect, who focuses on frameworks, designs and the complex fit between strategies and concepts, to ensure that there is a sound basis for change.

There is not necessarily any one right way of sequencing stepping into these roles, though it is generally thought that you do need a motivation to change (yourself or the situation) by understanding what is wrong, to have a clearly felt sense of purpose with a motivating vision, to have a high-level plan which incorporates a route map through the world, to understand the different stakeholders involved and their potentially conflicting agendas, and to have the determination and persistence to continue with the changes that you have initiated.

DIFFERENT ROLES FOR DIFFERENT CHANGE LEADERSHIP SITUATIONS

Our research suggests that each of the five roles is necessary in different proportions for different change leadership situations. This is true across all the sectors—private, public, and not-for-profit. A summary of results appears in Fig. 15.1, and the use of the five roles in an exemplary organizational restructure is described in Case Study 1.

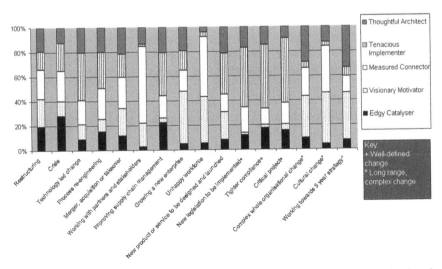

Figure 15.1. Most important roles for managers to adopt in various organizational situations

CASE STUDY 1

Leading a Restructuring Process

A quarter of all those completing the questionnaire on a potential restructuring process, mentioned restructuring as one of the top change priorities for their organization right now. This specifically corresponds to our experience with public sector organizations, where restructuring is a common solution to seemingly intractable organizational problems.

Our survey suggests that a balanced leadership approach is required, when tackling restructuring, with contributions from every one of the five roles. The Edgy Catalyzer role is needed to let everyone know why the restructuring is happening, and to enable those involved to experience the discomfort brought about by the current problems. In our experience, less successful restructures seem to happen in a cloud of mystery, without a clear rationale or existing problem outlined. The Visionary Motivator role is needed to engage the people to commit themselves to the future state. Restructurings are tough to endure, because they are often drawn-out processes if the leadership wants to be seen as fair and above board. This is especially true in the public sector, where rules about fair processes for the staff are generally adhered to. More successful restructuring exercises have been led by people who have been good at inspiring people to believe that once it is all over, a hopeful future will begin to emerge.

The Measured Connector role is especially important once the new structure is in place, because new relationships and a sense of purpose are extremely important to sustain success. New connections have to be established and new goals have to be agreed upon. This is something that seems harder in organizations, where there are mechanistic assumptions about each division's remit and a lack of natural connectivity.

During a restructure, the Tenacious Implementer role is important to ensure that plans are doable and deadlines are achieved. Restructurings with repeated delays and missed deadlines drain an organizational system's performance energy; people need to talk to each other at the water cooler to cope with uncertainty. Unsteadiness often interferes with even the most dedicated individual's productivity.

The Thoughtful Architect role is also needed to think through and explain new processes or ways of working. This leadership role is often undervalued, because Thoughtful Architects do not operate at

(Continued)

CASE STUDY 1 (*Continued*)

top speed, and may be comfortable with a level of complexity that leaves others feeling confused or anxious. However, in our experience, people in new posts often have absolutely no idea how the new organization is "supposed" to work, therefore the Thoughtful Architect is vital when thinking through and explaining a new structure.

Source: Based on Cameron & Green (2008).

THE FIVE ROLES IN MORE DEPTH

Edgy Catalyzers

Edgy Catalyzers cannot bear it when things are not right. They are passionate and proactive about letting people know that there is a problem which needs to be confronted. They have a clear understanding of what the leadership task is—moving people and processes forward to an end state–and they will not rest until this is accomplished. It is almost as if they cannot speak out. If the organization is committed, for example, to world-class customer satisfaction, then they will highlight the areas of the operation which do not subscribe to or demonstrate this in action. They are willing to confront shoddy performance or under-management.

They are very useful in kick-starting a project or initiative, because they are good at creating a sense of urgency needed and they have the energy and, perhaps, the thick skin required to confront people. They typically have a certain nervous energy and a sense that they want to be somewhere else. They do not shy away from saying what needs to be said. They can be abrasive, but only when taken to extremes would this role be described as bullying. However, it can sometimes be intimidating to be on the receiving end of an Edgy Catalyzer's tongue!

Alan Sugar is a good example of this role when he is centre stage on The Apprentice. He does not mince his words and is quite blunt. But one hopes it is always with the end goal in mind—of getting a good team working together, or a good business result.

Visionary Motivators

Visionary Motivators are more focused on the future than on the present or the past. Their role in life is to articulate a motivating vision (whether a shared vision or one of their own), and to engage with people to ensure buy-in. They are endlessly optimistic and emotionally resilient. The Visionary Motivator is a "glass half full" person who sees the positive in any situation, and is able to reframe situations to see the opportunities. Words such as inspiring, motivating, and visionary come to mind when describing the Visionary Motivator, but it does not necessarily mean that we all cannot step into this role. The words they use—"future focused", "positive", "proactive", and, often, "big picture"—are ways of communicating the direction in which they want people to be heading. Not only can they articulate this vision in a meaningful way, they also have a knack of connecting to the heart and to emotions.

Rather than being confrontational, Visionary Motivators more likely want to draw you into the vision, rather than push you towards it. They, too, have the energy but it is pervaded by optimism, and a sense of being on the front foot. The downside might be that they can come across as employing "spin" too much, and often do not want to hear about any downsides to their vision or its direction. Sometimes their visions have no substance behind them. The Visionary Motivator is someone whom the majority of people enjoy working for, and is their manager of choice. In the public sphere, politicians such as Ronald Reagan ("the great communicator") and Tony Blair (before Iraq!) come to mind as people who can get their message across, and can describe a better future state towards which we might be willing to pursue.

Measured Connectors

There was a time when organizations seemed to be hierarchical, were led in a command and control fashion, and had very few dealings with other organizations unless they were suppliers or direct customers. Life seemed to be much simpler then, with the rate of change a manageable phenomenon. Today, we have a complex world in which change is endemic, organizations' boundaries are permeable (with outsourcing, strategic partnerships, and so forth), and there are challenges which one sole leader (the heroic leader) cannot possibly hope to deal with.

Measured Connectors are the sort of leaders who exude confidence, as they walk through the turbulence of change as if they were in that calm center in the eye of the hurricane. They have a clear set of principles and a relaxed countenance. They do not expect to lead from the front, but they do expect to lead by example. They have the confidence and clarity to face difficult and complex challenges, and are more likely to articulate a set of underlying principles and a general direction of movement. They know their agenda well and seek to understand other people's agendas. In this sense, they wish to align other people's agendas with the overarching agenda. They do not believe that it is their responsibility to do all the work themselves—but are adept at getting disparate people and different stakeholders together, to deal with important issues. By linking people and their agendas and enabling them to get on with tasks, they are able to monitor progress with an inbuilt helicopter vision.

In today's world where outcomes will often be achieved by a number of different sections, departments, or indeed, organizations and agencies, Measured Connectors will step into their leadership role by demonstrating authoritative leadership and systems thinking. A good example of a Measured Connector is Tim Smit, who transformed a derelict Cornish quarry into the Eden Project, which has 1,00,000 plants from around the world and includes the world's largest greenhouse. He managed to connect people from all around the world and the local community, from the private, public and third sector, from individuals to governments, resulting in one of the UK's top tourist attractions, and a testament to creating a sustainable way of living on the planet to address the various environmental crises facing us.

Tenacious Implementers

The Tenacious Implementer role is probably the least "sexy" of all the roles. Books will often focus on the dynamic, motivating, and inspiring behaviors of *leaders* and leave the more mundane job of actually delivering things to the mere *manager*. However, the Tenacious Implementer is a crucial part of leadership. Those who step into this role are concerned with starting and finishing the job in hand. Typically associated with managing a project from inception to completion, this role is one of persistence and perseverance, and adhering to time schedules, quality controls and cost constraints.

Tenacious Implementers are determined and past masters, at getting the job done. They are definitely more task-focused than people-friendly, but are very clear that roles and responsibilities are important, and team processes need to function effectively to allow task achievement. Their 1% inspiration is definitely a result of their 99% perspiration! Their weakness can be rigid adherence to a plan, and they can become blinkered and dogmatic when new matters emerge, suggesting that a plan might need to be changed. Their focus on the here-and-now, and the short-term, means that they can sometimes lose sight of the final goal. Interestingly, all the other roles need Tenacious Implementers to some degree. Tim Smit, a Measured Connector, describes Evelyn Thurlby, appointed as chief executive officer (CEO) of the Eden project, as:*"Evelyn was just what the project needed: tough, driven and focused. While her full-blooded approach made me swallow hard on occasion, and her impatience to dispense with pleasantries sometimes felt like fingernails running down a blackboard, she was right that the project needed to become professional. What drove her mad were the myriad connections that were nurtured for no immediate gain, with a view to a bigger future at some indefinable point. Where I saw a campaign, she saw it broken down into individual battles that had to be won along the way. The truth is we were both right, and without both tactics being employed in tandem, we would never have made the progress we did."* (Cameron & Green 2008)

Thoughtful Architects

Thoughtful Architects are more reflective, more introverted leaders. They scan the horizon for the political, economic, societal and technological forces at play. They look for the drivers of change and the challenges which are emerging in the environment, and then scan and scrutinize the internal structures, systems, staff, and like to ascertain what needs to change now and in future, for the organization to survive and thrive. Thoughtful Architects can see the big picture and are able to develop all-encompassing strategies and plans, that act as route maps and compasses for the organization to follow. Their reflective nature means that the time taken to accomplish things can lengthen, but it also means that there are probably fewer disconnects in the overall strategy.

Although Thoughtful Architects are, like Visionary Motivators, focused on the future, they are, however, more concerned with the strategy, rather than the people side. They are more concerned with ensuring that the strategy "stacks up" than necessarily implementing it! The scientific world has produced many amazing Thoughtful Architects such as Einstein and Carl Sagan. In the business world, George Soros comes to mind: *"He is best known for his ability to make money from his strategic understanding of the world's financial markets. In order to survive during the post-war period of chaos in Europe, he had to use all of his imagination and ingenuity. He became a successful stock-broker by always anticipating the changes in the finance markets. He was able to out-manoeuvre conventional European financiers, using his imagination and power of logical thought in equal measure to understand the nature of markets and capitalize on that knowledge."* (Cameron & Green 2008)

CONCLUSIONS

What can these roles do for you personally? Whether you are a leader at the top of the organization, or in charge of a few members of staff, or whether you are a family member wanting to effect social or community change, having access to a variety of these roles will help you accomplish more.

The important point is to believe that, like an actor on a stage, you can step into any of these roles if you so desire.

Using a combination of these roles means that you are adjusting your leadership style to the situation and to your audience. In times of change, you will need all of the roles—as the research suggests. There are six exercises that follow. The first is to get you "warmed up", the next five will each take one role, and suggest a simple exercise that will get you stepping into that particular role or get you to think through that particular lens. When you step into any of the five roles, you need to be able to adopt the role's physical stance, the mental attitude that the role requires and demonstrate the behaviors that the role demands. The more you feel physically free, loose, and enabled, the better; the more you understand deeply where the role comes from, the better; and the more you have studied some of the behaviors, the more impact you will have.

Your Activities to Explore your Leadership Roles

Activity 1: The world: a stage.

This activity prepares you for all of the five roles. It is a generic exercise which will require you to step into the persona of one of the five roles. Stand up and take a minute to get in touch with your breathing, ensuring that you are breathing deeply. Upon inhaling, feel crisp clear air full of vitality filling your body, and on exhaling feel all of your muscles relaxing completely. Concentrate on both the inhalation and the exhalation for, say, 2 minutes. By combining the two, you become both relaxed and alert at the same time.

Look at the chart and decide on a particular role. Either by remembering a time when you demonstrated this role, or when you experienced or observed another person stepping into this role, begin to imagine what it is like to inhabit this role (see Table 15.1).

- Step into the physical stance of the roles.
- Start to think the thoughts that this particular role would have.
- Start to feel the feelings that this particular role would have.
- Start to say the things that this particular role would say.

Wherever you are doing this activity—in your living room or bedroom, or in your office at work—step into the role and just for 2 or 3 minutes practice what it is like being in the role.

Table 15.1.   The Five Roles

	Edgy Catalyser	Visionary Motivator	Measured Connector	Tenacious Implementer	Thoughtful Architect
How am I standing?	Assertively with focused eyes and finger ready to point	On the front foot, chest out, head high, looking at people	Feet firmly on the ground, open stance, taking in your surroundings	With the plan in your hand or in your mind's eye, determined, focused	In reflective mode, looking into the distance
What am I thinking?	What is not quite right? What needs to change? What do I need to say to bring about shifts?	Let us connect to the vision. How can I get these people on board?	What do we need to align? How can I connect these people to address the key issues together?	Who needs to be doing what by when? Is everyone clear about what their next task is? How is the plan progressing?	How does what we are doing here fit with where we need to get to? Have I thought through the whole strategy?
What am I feeling? Key descriptors	Annoyed, irritated, frustrated, determined	Positive, inspired, motivated, solution-focused	Calm, confident, engaged, open	Focused, persistent, resilient, here and now	Conceptual, perceptive, strategic, assured
What am I saying?	"This is a serious problem. Can you not you get a grip on this?"	"Let us work together towards a brighter future"	"Get together and take time to focus on this"	"Just follow the plan and we will get this done"	"Let me explain how it all fits together"
What is my outcome?	Creating a sense of urgency for change	Motivated people moving towards the vision	Aligned people working on the emerging issues	Achieving the project on time, on budget and with high quality	A longer-term strategy which fits together

Activity 2: Edgy Catalyzer.

Step into the Edgy Catalyser role by doing Activity 1. Think of a work or family situation which is not going as well as you would like. Write down or mentally list all the things which are wrong with the current situation, and also what is right with the current situation. Write and rehearse a statement outlining your current dissatisfaction, and why. Decide who you want to "discuss" this with (for example, the person you need to say it to or a friend or colleague) and book the appointment.

Activity 3: Visionary Motivator.

Step into the Visionary Motivator role by doing Activity 1. Think of a project or plan that you really want to succeed. Articulate a vision of the positive outcome of the project. Make it:

- Positive
- Passionate
- Personal
- Engaging

Write the script and rehearse. Practise with a friend or work colleague. Seek feedback and adjust accordingly. Repeat out, loud to yourself, whenever you need to. Ensure that you get your message across to all those concerned with the project.

Activity 4: Measured Connector.

Step into the Measured Connector role by doing Activity 1. Focus on a work-based situation, and identify two individuals in different parts of the organization who you think need to be talking to each other more to make the organization function more effectively. Rehearse different ways of encouraging them to get together. Think of sensible approaches and perhaps a few wacky ones too. Be clear about what you think they each might gain from the conversation and how it might be a good idea for the organization as a whole. Make connections between them and their challenges, as well as between people you know and information that you are aware of. Ask questions rather than giving advice.

- Have you thought of involving …?
- Do you know about …?
- You need to speak to …

Once you have rehearsed, try it out in reality.

Activity 5: Tenacious Implementer.

Step into the Tenacious Implementer role by doing Activity 1. Pick a specific short- to medium-term project, which you are having difficulty with. What moves you forward (including intrinsic and extrinsic motivators)? What holds you back (including what you say to yourself or think about yourself)? What tools and techniques do you normally use, and how effectively do you use them (project management methods, time management, and problem-solving/decision-making methods)? Have you identified and mapped the significant stakeholders, and do you have a plan to manage them? Using all this information develop a short-term plan with a clear next action.

Activity 6: Thoughtful Architect.

Step into the Thoughtful Architect role by doing Activity 1. Review the key contents of this book, and imagine how you might use some of the key methods to develop your future career. Write a 5 year career development plan. What elements of the book need to be incorporated into it? Identify how you will be using the five leadership roles, to achieve your outcomes in a better manner.

REFERENCES AND RECOMMENDED READING

Bandura, A. (1977). *Social Learning Theory*. Englewood Cliffs, NJ: Prentice Hall.

Cameron, E., & Green, M. (2008). *Making sense of leadership: Exploring the five key roles used by effective leaders*. London: Kogan Page.

Kotter, J. (1996). Why Transformation Efforts Fail. *Harvard Business Review*, 73(2) 59–67.

Schein, E. (2004). *Organizational culture and leadership*. San Francisco: Jossey-Bass.

Senge, P. *et al.*, (1999). *The dance of change*. London: Nicholas Brealey.

Shaw, P. (2002). *Changing conversations in organizations*. London: Routledge.

Todnem, R. (2007). Ready or Not. *Journal of Change Management*, 7(1) 3–11.

OTHER RESOURCES

Five leadership roles online questionnaire: http://www.transitionalspace.co.uk/Transitional%20Space%20leadership.php

View John Cleese in Fawlty Towers' Waldorf Salad episode

Listen to speeches by John F Kennedy, Martin Luther King, and other inspiring politicians, business people and actors.

Listen to Obama's Inaugural Speech for Measured Connector communication

Look at a YouTube clip of Carl Sagan talking about "the pale blue dot" which is Planet Earth http://www.youtube.com/watch?v=WmMUuR—Qvo

CHAPTER 16

LEADING IN A VIRTUAL ENVIRONMENT

Inger Buus

OBJECTIVE OF THIS CHAPTER

The main purpose of this chapter is to explore the nature of virtual leadership, as well as to discuss how you can communicate and operate effectively when leading a team separated by distance, and possibly time.

INTRODUCTION

Some of the mega-trends in today's society are changing how we work and collaborate. Projects are not only carried out by co-located teams, but increasingly by virtual, dispersed, or remote teams, who carry out their work in different locations and often in different regions and time zones. One therefore, has to consider that:

- Globalization means that employees and leaders in modern businesses come together, virtually, across regions and time zones, to run functions and projects.

Leadership and Personal Development: A Toolbox for the 21st Century Professional, pp. 287–299
Copyright © 2011 by Information Age Publishing

- Technological progress facilitates working remotely and virtually through multiple media and methods, for example, telephone, video and web conferences, Skype, telepresence conferences, and so forth. Some of the technology is free and compatible with multiple systems; so working virtually does not necessarily require expensive upfront investment in the infrastructure.

- New generations, whose technology fluency and ability to connect through virtual media vastly surpass that of the previous generations, are joining the workplace. Some would claim that their face-to-face social skills are not as advanced as those of the earlier generations, but they are certainly at home in the virtual world of games, Facebook, instant messaging, Second Life and thus, also modern business communication tools.

- The same generations are increasingly conscious of their work-life balance choices, as well as the environmental impact of the first wave of globalization's extensive commuting and global travel.

- Finally, the recent economic crisis has accelerated the move to cut travel costs and, in some cases, reduce the cost of physical office space in favor of working at home.

The above trends have rapidly changed the context for leadership in global businesses. Thus, you might find yourself leading virtually in this new set-up, without any real preparation.

New competencies that are not applicable to proximity management are required, while some classic leadership competencies need to be "amplified" in a virtual context.

VIRTUAL TEAMWORK

The pros and cons of virtual teamwork can be summarized as follows in Table 16.1.

VIRTUAL LEADERSHIP

As a general rule, if you are a virtual leader, you need to master the same skills, behaviors, and mindsets as a face-to-face or "proximity" leader, and be able to effectively manage the additional challenges of virtual leadership:

- Co-ordinate and monitor activities across time and space.
- Establish effective working relationships despite the lack of informal, daily contact.

Table 16.1.   Evaluating Virtual Teamwork

	Pros	*Cons*
Individual	• Higher flexibility • Empowerment and self-direction	• Feeling of isolation: out-of-sight, out of mind • Lack of interpersonal contact and sense of belonging: lack of networking and water-cooler philosophizing • Risk of misunderstandings and conflict escalation
Organizational	• Staff appointed for their expertise, not local availability • Work "around the clock" – using difference in time zones • Speed and flexibility in response to market needs • Closer links to suppliers and customers • Less travel and office costs	• Lack of strategy for virtual work, for example, vision, review of the business model, technology investments, and so forth • Lack of control/supervision of work • Costs of additional technology • Data security issues
Societal	• Develop regions with a low infrastructure • Integrate people with low mobility due to handicaps or family care duties • Reduce traffic and air pollution	• Increased isolation

- Communicate across cultural barriers—without verbal, social, and status cues.
- Compensate for the constraints of the technologies chosen.
- Build commitment—often dealing with competing commitments between your virtual colleagues/managers, and co-located colleagues/managers.

The potential for misunderstandings and multiple or contradictory interpretations of information, tensions, and conflicts is amplified by the lack of body language and facial expressions in virtual communication. This means that, as a leader, you need to amplify good leadership practices, such as listening with intent and care, recognizing contributions, acknowledging and reinforcing good behaviors, summarizing actions and decisions, and seeking feedback to an even greater extent than in the proximity management context.

Jaclyn Kostner (1996) has written an entertaining and easily accessible story on the distinctiveness of virtual leadership, using the lessons from King Arthur's table. In this story, she has a modern remote team leader, Jim connect with King Arthur, who acts as his mentor. King Arthur teaches Jim how, as a remote leader, he has little power and control over his team, and that the key to building high performance across a distance is to build trust. In this regard, every word, action, and initiative in the virtual team can help to build trust.

TRUST

As mentioned, trust is the core ingredient of success for effective virtual teams. It is this element which keeps the team on track when the leader is not there. How do you build trust when you are not face-to-face? Let us consider the core components of trust as defined by Maister (2000): Reliability, credibility, and intimacy as trust enhancers but self-orientation as a destroyer of trust.

You can demonstrate reliability by, for instance, delivering on your promises. In a virtual team, this means being very clear about who does what by when. Credibility is as important, and concerns everybody recognizing the competencies available in the team, and the contributions that the various team members make. While credibility and reliability can easily be recognized in virtual collaboration, being able to build intimacy and to show empathy are trickier. Many virtual project leaders have found that investing upfront in face-to-face kick-off meetings, where relationships are allowed to form before going into a fully virtual format is well worthwhile. If this is not an option, you need to consider how you can create the informal, personal touch in a virtual world; how you can allow people to get to know each other better, for example, by having a shared e-platform with profiles, pictures, chat rooms, and so forth. You can also allow people to get to know each other by pairing them up or letting them complete some tasks in sub-groups.

As a leader, you should prioritize socializing with all the team members, particularly with those who are not on the same site as you are. Use every opportunity, for example, if you are passing through a location, to meet, or have lunch with the team members there. Encourage your team members to do the same so that any opportunity for informal communication is exploited.

You will destroy trust if your self-orientation is too high. For a virtual leader—as indeed for any leader–this means working for the greater good of the team, rather than for your own agenda and career ambitions.

Interesting research by Ghislaine Caulat (2010) at Ashridge shows that some teams have managed to build very high levels of trust without ever meeting face-to-face. The anonymity of the virtual world has allowed some individuals to share more openly, and achieve higher levels of intimacy.

A measure of trust may be the extent to which the team is comfortable expressing disagreement with the leader, or with each other. In virtual teams such as co-located teams, the risk of "group think" is real, and needs to be avoided. More productive teams tend to allow disagreement to be expressed constructively.

MEANING MAKING

One of the virtual leader's most important roles is to create a meaning for the team. Having a shared vision and a sense of purpose for a virtual team is even more critical if the leader is not physically present every day and the team members have split loyalties. We tend to feel more committed to tasks and the people based locally and often need additional encouragement and continuous reminders to stay focussed on our virtual colleagues and tasks. Using a knowledge sharing platform, a project management or online collaboration tool will allow people to track the team's progress easily (Link 1), and stay aligned to the task.

COMMUNICATING EFFECTIVELY IN THE VIRTUAL WORLD

Trust building is made more difficult by the nature of virtual teams' means of communication. The balance of formal and informal communication is particularly important.

All research to date stresses the importance of informal communication as a major trust-building tool for virtual teams. In the absence of water-coolers, coffee corners, and smokers' corners, and so forth, virtual teams need to find pockets of time for free-flowing, informal exchanges. Traditional conference call rules advise the use of a strict agenda, with people taking turns to talk. In fact, trust building might require an item on the agenda for small talk and informal catch up, with people contributing spontaneously in an improvised format. At the end of the meeting, you can also debrief regarding how the meeting went, and have a "battery check" regarding how everybody is feeling. Secondly, the balance of directive and consultative exchanges will significantly impact the team's productiveness. Some claim that the average attention span of business professionals listening to a conference call is only 3–5 minutes. This clearly means that dialogue and co-creation of content will determine the call's productiveness. Co-creation and collaborative work create commitment rather than mere compliance, which directive, one-way information might achieve. Thirdly, the frequency of communication is important (Hofner, Kappler, and DeVries, 2005). Short but frequent meetings allow the virtual teams to build relationships, and are more effective than longer or infrequent interaction. Finally, teams need to agree on a code of conduct for virtual communication. The rules will vary depending on the media:

- When using audio communication such as phone/Skype and telephone conferences, those participating need to pay intense attention to audio cues such as silence, voice tone, inflection, and the pitch of a voice. Silence speaks volumes but is difficult to maintain, particularly for the more extroverted types. Research done by Professor Mehrabian at the University of California showed that words account only for 7% of the meaning in face-to-face communication, voice for 38%, and body language for 55%. In audio communication, words account for 16% and voice for the remaining 84%. It is easy to see how vulnerable we are in audio communication, compared to being face-to-face. When presenting, face-to-face team members will continuously read the body language of the leader and adapt to their communication. This is not possible in, for example, a conference call, which is why it is important that the leader in particular, responds with "virtual nods" and sounds of approval (Caulat, 2010).
- E-mail communication deserves a chapter on its own since research has documented the power games in e-mail communication, as well as standards for "good" e-mail communication. Virtual teams need to decide how they want to use e-mails, whom and when to carbon copy (c.c.), and so forth. E-mail is an effective and quick way of sharing information, but is not recommended for discussions or brainstorming. As a leader, the main rule is "less is more."

Cultural Sensitivity

This is yet another competency which the virtual team leader needs to hone in order to be effective. At a distance, subtle cultural cues can be difficult to detect, so knowing the individual team members, their cultural background, and their communication preferences is critical (see Chapter 12 on building relationships and working in teams across cultures). Equally, communication between the non-native speakers requires particular attention. Speaking slowly with frequent summaries, checking for understanding, and offering clarifications helps prevent misunderstandings, and balance a discussion which native speakers can sometimes dominate.

Work-life Balance in Virtual Teams

Finally, a word of warning on the risk of work across time zones: While virtual teams can work the time zone differences to their advantage and allow tasks to travel with the world clock, there is also an inherent risk of the team members continuously working at inconvenient times, in order to connect with their colleagues in other time zones. Several free Internet tools are now available to allow you to take normal working hours into account, when scheduling activities across the time zones (see the recommended links at the end of this chapter). It is particularly important that the leader adapts to meeting times to the different time zones, to minimize the feeling that the team members in the same time zone as the leader are being favored.

As a leader, be mindful that you are also acting as a role model, with regard to the way you use the virtual media for your day-to-day management and communication. Consider people's work-life balance and do not travel the world if you ask your team not to. To support your leadership task and minimize your need to travel, you may want to appoint a "team of deputies" in the different locations, that is, a team members or other managers who can support your virtual project, or function on an ongoing basis (Thomassen & Villumsen, 2006).

CASE STUDY 1

On Suzan—A Global Training Manager

Suzan, (37), Dutch, Global Training Manager, London, UK.

Suzan was responsible for a global training program for business partners from finance, marketing, and human resource (HR) in a global high tech company. Previously, she would ask people to fly in for a 3 day, off-site training program in a beautiful chateau. However, general travel bans forced her to think differently, and she designed a solution which combined telephone coaching and local sub-group face-to-face meetings, with gatherings in the telepresence suites her company had invested in. To her surprise, the telepresence environment allowed people to build trust in a way the conference calls could not.

Since people were "face-to-face" on life-size screens meant that they felt more comfortable sharing their experiences and thoughts on their development needs. Her target audience for this training were people from functions, with responsibility for corporate policies'

(Continued)

CASE STUDY 1 (*Continued*)

global coordination, typically, cutting across the local policies and preferences. The experience of engaging in personal development in a virtual setting, taught the participants how to use the medium for their teams and their daily work. This was probably the greatest value that the training program added–it very clearly demonstrated the benefits of using a mixture of technologies to communicate in a virtual team setting.

CONCLUSION

Finally, virtual work is relatively new to most of the people and joint learning reviews will go a long way to set the team up for success. Team members need to be trained in technology, and the teams need to work out the best way that they can collaborate virtually. As a leader, you should allow time to track learning concerning virtual collaboration—and celebrate even small successes.

Your Activities to Practice your Virtual Leadership Skills

Activity 1: Setting your virtual team up for success.

Analyze the work styles and communication preferences in your team.

_____

_____

Reflect on how you can adapt to each individual's style and preference.

_____

_____

What else do you know about the individuals in your team? What motivates them?

_____

_____

When are they at their happiest and most productive?

_____

_____

What critical tasks and/or roles do you need to fulfil to be successful as a team?

_____

_____

What strengths do you have in the team?

_____

_____

Undertake a gap analysis and, with the team, discuss how to leverage their strengths and compensate for the gaps.

_____

_____

Clearly define each team member's roles and responsibilities (or those of the team if this is appropriate).

_____

_____

Determine etiquettes for written and verbal communication with the team.

_____

_____

Define a knowledge management and knowledge sharing strategy. How should the team share knowledge?

_____

_____

Agree with the team on how you will allow space for informal communication.

_____

_____

Do regular process checks in the meetings to capture collective learning and surface any tensions:

- What are we learning from this way of working?
- What works well? What should we start or continue doing?
- What can we improve?
- What should we do differently?

Activity 2: Simulate a virtual leadership situation—and obtain feedback.

Practice makes perfect. You can practice virtual management by running a simulation with your team and asking them for feedback. Here is an exercise for you to try:

In one of the first face-to-face team meetings, ask a couple of people to move to a corner and turn their backs to the rest, but keeping their computers connected to all of those present, if possible.

Ask a couple of people to be observers and pay close attention to the tone of interaction, level of contribution, and so forth in the room.

As the leader, undertake a few team interactions, simulating conference calls or Web conferences (whichever is appropriate), with those at your table and the others in their corner.

Ask everybody to reflect on what happened in the interaction:

How much did they contribute?

_____

_____

When and what?

_____

_____

Who spoke?

_____

_____

How did they feel?

_____

_____

How did you, as a leader, interact with the team at your table? With the "remote people"?

_____

_____

Use the exercise to derive simple guiding principles for future team meetings/conference calls.

_____

_____

Activity 3: Assessing your virtual leadership competencies.

Use the below table to rate yourself regarding key virtual leadership competencies on a scale from 1–5, with 5 being the highest absolute strength. Be as honest as possible, and validate your responses with others.

Competency	*Score (1–5)*	*How could you use this strength more or improve in this area?*
Coach and manage performance without traditional forms of feedback		
Recognize and acknowledge contributions		
Invite co-creation of content		
Listen with intent and care—pick up audio cues		
Socialize appropriately and equally with the entire team		
Encourage debate, disagreement, and constructive criticism		
Select and appropriately use electronic communication and collaboration technology		
Lead in a cross-cultural environment		
Manage team members' development and career development		
Building and maintaining trust		
Build commitment to a common vision		
Support team members in dealing with competing local commitments		
Gather learning about virtual team work		

RECOMMENDED LINKS

- Basecamphq.com—an example of affordable virtual collaboration software.
  http://basecamphq.com/
- Timeanddate.com—a free Web-site with a meeting planner, time conversion and other useful tools for planning virtual meetings across time zones.
  http://timeanddate.com/
- Link to Mannaz Newsletter articles.
  http://www.mannaz.com/newsletter.asp

REFERENCES AND FURTHER READING

Kostner, J. (1996). *Virtual leadership: Secrets from the round table for the multi-side manager*. NY: Warner Books.

Caulat, G. (2010, January). Virtual leadership requires a systemic change of mindset. Ashridge Faculty Publications, *HR Magazine*. http://www.hrmagazine.co.uk/news/features/978351/Virtual-leadership-requires-systemic-change-mindset%20target.

Hofner Saphiere, D., Kappler Mikk, B., & DeVries, B. I. (2005). *Communication Highwire: Leveraging the Power of Diverse Communication Styles*. MA: Intercultural Press.

Kostner, J. (1996). *Virtual leadership: Secrets from the round table for the multi-side manager*. NY: Warner Books.

Maister, D., Green Ch. H., & Galford R. M. (2000). *The Trusted Advisor*. NY: Simon & Schuster.

Thomassen, B., & Villumsen, H. (2006). Distant management—practical philosophical perspectives, *Mannaz Newsletter*. http://www.mannaz.com/Mail.asp?MailID=92&TopicID=1022

CHAPTER 17

LEADING MORE EFFECTIVELY THROUGH FEEDBACK

Phil Cullen

OBJECTIVE OF THIS CHAPTER

The main goal of this chapter is to help you understand the best ways to provide feedback to your colleagues, and avoid some of the pitfalls usually associated with the fallout from poor feedback. Ask people for an example of poor feedback that they have received, and they can usually provide one instantly!

INTRODUCTION

There is little doubt that, in the 21st century, a leader's work in any organization is more complicated or makes more demands on his/her time, than ever before. There are demands to satisfy operational targets, customers and suppliers' needs, and—perhaps of most importance, given that none of these can be achieved without them—there are the team members who directly report to such a leader. The importance of monitoring and reviewing the performance of those around us has never been more crucial.

Leadership and Personal Development: A Toolbox for the 21st Century Professional, pp. 301–313
Copyright © 2011 by Information Age Publishing

The same is true of the need to constantly drive improvements in organizational performance while seeking to reduce costs and ensure appropriate rewards for those in organizations—usually based on what they have delivered.

In this chapter, we will examine how leaders can improve their employees' performance by giving them timely and appropriate feedback. We will look at the way in which to give feedback, investigating some of the best approaches, and also focussing on some of the poor practices that are still very evident in the workplace. Let us start by looking at where feedback falls in the role of the leader. The Fig. 17.1 is similar to a typical hierarchy in an organization, and the doubled-headed arrows are the places where feedback can typically take place.

You see that a manager has a relationship with his/her own line manager and his/her team, which involves a two-way feedback. It is arguable that the feedback given to the team could be one-way in some situations, for example, the setting of business objectives or goals. However, the manager must, then, have regular feedback processes in place to secure information that explains performance in terms of those objectives or goals.

The same applies to the line manager. Feedback on performance is a necessary part of their relationship and, very importantly, a leader needs to take that feedback on board, and to act on it. Many organizations now accept that feedback across the organization, in which peers are treated as internal customers, helps to improve the overall performance. Here, feedback is provided along the "value chain," to improve performance and responsiveness to internal and external customer needs.

Finally, there are relationships with suppliers and customers outside the organization; these may require a two-way feedback. Where organizations have out-sourced parts of their operations, for example, order fulfilment

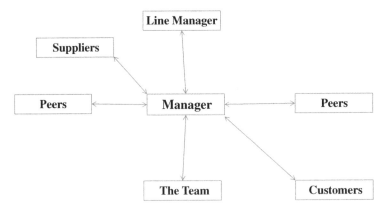

Figure 17.1. Flows of feedback

and payroll, the problems can be more acute and even more critical to the organization's success. Out of sight should not mean out of mind.

All of the stakeholders mentioned rely on good communication skills and, more importantly, on good feedback in a two-way approach. There is also the issue of what to give feedback on. The approach and amount of feedback may mostly depend on the situation and the recipient. Much of this chapter will therefore, focus on the relationship between the leader and a team member, although the good practices discussed are appropriate for many of the other relationships in the Fig. 17.1.

WHAT IS FEEDBACK?

Feedback can be best understood as communication with an individual and/or team to provide them with the information on how you and others perceive their performance or behavior, and the effect of this on them, others, and the organization as a whole. The main reason for providing feedback is to help employees improve their work by increasing their level of awareness, of what they do and how they do it. When undertaken properly and as a part of a framework for providing feedback, feedback can have a number of very helpful benefits for individuals:

- They learn about themselves, their strengths, their areas for improvement and future goals.
- They will be provided with specific advice concerning their performance.
- They will be able to build relationships in the workplace and beyond.
- They will be able to identify differences between themselves and others.
- They can use this knowledge to build relationships.
- They can improve their communication skills.
- They can develop greater levels of rapport.
- They learn about things such as organizational values.

Giving feedback is not the easiest of tasks; despite many years of experience, there are many leaders who still feel uncomfortable about talking to their team members in a meaningful way. Being frank with poorly performing members of the team can be an issue, particularly if there are other factors like health to take into consideration. Conversely, those receiving good feedback can also have difficulty in accepting it.

Some leaders simply feel that it is better to avoid embarrassing situations and not bother at all. Nonetheless, providing feedback to team members is critical, and it is particularly important as part of a formal appraisal or dealing effectively with performance management issues. The author's

Table 17.1.   Types of Feedback

Feedback	Polite	Impolite
Positive	Praise	Patronizing feedback
Negative	Constructive criticism	Destructive criticism

Source: Author.

model illustrated in Table 17.1 which introduces the concept of feedback as either "polite" or "not polite", summarizes one of the reasons for that feeling of embarrassment.

Let's examine at each one in turn.

- Positive, polite feedback makes the recipients want to repeat their performance, or improve it. *Praise is an example of positive feedback.*
- Positive, impolite feedback diminishes the sense of achievement team members may feel. *Patronizing feedback is an instance of such feedback.*
- Negative, polite feedback makes the recipients want to do things differently next time, to improve their performance. *Constructive criticism falls into this category.*
- Negative, impolite feedback is destructive and may make the recipients embarrassed or angry. Such feedback does not enable the recipients to identify ways by which they can improve their performance. *Expressions like "What a stupid thing to do!" fall into this category.*

Throughout the monitoring process, feedback can act as a great motivator and it works both ways—get it wrong and motivation regresses fast; get it right and motivation progresses steadily towards achieving both your and your teams' performance objectives.

DEVELOPING A CULTURE OF GIVING FEEDBACK

The ability and need to interact are indispensable parts of a good leader, which also includes giving and receiving feedback. Feedback for a job done well is a reward in itself. Given appropriately, feedback shows your team that what they do is important enough for you to comment on it, and that you do not take their efforts for granted, simply because they are doing only what they are paid for.

Feedback should not be limited to the annual formal performance appraisal. Give feedback as quickly after a task or activity, as possible. Be very specific, focussing on the opportunity to provide feedback on a recent incident and not focussing on previous incidents, which will act as a distraction.

Stick to descriptions of what you saw. The acronym BOOSTER below is a checklist that you could follow to remember that feedback should be:

- **Balanced**—focus on things done well, not so well and things that can be improved.
- **Observed**—use examples of those tasks and activities for which you have direct evidence, and do not rely on hearsay.
- **Objective**—avoid subjective, evaluative comments.
- **Specific**—do not waffle! Give examples of what you have seen or heard.
- **Timely**—give feedback as soon as possible after an incident.
- **Enhances performance**—the purpose of your feedback is to increase the team members' contribution.
- **Relevant**—focus on the things that are appropriate for their job.

The persons receiving the feedback must have the opportunity to reply and be encouraged to respond. After they have done so, accept their feedback and, if necessary, explain what will happen next. We have assumed that most of the feedback communication is done verbally, which mostly works the best. Do pay special attention to the method of communication that you decide to use, as it may be beneficial to do so in writing where there might be disagreement, questions, other points of view, or where clarification is needed.

Remember that your team members often avoid feedback because they may have had bad experiences in the past, and are concerned about what they might hear from you again. Part of effective feedback is that you are seen to act on those actions that you have agreed on. This works both ways of course. Establishing rapport and a sense of trust between a leader and his/her team members is essential for the organization to function effectively. If there is mistrust in any of the relationships, this will inevitably lead to a worsening of working relationships. If all of you trust each other, you will have the beginning of a sound working relationship that will not only be of benefit to the individuals concerned, but also to the business.

WHERE DO WE USE FEEDBACK?

There are obvious places where it is natural to provide feedback. We will take a look at each in turn, and then move on to identify best practice approaches to each.

Informal Feedback

At the best, formal performance review systems provide infrequent, but focussed feedback. However, the best opportunity to provide very regular feedback lies in the leaders' ability to use informal feedback mechanisms, to keep in touch with their team. Feedback provided in this way can work very well. Congratulating someone on a job well done, a positive comment on someone meeting a target or for covering for a sick colleague will demonstrate that you have a good idea of what is happening within your team. This type of informal feedback can be very positive, and is important for the effective working of the business.

A good way of looking at this approach is to focus on "catching people doing things right." If you have good performance management systems in place, you should be in a position to know how good your team is at achieving its targets. It would therefore be really effective to find out what they are doing, and how. Once this has been established, ensure that you take the opportunity to provide individual team members with some feedback or, if the team is doing a good job, to focus your attention on the team. You may also be the recipient of informal feedback. This allows you to seek feedback on your performance frequently and actively, and once you have received this feedback, be willing to use it to make improvements to your role as a leader. Being a good role model demonstrates how important it is to use the feedback that you receive. Finally, it is a good practice to create a culture of seeking feedback, although there is little point in seeking feedback if anything you do not like results in you responding assertively, or seeking to blame others.

Formal Feedback

Many large and sophisticated organizations have formal annual appraisal systems in place, through which employees work with their line manager on a one-to-one basis, to assess their individual performances against objectives ideally agreed on at the start of the operational year. In the light of this, regular reviews with these objectives and other organizational priorities in mind provide an opportunity for a two-way feedback process. The line manager can provide evidence of performance in terms of the agreed objectives, and the team members can be encouraged to specify what their line manager and the organization might do to assist further.

The performance appraisal process should give individuals supporting feedback on their strengths and areas for development. It can help them track how they develop their skills to respond to changes in the organization and to further their career. At the end of the year, a more formal annual performance review can follow. Some of the features of this are:

- A discussion of the improvements in personal performance, team performance, and organizational contribution.
- A review of the previous performance review.

- It is a formal, two-way meeting, usually with a process defined by the organization.
- Time must be allowed for discussion and two-way feedback from the line manager and the team members.
- Positive, supportive feedback is used, so that joint problem solving and continuous improvement will result.
- A series of action points are agreed on that needs to be followed up during the year in informal review processes.
- The date of the next performance review needs to be agreed on.

360° Appraisal

In some organizations, it became apparent that line managers might not be the best persons to provide sole input with regard to a team member's performance, as determined by a traditional appraisal process. The 360° appraisal widens the scope of the appraisal process, and may involve others also, including their peers or subordinates, who provide feedback on the team members. The 360° appraisal may provide managers with a more rounded assessment of performance, than is possible with traditional appraisal. In many organizations, the process is reserved for the management only. To allow for the process to be as objective as possible, it is done confidentially in some cases, with forms being sent out centrally and returned with "composite" reports that do not show the names of those providing the feedback. If your company is not ready to embark on a costly 360° feedback process, you could consider the 361° feedback approach described below.

CASE STUDY 1

The 361° Feedback: A Cost Efficient Way to Produce High-Quality, In-depth Feedback

Vitor Sevilhano (Portuguese), chief executive officer (CEO) of Labform (www.labform.pt), Lisbon, Portugal.

What it is:
Our experience tells us that in organizations everybody talks about everybody and everybody evaluates everybody at the coffee corner. Consequently, why not capture, those talks, those perceptions, those evaluative comments in an organized way?

(Continued)

CASE STUDY 1 (*Continued*)

That was when, my business partners at European Learning Alliance (ELAN), and I thought of a very simple but powerful questionnaire that we call the public identity questionnaire.

How it works:
Purpose: To find out more about the impact you have on your closest colleagues and the organization as a whole, with the aim of improving your performance in the organization.

Who should participate in the feedback process:
Self, the boss, peers (a minimum of 3) and subordinates (a minimum of 3)

Questions and comments asked in the 361° feedback:

- To Self
  - What reputation do you think you have within the organization?
  - What reputation would you like to have?
- To All the Others
  - The way I see you (strengths and weaknesses).
  - The reputation I think you have within the organization.
  - The advice I can give you.

Output:
A personal report with four sections: (1) your responses; (2) your boss's feedback; (3) the consolidated feedback from your peers; and (4) the consolidated feedback from your subordinates.

As with any questionnaire of this kind, some caution should be taken when using it. Some loose comments on the process:

- The evaluated person should invite people to answer the questionnaire;
- The peers and subordinates should keep all comments strictly confidential;
- This tool should not be used in environments where there is conflict;
- A positive approach should be emphasized throughout the process.

This approach has been implemented in companies in Latin America and across Europe and has worked extremely well, producing high-quality feedback while saving huge costs.

Preparation of Feedback: What will I Say, and How will I Say it?

If you are not used to providing higher levels of feedback, it can be difficult to think of what to say to your team. The following checklist can help you get started in a more professional way.

- Prepare for the feedback
- Establish rapport
- Give encouragement
- Express feelings
- Listen actively
- Give feedback
- Receive feedback
- Give honest praise
- Ask open questions
- Clarify misunderstandings
- Observe body language
- Identify problems
- Identify training needs
- Solve problems
- Set standards
- Set targets and/or goals
- Draw up a plan of action
- Summarize—throughout the process look for opportunities to summarize what has been said before moving on.

BARRIERS TO EFFECTIVE FEEDBACK

You might be wondering whether it is really so easy, and whether it can go wrong for you. Well, yes, it can and there are a number of reasons why this might happen. The first of these is that feedback can sometimes surprise or shock, if no clearly defined objectives has been set for job, or the performed task. This could be because the leader and his/her team members did not share the same view of what the job entailed. You need to summarize the objectives after they have been set, and check your team members' understanding by asking them to repeat these in their own words. Unless you do this, issues about your credibility to provide feedback may later be raised, so work on developing your competence so that your team members respect your feedback. Even when you develop the confidence, your team members may be reluctant to accept your feedback, because other managers have previously provided feedback poorly. Finally, your lack of confidence when giving feedback may become evident during the discussion.

THE FEEDBACK SANDWICH

Leaders need to bear in mind that negative feedback is not always acceptable to team members. It can often be rejected out of hand. One way of tackling this is to use a feedback sandwich, in which the negative feedback is placed between two pieces of positive feedback. The approach is therefore:

- Explain what was done well.
- What might need to be improved?
- Provide an overall positive comment about the team members' performance.

In moving from the first to the second statement, use the word "and" and not "but". This is because the team member will often immediately delete the first positive statement and will instead focus on the negative feedback. To see the effect of this, see the following:

> *I think you are doing a good job but ...*

The initial statement is forgotten and the recipient is now waiting for the negative feedback. Once he/she has received that negative feedback, he/she will not focus on the final positive statement.
Another approach is to say:

- These are the things I would like you to keep doing ...(then list them).
- These are the things I would like you to change ...(then list them).
- These are the things I would like you to stop doing ... (then list them).

To confirm that the recipient understands, and to start the process of gaining his/her commitment to the change, you can then ask your conversation partner to tell you how he/she will do this next time.

RECOMMENDATIONS FOR THE PERSON RECEIVING FEEDBACK

The feedback receiver must be in a position to act on the feedback. To make this happen, it can be helpful to brief the team member with the following rules for receiving feedback:

1. Listen carefully to the feedback.
2. Do not get defensive.
3. Summarize and repeat what he/she has heard to check his/her understanding.
4. Ask questions checking for understanding to help him/her have a better idea of what he/she needs to do.
5. Clarify the accuracy of what has been said.
6. Suggest he/she seeks further feedback from others.

CONCLUSION

You are now in the best position to manage your team by using feedback as a rewarding and constructive experience for all of those concerned. Remember, that at the beginning of this chapter we ascertained that there were many other people who could also benefit from your feedback. We have not only concentrated many of the lessons on your team members, but also used these approaches with your line manager, peers, customers, and suppliers.

Your Activities for Improving your Feedback Skills

Activity 1: Stakeholder Analysis.

In the Fig. 17.1 in the chapter, we identified that you have many stakeholders. Create a stakeholder analysis by recreating the diagram and adding names in the boxes.

Consider the quantity and quality of the interaction that you have with these stakeholders. Using a scale of 1–5 rate each one, for example:

Name:
Quantity of interactions:
Quality of interaction:

Is there a need for a different communication style with any of these people, while using a feedback-oriented approach?

_____

_____

_____

Activity 2: Practice your feedback skills.

Choose at least three skills that you can put into action within the next week.

_____

_____

_____

Now "catch people having done something well" and using the BOOSTER model to provide them with feedback on what you have seen.

Do this regularly and you will soon see a difference in performance, and will also feel more confident with the process of providing feedback.

FURTHER RESOURCES

Web-sites

- Chartered Institute of Personnel and Development: www.cipd.co.uk
- Chartered Management Institute: www.managers.org.uk
- Society of Human Resource Management: www.shrm.org
- Chartered Institute of Personnel and Development Newsletter: www.peoplemanagement.co.uk

RECOMMENDED VIDEO LINKS

- Ralph Watson: http://www.youtube.com/user/ralphrwatson
- Mike Pagan: http://www.youtube.com/user/mikepagan#p/search/0/RYv7Xuiz-G4
- Joy Huber: http://www.youtube.com/user/MsEnjoyable#p/u/7/iWnFkmOJOyk

REFERENCES

Hughes, S. Ginnett, R., & Curphy, G. (2009). *Leadership: Enhancing the Lessons of Experience.* New York: McGraw Hill.

Peters, T., & Waterman, R. (1982). *In Search Of Excellence: Lessons from America's Best-Run Companies.* New York: Harper Business.

Torrington, D. F., & Hall, L. T. (2005). *Human Resource Management* (6th ed.). Upper Saddle River: Prentice Hall.

PART VI

LEADING YOURSELF AND OTHERS
THROUGH COMPLEXITY

CHAPTER 18

COMPLEXITY SKILLS

Wolfgang Amann, Christoph Nedopil, and Shiban Khan

OBJECTIVE OF THIS CHAPTER

The objective of this chapter is to introduce complexity as one of the main drivers of the need for personal development. Since the current and future tasks of managers and leaders continue to become more complex, we have to prepare for what causes complexity. We have to understand how to manage it proactively.

INTRODUCTION

No book on leadership and personal development in the 21st century would be complete, without preparing the reader for what can easily be deemed the number one factor overwhelming managers in internationally active companies–complexity. There is no need to prove the interconnectedness of our global economy, as the biggest financial and economic crisis since the Great Depression has just provided this evidence. Nevertheless, experts continue to disagree on what kind of crisis we are actually facing— whether it is U-shaped (time-wise a longer economic downturn with an

Leadership and Personal Development: A Toolbox for the 21st Century Professional, pp. 317–329
Copyright © 2011 by Information Age Publishing

eventual upward development), L-shaped (a lasting economic crisis), or V-shaped (the crisis hitting and the recovery following rapidly). After Greece, the financial situation in Portugal, Ireland, and a number of other countries is yet to be understood and mastered. In addition, the gamblers are back in basically every market as well, making future speculation bubbles and system shocks a certainty.

Granted, global economic crises have happened before. However, the amazing speed of current political and economic changes is unprecedented. Previous crises were slower and more limited due to a variety of boundaries. The latter separated industries, nations, or at least regions, much more than in our current integrated world. While these developments have not created complexity in the institutions in the past years, they have certainly increased it.

Smart managers do not regard the current developments fatalistically, as something to merely accept, and that offers no opportunities to act upon. The application of complexity to personal development is intensifying. What we have experienced, is that managers and graduate students with some work experience can easily relate to the managerial complexity concept, and apply complexity's core meaning to their real life issues and dilemmas. Another observation is that some businesses and managers are overwhelmed by this increased complexity, while others find ways of identifying the relevant complexity drivers, in their particular business environments, build or enhance the right skills to manage them and, finally, outperform others. However, through our research and coaching, we have–unfortunately—also discovered that there is no panacea to help those determined to overcome complexity. We openly admit that some managers and businesses simply got lucky and we do not really know what they did correctly to contribute to their success. However, most successful business managers have worked rigorously to understand the factors shaping their business, have kept the company's values in mind when defining clear strategies that everyone can understand, have fully focussed on executing their main projects carefully, and have also taken bold steps when these were required. We thus invite the reader on a journey of discovery. Allow us to share what really drives complexity.

FOUR CRUCIAL DRIVERS OF COMPLEXITY

In our coaching sessions, executive education seminars, and research (Nedopil *et al.*, 2011), we have identified four fundamental drivers of complexity, that are of relevance to a broad variety of industries and career paths. Although we describe them sequentially, you must remember that they are often interrelated, and can "strike" simultaneously.

1. Diversity is the first driver of complexity. Especially, the internationally active companies face challenges due to the diversity in their internal and external environments. Diversity can best be understood as a plurality of elements, that is, a high number of relevant factors in a system, which also shows noteworthy amounts of dissimilarity. The following example illustrates what we mean. Diversity in firms, can materialize in the following way:

- On the corporate goal level, many companies have an expanding goal system. Fortunately, many firms now aim to achieve environmental and social goals beyond mere financial ones. Unfortunately, however, many companies have tremendous problems achieving positive financial results on an ongoing basis. Achieving one goal—a pure financial one—is difficult enough. How can one achieve two or more goals, and do so continuously?

- On the stakeholder level, complexity includes the multiplicity and dissimilarity of the stakeholders, for example, employees, customers, suppliers, investors, competitors, and other organizations (for example, NGOs or regulators) with interests in the company's operations. You will need to find—increasingly, as you climb the career ladder—ways to handle the different demands from these stakeholders, which are also expressed in various and changing ways.

- On the market level, reflect on the differences in customer tastes in the dozens of markets in which a company is usually active. Bear in mind that no past success, either yours or that of your employer, guarantees immediate success in the future. Too frequently, the logic of business models and value generation, changes in the markets.

- With regard to the human resource (HR) systems, think about the vast differences between traditions around the globe. From a (vanishing) tradition of life-long employment to "hire-and-fire-at-will."

2. Interdependence is the second driver of complexity. Interdependencies are primarily caused by scarcity of resources, and market boundaries disappearing. Companies aiming to integrate activities in different countries for synergy reasons are especially affected. Reflect on how a politically motivated lax loan system for housing the American poor paralyzed economies and companies in geographically distant areas due to sudden capital restrictions (scarcity of resources) and exposure, and interconnectedness to new players.

3. Ambiguity is our third driver. Ambiguity describes the realities in companies where clear cause-and-effect relationships are lacking. Is your company profitable because it is innovative, or is it profitable, and therefore innovative? Does market share lead to profitability or the other way around? What are your true levers for operating the business machine? Or are the times when businesses and markets could be understood and controlled like machines, long gone? The Shell scenarios of 2001 are a sad, spot-on example of ambiguity. At that time, oil company Shell had the most experienced, biggest and most expensive scenario development team on the planet. In 2001, the experts proudly presented two major scenarios about the future of globalization. The major problem was that none of them foresaw what was to happen only a few months later. Neither the tremendous corporate governance scandals, nor the terrorist attacks of September 9, or their far-reaching consequences were anticipated in the presented scenarios. When the best experts working on scenarios for the future, overlooked not one, but two major developments in the short term, let alone the financial and economic crises that were to follow only shortly after, then this is perhaps telling of the uncertainty in our business environments.

4. Fast Flux is the fourth driver of complexity. It depicts a reality in which not only the overall speed of change is accelerating, but the number of directions and areas in which we see change, is multiplying. Fast flux materializes in increasingly shorter product life-cycles. In the automobile industry, for example, product life-cycles and, thus, windows of opportunities to amortize the increasing development costs have been cut in half, over the last 10 years. In the mobile phone market, the main cycles are less than a year. Apple had only a few weeks in which to be the only provider of IPad-style tablet PCs. Fast flux is the meanest drivers of complexity. Even if you have figured out an answer to dealing with diversity, interdependence, and ambiguity, these solutions may be outdated the next day. There is an old saying that applies to almost every market: Some make things happen, some watch what happens, some wonder what happened!

MANAGING COMPLEXITY IN REAL LIFE

Accepting fast flux, embracing it, possibly learning how to proactively trigger fast flux for the competitors will be the key for rapid and healthy career advancement—and most certainly for survival. Such activities indicate the superiority of a mental stance, while merely exploring what can be done about complexity. With very few exceptions, such as the undertaker business, all jobs and firms have seen complexity increasing. Many firms cannot cope up with this increase. Across all the industries, industry consolidation, which occurs sooner or later, wiped out 80% of the independently operating companies. In the wind power industry, which has really taken off only over the last 5 years, this consolidation is already in full swing. Embracing this reality is the first step to coping up with it.

The second key element is aiming to relocate complexity to areas where either the company draws exceptional benefits from it, or where customers enjoy the best advantages possible. If there is no such opportunity, simplification is the key. Think about the low-cost carrier easyJet. Its business model was built on simplicity: Only one type of airplane to make maintenance cheaper and pilots' job easier, only point-to-point flights to keep operations simple, and as much online work by customers as possible, to decrease the costs further. If easyJet had any complexity whatsoever in its system, it was in the airport negotiation teams. Perfectly trained specialists were let loose on secondary sites to negotiate the best deal—an uneven distribution of power. Only after smartly investing in perfecting its business model and in eliminating any inefficiency for years, did easyJet start with lounge access, loyalty programs, and bookings, and so forth. It clearly saw that the benefits of consciously adding more complexity to some fields would compensate for the drawbacks. Few companies can claim that they have avoided complexity as smartly as easyJet did, which is why we add simplifying to our generic strategies.

Looking now at the ways to truly manage complexity, we identify four simplifiers. The first of them is to set **common goals** and behaviors. Take the example of many a company that emerged from mergers and acquisitions, to find themselves running different sub-cultures in different departments. It is therefore of the utmost necessity to explore common goals and behaviors. Which are the sets of goals and behaviors that are easily understandable and applicable to your business, and that can help in today's hectic environments? How can we create transparency about our guiding compass, although all our schedules tend to be too full? Ninety-five percent of the managers in mid-sized to large companies do not know the specific part of the overall company strategy that is relevant for them. The current crises and possible changes in the ownership structures add further complications and "flux." From our exploration of highly successfully individuals and well-managed companies, we have learned that they rarely have more than four fundamental key values. In turn, more poorly managed and underperforming companies often have so long laundry lists that they could easily serve as bingo for managers.

We suggest a clear **focus** as the next simplifier. Our colleague Heike Bruch at the University of St. Gallen found, that only 10% of the individual managers in mid-sized to larger companies actually have sufficient positive energy for, and a strong enough focus on the very few projects, that could increase their team's and their company's performance. Management guru

Peter Drucker (2001) reminds us that "if what looks like an opportunity does not advance the strategic goal of the institution, it is not an opportunity. It is a distraction." Employees and managers should focus their work on the actions they can learn and do. We too often promote people to their level of incompetence. We strive towards the next level, fancier titles, higher pay, and more responsibilities—opportunities to amortize our investments in our education and careers. We may thus even drive our promotion to our level of incompetence and, thus, cause failure. No doctor in a hospital is naturally a good hospital leader, and no great engineer will necessarily excel after being promoted to white collar management tasks, where different types of abstract numbers and people have to be managed. Hence, in line with our opening chapters on personal development focusing on our strengths, we encourage you to reflect on what you are best at, and what skill gaps might emerge while climbing the career ladder. Bear in mind that members of the generation Y are not unlikely to have had 14 different jobs by age 38. Beyond this personal level, contemplate the possibilities of focussing your business projects proactively, new initiatives and overall company on the few ideas, which will have an above-average impact.

Decentralization is a third generic strategy that also indicates how focused projects should be managed. Are you empowering those with the most information, who are actually interacting with the customers, to implement the "big picture" strategy? Are you generating opportunities for growth and new motivation by means of decentralization? Would you rather have more decentralization—for the sake of the overall company performance—than you have now? According to our experience, receiving more freedom to design answers and implement them leads to above-average motivation, and employee loyalty. In mid-sized to larger companies, 75% of the employees suffer from inner withdrawal—a lack of real care about the company. Decentralization can help to keep your colleagues more motivated. Learning how to decentralize smartly also allows for more opportunities to reflect on bigger developments and risks as it frees time and energy capacities.

Standardization of core processes can help you, as a fourth way, to simplify complexity in your teams and organizations. But it is crucial to first understand what really can and should count as a core process. Each company and industry may have its own opportunities for core processes. Think of one accepted way of capturing and sharing knowledge in management consulting companies. Different standards lead to unacceptable inefficiencies. Usually, the unbearable feeling of having to re-invent the wheel time and again can be a good indicator of where to start looking for the possibilities to implement the core processes.

LEARNING HOW TO MANAGING YOUR PERSONAL DEVELOPMENT CHANNEL FOR PEAK PERFORMANCE

The above managerial concepts and advice can best be summarized with a perspective on your development channel as portrayed in Fig. 18.1. It juxtaposes two key dimensions:

- Your professional role's complexity (leadership span, budgeting responsibilities in times of increasing environmental volatility, amount of trouble-shooting, diversity between countries, market or customer segments served, and so forth).
- Your experience (with solving problems, managing teams, units and larger systems, and so forth).

The development channel concept invites you to reflect on your position regarding these two dimensions over time. Three situations can be distinguished:

- **You are currently in the "bore-out" zone:** Your current experience noticeably outweighs the role requirements you currently have to fulfil—the zone below the depicted development channel in the form of the upward bar. If you do not have many other important responsibilities or tasks besides your work, for example, a young family, positions in sports or service clubs, it may just be a question of time until your performance drops. Personal challenges are missing at

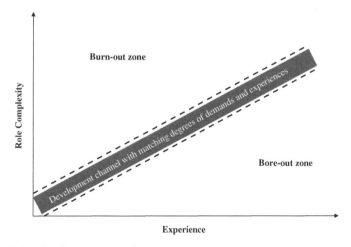

Figure 18.1. The development channel

work. There are no growth opportunities. Your previous investments in hard work or education could suddenly seem the wrong decisions. Action needs to be taken to move back into the right position within the development channel, for example, by changing your position or taking on additional projects.

- **You are currently in the "burn-out" zone:** There are constantly more projects, requests, problems, and e-mails than you can handle—the zone above the depicted development channel. Management holds you accountable for results, but the resources to achieve these are lacking. While the designed solutions to challenges may have looked good on paper, something unexpected occurs all the time. A bigger budget is needed, or, currently, budgets are cut without the goals being adapted. Blackberries and their likes make you accessible even in traditional recreation periods such as in the evenings, on the weekends, or simply during commuting home from work when exhaling, reflecting, and distancing you from your work issues should be possible, but have become increasingly impossible. The repercussions of this on sound sleeping patterns, perhaps relationships and even your physical health cannot be ignored any more. It is time to trigger change once again to find a healthy balance and the right position within the development challenge. Working with mentors, coaches, and peers is the key in trying to find the way forward—before it is too late.
- **You are spot-on in the development channel:** Sound personal career management, work-life balance considerations are good, and a healthy mix of patience and ambitions will ensure professional and personal growth over time.

On your way up the career ladder, it is crucial to comprehend, that managing the development channel is not only a responsibility you have in respect of yourself, but also in respect of selected colleagues and team members. Teaching others the relevant observation and coaching skills over time, is the responsible manager's homework.

CASE STUDY 1

Dealing with Leadership Complexity in Matrix Organizations

Dr. Bertolt Stein (49), German, expert on leadership in matrix organizations, Berlin, Germany.

(Continued)

CASE STUDY 1 (*Continued*)

From our experience of working with managers and leaders around the globe, we know that people find it increasingly challenging to be a leader and manager, working in a matrix organization. Do you agree that the level of complexity is higher in a matrix organization, than in more traditionally structured organizations? If yes, why is this so?

First of all, it is very important to distinguish the kind of a matrix structure in which we are working. Traditionally, we distinguish between a functional matrix, a balanced matrix, and a project or process matrix. The functional matrix occurs when an individual is designated either as a project manager or project administrator, and is assigned to oversee a project's cross-functional aspects, while the organization retains most of the characteristics of a purely functional organization and follows the classical hierarchical management model. In a balanced matrix, the decision-making authority lies equally with the project managers and functional managers, therefore, the employees are actually members of two organizing dimensions within the company, and two bosses evaluate each staff member.

Finally, in a project/process matrix the center of authority is the project/process manager and—similar to the balanced matrix—there is a need for horizontal and vertical coordination. The idea behind any kind of matrix organization is to support business processes and projects, which in turn create products and services and by doing so, serve the customer. Consequently, the increase in complexity is expected to pay off through a better service to the customer, and from my perspective, this is the only reason why we should increase complexity.

In some organizations I have observed structures which I polemically call a "freak matrix." It is usually the result of continuous restructuring exercises; in the course of those, a set-up's rational purpose—if there were one–somehow got lost, or was sacrificed for the fulfilment of the individuals' narcissistic or power needs. The best way forward in such a situation is to abolish the structure completely, and go through the exercise of defining the best organizational set-up from the strict perspective of optimal business processes, that lead to services and products that the customer appreciates.

The challenges of leading in a matrix organization are generally about influencing people with limited or no formal authority, dealing with colleagues who are working towards different, sometimes contradicting goals, than you are and finally, managing/leading dispersed teams.

(Continued)

CASE STUDY 1 (*Continued*)

How can professionals prepare themselves for dealing more effectively with these leadership challenges? Are there any tools and techniques that support leaders in this context?

Leading in a matrix organization requires managers who are equipped with influencing skills that fall into the "pull styles" rather than "push styles" category. We are therefore, for all means and purposes, talking about replacing persuasion and control—which work quite well in vertical organizations—with vision and trust. In this context, specific skills are, for instance, the ability to estimate other's style, to clarify the other party's needs and issues and to demonstrate attentiveness to other's needs. It is the key to maintain two-way communication and to continuously investigate the involved people's perception and understanding. A very basic skill is the ability to create a vision for people by formulating the "what" and "how", the purpose and the means, the goal and the strategy, in such a way, that everybody fully understands and commits to them. This usually goes hand-in-hand with the ability to reduce complexity to the core, and to use different communication approaches that appeal to the different types of people we usually deal with. It leads us again to the old issue of knowing the preferences of the people around you, and adapting your behavior accordingly.

Another set of skills is dealing with conflict, and creating a problem-solving environment. In a matrix structure, the manager depends heavily on people who commit actively to contributing to collective achievements. Even if you were able to impose your choices on others, it would at the best lead to compliant behaviors, which is simply not sufficient—you are looking for other's active involvement!

It all starts with you, of course. How could you possibly provide others with orientation and a sense of purpose if you have not established these for yourself first? There are mental tools that may help you to do this and are easily applicable, but there is one pre-condition: You need to have time on your agenda for thinking. If you are drowning in operative work, you will not invest in things that can keep you floating.

For example, examine "reflective structuring"— a systematic process aimed at identifying an organization's (company's, department's, project's, process's, and so forth) purpose and business goals, and the underlying influencing variables. It is an approach to identify the most relevant dimensions for your business success—and will, consequently, focus your efforts on those, and simply ignore the rest.

As far as projects are concerned, it is very helpful to apply systemic theory to prevent us from believing that we can plan and control, for

(*Continued*)

CASE STUDY 1 (*Continued*)

example, a development, or change project fully. Only if we learn to accept that we are equipped with only one interpretation of multiple realities, will we start listening to others, start being curious about those other interpretations of reality. That will help us to stop imposing our views and beliefs, and rather start modulating projects along the dimensions we can collectively influence.

Can you share examples from your consultancy and coaching experience, on how you have supported people to overcome these challenges?

In my consulting work, a combination of structuring tools and executive coaching has shown to be most helpful for managers in a matrix organization, as these increase their effectiveness. This is perhaps because reflection simply works better with a mirror (a coach) and most of the managers were probably not equipped with the relevant methodologies for complexity reduction, scaling, and systematic approaches for improvement during their education. Let me close with another skill I find extremely important for effective managers in matrix organizations: Daring to clean up your area of responsibility of everything that may have been purposeful in the past, but no longer is. This means investigating whether or not rules, processes, procedures, and so forth contribute to making our products or services better or more efficient and, if they do not contribute, to abolish them totally. That again frees time for doing the right things.

My message is: The more complex your job, the more important good and sound leadership and personal development are. Success comes through focus! Complexity demands a focus on business and on personal development.

Bertolt Stein's insights leave no doubt that whoever works in a matrix structure, no matter which type, needs to complement their hard skills with the corresponding soft skills. In other words, managers need to remain in their development channel, if they want to reach peak performance in all areas. The soft skills portfolio should also include honed networking skills, as the following section illustrates.

NETWORKING SKILLS

A separate chapter in this book focuses only on networking skills. In the context of complexity, however, it is worthwhile sharing two key insights. One big advantage of a greater density of professional networks in the wider

Case A   **Case B**

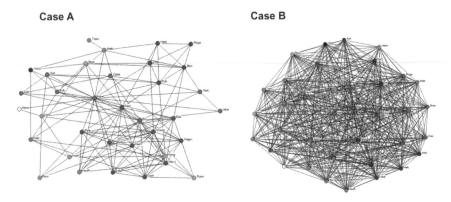

Figure 18.2. Network density as intended, desirable complexity

sense is that it can serve as an early warning system. Compare, for example, the two organizational settings portrayed in Fig. 18. 2: Case A has a number of relationships, while case B is much better connected. The information may travel faster between friends and colleagues with whom you have better relationships. This exchange—always in compliance with ethical and legal standards, as well as office policies—can prevent disasters. Information exchange and support are however, not, a one-way street. Second, the quality of decisions can improve drastically if more experts can provide relevant input. This holds for situations of uncertainty, of course, and where there is time to gather feedback. Reflect on the insight, that being a member of the Rotary Club will expose regular meeting attendees to as many lectures as a full Master's degree would, the only difference being that the lectures are of a broad nature, which can be an advantage. Add the many meeting opportunities with people in other industries, and one can not only draw early warning signals from them, but also their voluntarily shared set of perspectives. One may at first think that networking skills are something innate and that, to some extent, some people find it easier to become connected. The strategic relevance of actually becoming better connected and to build the right skills to network are crucial for future performance. It is one of those, admittedly few areas, where more complexity in the form of a diverse, interdependent network adds tremendous value.

CONCLUSION

As you know, it is reflection on experience that builds competence. Experience alone often leads only to (frequently unfounded) confidence. Unhappy stakeholders—in the wider sense of the word, include our private contacts—then pay the price of this unfounded confidence. We have outlined what drives complexity, and where we can build skills to manage it. Complexity, too, can easily overwhelm, and precaution and proactive action must be taken. Reflection on experience comes in two forms—after the main event or beforehand. We thus encourage you to do the subsequent exercises also.

Your Activities for Honed Complexity Skills

Activity 1: Reflection exercise on your development channel.

Please take 15 minutes to reflect on where you have been in different positions with regard to your development channel over the last years. Also map where you would like to be 3–5 years down the road. Were there phases where you were in the boredom zone? Were you in the burn-out zone? How did you trigger change in order to ensure a constant match between your profile and the role complexity? After analyzing your case, how should your team and its individual members be positioned? Honesty in this analysis is crucial, as it prevents future disasters. Management is a 360^0 job. If in these times of cost cutting and lay-offs, resources do not suffice to prevent burn-out or further skill development, the development channel helps you to communicate with those above you, and serves as an early warning sign.

Activity 2: Reflection exercise on the four drivers
of complexity.

Reflect on the four drivers of complexity. Which ones matter the most in your industry and position? How do you, or your organization, actually tackle them? How should you tackle them?

REFERENCES AND FURTHER READING

Drucker, P. (2001). *Essential Drucker: Management, the Individual and Society.* Oxford: Butterworth-Heinemann.

Nedopil, C., & Steger, U., Amann, W. (2011). *Managing Complexity in Organizations: Text and Cases.* UK: Palgrave Macmillan.

CHAPTER 19

CRISIS MANAGEMENT SKILLS

Wolfgang Amann, Shiban Khan, and Christoph Nedopil

OBJECTIVE OF THIS CHAPTER

The main aim of this chapter is to prepare you proactively for what every manager and leader will inevitably have to do throughout their careers—managing crises. Some managers and consultants even see the true future of the management task as lying in managing crisis after the crisis. It will happen to the best, not just once, but repeatedly. It is not a sign of incompetence or weakness. Given the bursting of the Internet speculation bubble, the corporate governance scandals, and the financial crises—all of these in just the last 9 years—it is worthwhile reflecting on, and learning more about crisis management skills.

INTRODUCTION

In today's volatile business environments, personal development needs to comprise crisis management skills. Few strategies, projects, change initiatives, or career plans are implemented as planned. If you work in the strategy department, then be aware that 80% of the "big picture" strategies are not implemented as planned. 95% of the new strategic initiatives fail.

Leadership and Personal Development: A Toolbox for the
21st Century Professional, pp. 331–342
Copyright © 2011 by Information Age Publishing

Furthermore, corporate idea management reveals that only one of every 300,000 ideas presented by mid-size to large companies' staff members, ends up as a product. If you work in information technology (IT), it may not be new to you that 75% of the IT projects either exceed their financial, or time budget—or both. If you work in mergers and acquisitions, 75% of all the deals do not deliver the value they were initially supposed to. In today's world, hundreds of thousands of people are laid off around the globe—often not due to any fault of their own. The survivors may believe they are lucky, but they are not necessarily better off as they have to shoulder all of the work, which potentially entails other risks and crises. And if business challenges were not tough enough, they now emerge jointly with economic and financial crises.

We, like many of our colleagues, propose a multi-step crisis management approach (see Fig. 19.1). This approach first focuses on honing your mental readiness for crises, which is followed by teaching crisis prevention skills, crisis detection skills, and actual crisis management skills as well as skills to allow you to benefit from the crises, before this cycle starts anew at a different time and place.

Figure 19.1. The art and science of crisis management

PREPARING MENTALLY FOR TIMES OF CRISES

Great and successful crisis prevention and management start by mentally embracing the "Zeitgeist"—the fact that we live in turbulent times with one crisis following another. Nowadays, crises never arise as isolated cases and usually come at the most inconvenient times. If a number of managerial initiatives fail, the first key to success is to accept this reality. Owing to the financial constraints, fast-paced changes in the economic environments, aggressive moves by competitors, regulators, NGOs, and investors, we often do not have time to implement strategies without interruptions, distractions, and crises. But mental exercises in re-framing or re-interpreting reality are not our main message here. Instead, we encourage you to accept the fact that crises will occur. They happen to Juergen Schrempp, designated as Manager of the Year, three times, just as they do to others. Also bear in mind that there are managers who deliberately start 25% more projects than they can handle. They know that a portion of their projects will fail but not which ones, and therefore want to ensure that more projects actually survive. Others deliberately embark on high risk projects that could endanger the company ("bet-the-company" projects), to ensure faster careers. Such managers do not make crises less likely, and thus force others to live with the consequences of their choices!

PREVENTING THE CRISIS

Key aspects of preventing crises (which are at least partially triggered by your decisions and styles) include:

- Firstly, be realistic when it comes to goals for a given time period, and have resources available to manage unexpected events.
- Secondly, focus on a few very important priorities. And remember, if you have more than three priorities, you might as well have none. While it is true that taking on risky projects can give you visibility, you will also gain visibility if they fail.
- Thirdly, resist the temptation to play a daily role in too many projects. Being asked for help or for your contribution may be flattering, but too many meetings, phone calls, and advice are distracting.
- Fourthly, organize a few quick wins. If projects or initiatives are planned not to show results for the first 2 years, your superiors and team members may become impatient. Two years down the road, some of them will already have left.

- Fifthly, proactively clarify your values and principles. When hell breaks loose, it is an advantage if you have principles to depend on. Decide proactively when you will pull the plug on yourself, for example, taking conscious decisions not to sacrifice your health or a good relationship with partners and family members for a company, which maximizes profits for anonymous shareholders. Walk the talk regarding your principles even when there are no crises to educate those in your environment, regarding what they can expect from you when the going gets tough. Doing so, helps build the social capital which will come in handy later on.
- Sixthly, do your homework regarding crisis prevention in terms of communication policies, routines to allow conflicts to escalate in a channeled way, and sending high potentials as well as senior managers to crisis management seminars in "times of peace".

With more than 80% of the strategies and 95% of the new product initiatives failing, individuals must focus on the essentials, and be allowed to keep their activity portfolio lean. This means that managers' resources should not be fully spent on planning alone. Keep the key resources for the implementation phase, and ensure that early warning indicators are constantly checked. They are a part of the next crucial phase in crisis management.

DETECTING AND COMPREHENDING CRISES

(Early) warning systems and crisis indicators have been developed over decades, by and large, spanning four main generations:

1. Generation:

- Mainly detected the actual figures from a plan.
- Was too frequently past-oriented.
- Key performance indicators were often too reductionist, and thus already problematic. ´

2. Generation:

- The first generation of real early warning indicators based on the assumption, that information had to be available on the latent and pending crises.
- However, factors had to exceed a certain critical level to be noticed.
- The lack of clarity regarding cause-and-effect pattern, remained a concern.

3. Generation:

- More comprehensive early warning systems in the form of strategic radars, and steering cockpits within executive decision support systems.
- Explicit inclusion of qualitative data.

4. Generation:

- Far-reaching personalization of systems, even for the individual members of one top management team or board.

There are additional factors which are the key to understanding crises. Perception is reality—we should accept this. Although it may seem unfair, or there may be no rational foundations for it, you have to live with the reality, that if someone says the word crisis, there is one. Investors will shy away, customers will become wary, and enemies will indulge in "schadenfreude," misuse this moment as payback time, or undertake other unwanted attacks. We suggest that the following criteria should be considered when analyzing risk potentials (compare also Steger, 2003 for a fuller review of such criteria and a number of examples):

- Is there an adversarial advocate, constantly triggering the action steps?
- Do special, unusual events occur, or are new "actors" emerging on the scene?
- Is there a credible human side to the story, besides an easily identifiable, dislikeable enemy, and a straightforward solution? The question is thus: How media friendly is the topic? Remember, bad news is the best news for the media.
- Is there damage, even if it is "just" corruption or a neglected public interest?

These factors contribute to the unfolding of the crisis, especially if they exceed a specific threshold of awareness. Managers should, therefore, examine the issue at hand—from both the sides—according to the following checkpoints:

- Is the issue serious and believable?
- Does the issue evoke emotions? Is it understandable, visual, touching?
- Is the issue media-friendly? Syndicate or works council friendly?
- Are there interconnections with the other company or industry issues?

- How strong are the opponents from within, or outside, as potential adversaries?
- How isolated is the person, team, company in the center of the crisis? Have the players and support groups been identified?
- How far has the dynamics already evolved?
- How easily can it be solved?

As Steger and Nedopil (2010, pp. 41–42) rightly point out, above questions can help characterize the nature of a crisis - with a bullet crisis versus a bomb crisis being two extreme ends of a continuum. A bullet crisis has is defined as more specific, focused on a limited area, although it can have considerable impact there. A bomb crisis hits an organization more fundamentally and broadly. It affects the business model, the underlying logic of success.

It is crucial to distinguish different phenomena. A general risk is not a crisis. A risk refers to a potential threat to the achievement of goals. A conflict is, more or less, a latent tension between two parties. A mere disturbance is a dysfunctionality, without the latter exceeding an individual or a company's, problem-solving skill capability. A true crisis is a process which actually endangers goals. This is subsequently linked to the continuation of projects, careers, or companies. It is a truly decisive, difficult situation from which two drastically different futures may emerge. Further characteristics of a crisis are its ambivalent potential outcome, time pressure, and the (at first glance) limited range of options, to influence the way forward. Some crises—fortunately, not all—turn into catastrophes: inevitable, large-scale crises with very few possibilities of achieving the original goals. The above pointers can help you detect a crisis.

MANAGING THE CRISIS

The nature of the crisis influences the way forward heavily. Financial crises call for cash-flow and liquidity-based solutions. If a marketing plan does not work out as planned, adaptations to the success recipe are the key. There is no doubt that expertise and experts, even in the form of external management consultants or business school representatives, are required to fix the core of the crises. In the context of this chapter, allow us to focus on additional pointers beyond the hard skills on the business side, when it comes to managing crises. Here are some key pointers:

Keep a Cool Head, a Warm Heart, and Working Hands at all Times

The 18th century Swiss pedagogue and educational reformer, Heinrich Pestalozzi's advice on how to think is still relevant today. Whenever possible, you should try to prevent that you or others get too emotional, as these emotions might be the main reason for not moving towards a mindset, which enables you to work on solutions much better. In this book's chapter on Dan Goleman's concept of emotional intelligence, we describe how personal competence comes from being aware of, and regulating one's emotions; social competence is awareness, and regulation of others' emotions. Crises are the ultimate moment of truth for these competencies.

Allow us to add a few thoughts on who should manage the crisis and adhere to Pestalozzi's guidelines. Steger and Nedopil (2010, p. 56) suggest a separate team to be formed, if, for example, managers can not affort to ignore their regular tasks, if potential conflicts of interest might occur, or even worse, if possible legal repercussions including impeachments of the management deserve an as professional crisis response team as possible. Organizational design alternatives vary, though, with the nature of the crises. Some crisis management teams may work closely with the board. Other fire fighting teams may well focus on lower parts of the organizations.

Dissect the Crisis

Managing a crisis requires focus as almost every resource—from time to energy and money—becomes limited. Screening the problem at hand creatively and your environment for simplifiers is the key. Dissect problems. At times, problems seem to be piled on top of each other. Besides experiencing energy-draining discussions and emotions, remember, that disappearing trust, broken bonds, and uncertainty about your future, can easily become an overwhelming number of challenges. Do you see ways that you can separate or dissect them? Where can you buy time? Where can you settle out of court? Which battle can you end—accepting minor losses in peripheral areas, rather than in real core issues? Would giving in or compromising now, give you the opportunity to create a better solution later on? And, at all cost, prevents a situation, in which professional trouble and crises spill over into your private life on a massive scale—or *vice versa*. This would be the exact opposite of dissecting. It would pile more challenges on top of the existing ones, leading to additional, self-created, but hard to control, dynamics, and distractions.

Watch Your Communication

According to the Harvard negotiation principles, it is the key to separate problems, from the people involved. Consequently, adding interpersonal problems to the matter at hand can only be counterproductive, and accelerate downward spirals. Instead of creating a vicious cycle which forces you to remain in crisis mode, ensure you practice proper hygiene in your communication patterns at all times. Never attack a person as such, as the latter can only become defensive, which breaks bonds that are a crucial for helpful dialogues. Avoid discounting others in terms of talking negatively about them. Keeping a positive attitude and creating the impression of being on top of things, may attract helpers and admirers. In line with the communication hygiene, reflect on how harshly you need to act and react. Overly hard, uncompromising stances may lead to delays in reaching solutions. This holds especially true for those groups and individuals on whom we depend heavily, as this could entail biting the hand that feeds us. Proper communication hygiene also includes leaving the scene in a way which allows others not to lose face and allows pleasant meetings in future, if the issue at hand does not categorically exclude this. Choose your opportunities to communicate wisely. Only a small percentage of human communication consists of words. The rest comprises body language, tonality, and so forth. Solving problems and crises via e-mails, does not therefore allow, for clarity on contextual information.

Look for Allies

Crises and problems can be handled more easily if they become the responsibility of a larger group. Asking others for support can lead to fresh ideas, more resources, and a feeling of strength now, that support has been secured. In a corporate setting, help may come from, for example, mentors, other departments which do not want the crisis to spill over to them, whether directly or indirectly, and the legal affairs department. An increasingly common way of corporate governance also allows for decentralization and empowerment, as long as someone's performance is high. Otherwise, bosses or (project) boards may have to step in. They may not have picked up the signals immediately, but can, and have to become active. Help can also come from hiring lawyers or coaches, as they can provide certainty regarding specific information and additional perspectives. Again, it is not a sign of weakness or incompetence to ask for help, but the opposite—ignoring potential allies—may well be.

LEARNING FROM A CRISIS

When the going gets tough, the tough get going. Allow yourself to feel that you are being challenged and tested in times of crises. These times provide evidence that your education and the trust others have in you are justified. The sooner the managers start looking for opportunities to turn crises into the start of something great and new, the more do they increase the likelihood of success. Many companies and individuals have managed to emerge stronger than before, after being hit by a crisis. Crises are often the beginning of transformation, and of a new solution, which works even if temporarily. Business academics have been believing for decades that no progress can be made, no next level of professionalism reached, without first experiencing a latent and then a full-blown crisis (compare Greiner, 1972). There are tremendous learning and growth opportunities. In fact, some companies—and Hyundai, GE, and Microsoft are the best practice example—now purposefully create artificial crises to harvest the benefits. They may also use the current financial crisis to lay off more people than necessary, as there is a wide-spread notice of the need for lay-offs in companies in a society.

To encourage crisis management skills, the staff can be kept on their toes by, for example, assigning unrealistic deadlines, creating certain resource limitations, letting two teams compete with each other for future funding and project responsibilities, and—like GE and other firms—by firing the bottom 10% of a team. Reflect on the real reason why many car manufacturers became active in Formula 1 racing. Neither Mercedes nor Toyota needed the publicity for sustained brand recognition, and the VIP parties with celebrities are also not the primary motivators for the executives. There is literally no better way to train key engineers for subsequent assignments, than in Formula 1 racing. The high potentials may have weeks to fix problems if they are lucky, but they regularly have only hours or days. This is where crisis management skills are honed, and the survivors become invaluable for future assignments.

CASE STUDY 1

The Crisis You Do Not want to Manage

Recently, McDonald's country manager in Argentina woke up to what must have at first appeared to be his worst nightmare. While business had been growing steadily and its strategy of becoming "the family place to eat" showed success, a scandalous piece of news hit the press: A customer claimed that eating in one of McDonald's restaurants resulted in her contracting a bacterial infection. Before the country manager could figure out what happened, when and why, the customer demanded compensation, and the health authorities threatened to shut down all the restaurants in the region to prevent others from falling ill. The news spread like wildfire and sales dropped as worried mothers shied away from visiting the restaurants. Voices emerged that bribing the local health authority officials was a good

(Continued)

CASE STUDY 1 (*Continued*)

idea to prevent the outlets from being shut down. What was the country manager to do? Before he could do his homework, he was confronted with a fully-fledged crisis. Even gathering intelligence would take days, if not weeks. Consulting with public relation (PR) experts would also take days for the briefing alone. The media kept calling him for statements, and the other local restaurant managers kept badgering as they feared for their revenue stream, since their margin was fairly low to begin with.

While valuable time passed, new evidence emerged that the bacteria, which the customer and her doctors claimed to be the source of her sickness, actually needed several days to incubate. There was no way the customer could have immediately become ill due to eating at a McDonald's restaurant. The only other explanation was that the country manager was confronted with a clever scheme to defraud the company. But how smart were his opponents exactly? How many were there? How big could this get? What would come next? And how could the company deal with the already formed public opinion, that the careless foreign multinational must have sacrificed the food quality and hygienic conditions, to achieve even higher profit margins? How could the company deal with the health authorities? Would not bribery perhaps cause a whole new set of problems and risks for the country manager, and this time truly due to poor judgment and misdeeds? How could the company convince worried mothers that McDonald's was really safe? One sleepless night followed another for the country manager. The crisis in Argentina reached the US headquarters, which demanded that attention be paid and for fast, as well as, professional solutions before the news spilled over to other countries and triggered a domino effect. The country manager wished he had built proactive relationships with the health authorities himself. He wished he knew someone in the media, who would not attack the big brand McDonald's, as an easy target. There also were no crisis management policies in place, and no buffers built into the busy schedules and staff capabilities, especially regarding professional, but expensive, top managers who were now so desperately needed.

Fortunately, the hype climaxed, and the media had to report that a scam was the real cause of the problem. The customer had actually gone from one industry to another trying to win settlements and compensation. But as the industries were not connected and did not communicate with each other, no one had noticed this for a

(Continued)

CASE STUDY 1 (*Continued*)

while. Once the dust settled, the country manager organized sufficient resources, held stakeholder meetings, and managed to open
the restaurants again after only a few days. He did, however, promise
himself that history would not repeat itself, and that other branches,
country organizations and headquarters could gain substantial
insights from this incident. McDonald's updated its crisis management policies and training opportunities, and emerged stronger in
this field than it had ever been. Since the organization is still perceived as an easy target, this will most certainly help in future.

CONCLUSIONS

Management can be defined as the constant solution and prevention of crises. In that sense, calling the flagship business title—the—Master of Business
Administration (MBA) is actually quite false, as we have hardly any need of
administrators. At the same point in time, management is a craft where we,
of course, can talk or write about how to do it, but actually practising is the
key. In this regard, encountering a crisis is, by no means, something negative.
It is a great learning opportunity, and a test of your strengths. The more your
career progresses, the bigger and more complex the crises you have to deal
with. It is, therefore, crucial to learn and reflect about how to master crises on
a constant basis. The following exercises can be a good start. Also watch out
for key leaders in newspapers and how they solve crises (or failed to do so) to
enhance your crisis management acumen, at least on the abstract level.

Your Activities for Honed Crisis Management Skills

Activity 1: Application and reflection exercise.

Besides these conceptual pointers on how to manage crises professionally, we encourage you to answer the following three questions.

1. Draw up your list of current priorities and challenges. Reflect
   on the following questions: Are you already on the point of
   being overburdened with projects and expectations at work? Is

there room to deal with unexpected events that could distract you, while still ensuring winning the key "battles"?

_____

_____

2.   According to Murphy's Law (and remember, Murphy was an optimist), things that can go wrong, will go wrong. Reflect on your social capital, that is, the relationships you built in the past. Will your environment "forgive" mistakes? Help readily? Will you have enough resources in terms of time, funds, team, and management capacity, experts to draw on in case of unexpected events? Does your setting resemble McDonald's before or after the incident mentioned the above in terms of readiness for the next big crisis?

_____

_____

3.   Have you installed early warning systems to interpret weak signals of the emerging crises? What are the signs of crises threatening your organization's business model and immediate sales success, your team, your own career, your happiness, and well-being?

_____

_____

REFERENCES AND FURTHER READING

Greiner, L. (1972). Evolution and Revolution as Organizations Grow. *Harvard Business Review*. July–August.

Steger, U. (2003). *Corporate diplomacy*. Chichester: Wiley.

Steger, U., & Nedopil Chr. (2010). *Navigating through criser – a handbook for boards*. Washington: IFC.

CHAPTER 20

CREATIVITY SKILLS FOR THE 21ST CENTURY PROFESSIONAL

Mike Green, Katja Kruckeberg, and Wolfgang Amann

OBJECTIVE OF THE CHAPTER

The objectives of this chapter are to emphasize the importance of creative thinking, to describe the characteristics of the creative mind, to show how important creativity is, especially in complex and changing situations, and to offer selected tools and techniques to enhance creativity.

INTRODUCTION

Allow us first to create a shared understanding of what the term creativity means. "Creativity occurs when—and only when—an individual or a group product generated in a particular domain is recognized by the relevant field as innovative and, in turn, sooner or later, exerts a genuine, detectable influence on the subsequent work in that domain. (...) the creator stands out in terms of temperament, personality, and stance. She is perennially dissatisfied with current work, current standards, current questions, current

Leadership and Personal Development: A Toolbox for the
21st Century Professional, pp. 343–355
Copyright © 2011 by Information Age Publishing
All rights of reproduction in any form reserved.

answers" (Gardener, 2006, p. 81). This quote comes from Gardner's book *"The Five Minds for the Future"*, in which he describes the crucial importance of developing the creative mind which builds capacity and capability to uncover, and clarify new problems, questions and phenomena. He begins his book by showing that societies have not always encouraged creativity, as the most important human attribute. Indeed, in many societies, creativity produced ideas and concepts which were definitely regarded as counterculture, and were actively discouraged or punished. And even those societies, which we admire and label "creative", for example, the Egyptians and ancient Greeks, actually progressed incredibly slowly over time.

However, times are changing. With change taking place exponentially over the past decades, we have witnessed the blossoming of creativity in every walk of life, impacting every person on the planet through new products and services, as well as different ways of doing things. Creativity, as well as the associated innovation has become quintessential, especially since World War II. After the latter, there was a lack of resources in many countries. Production facilities needed to be reconfigured to non-military products. At that time, creativity was merely focused on producing goods and distributing them. We refer to this as the first post-war paradigm.

The second post-war paradigm emerged largely in the 1980s when markets were saturated, and the post-war replenishment and reconstruction needs had been satisfied. The markets were so oversaturated that companies sometimes spent a considerable percentage of their overall costs on analyzing, segmenting, and smartly managing markets through their marketing mix. At times, and in certain industries, these costs exceeded the ones incurred for the actual production of goods. However, marketing, not production, was the bottleneck. Only intense advertising would allow companies to push their products on to the markets—often at the cost of the other players. A new form of creativity was needed, as many industries had turned into zero-sum games—you can only win if someone loses. This second post-war paradigm "market orientation" required creative ways. Advertising agencies grew big by selling their creativity talents. Marketing became the primary function in business, attracting the best paid and the most creative human resources.

From the 1990s onward, however, the third post-war paradigm arose for our corporate world, which is best labeled as "creative destruction". Originally a concept of the Austrian economist Schumpeter, it best characterises the type of creativity most needed today. Companies and individuals can win if they creatively destroy the competitors, or the logic in an entire industry's value proposition. Remember how low-cost carriers in Europe suddenly focussed on offering flights costing only as much as a train ticket? Remember how Apple built an empire of integrated products over the last year that includes computers, handheld devices, music, and video distribution in a closed Apple world system? Reflect on how Google creatively and constantly attacks Microsoft in the search engine and office product markets. Within a matter of years, the situation has changed drastically. While the authorities scrutinized Microsoft for misusing market power, it is now Google's turn to be creative. Fortunately, the company continues to send countering messages regarding its intentions. "Do no evil" is the official motto. And what is really so bad about offering free products? These are creative communication patterns and business models that allowed Google to generate more than 22 billion United State dollar (USD) in sales in 2010.

To sum up, the main business logics have changed over the last 70 years—at least three times on the large-scale picture. For companies in developed countries, constant innovation and the exploration of new opportunities have become the name of the game to have some chance against the increasingly strong competitors from the emerging countries. The latter, however, grew through their different type of creativity. Often exploiting the availability of solutions or concentrating on niches, they, too, built managers and leader capabilities in order to join the exploration game.

To be clear, this does not mean that we all have to be creative at all times, in all aspects of our jobs. Indeed, one of the major criticisms of organizational leaders is the degree to which they want to and can innovate. More cynically, some top managers refer to the groups most resistant to change, when they mention that, in the old days, whenever someone had a good idea, the others slaughtered a donkey—ever since then all donkeys are afraid of change!

But for quite a number of people there could well be a good reason for less creativity, innovation, and change. Some companies undergo so many reorganizations that none of the previous restructuring efforts will have had time to bear fruit. The key dilemma for today's manager could well be to know, when to be creative and when not to be!

Our turbulent times have also had a tremendous impact on how to reason. As Snowden & Boone point out in their article on "A Leader's Framework for Decision Making" (2007), we need to approach various situations in fundamentally different ways, depending on the levels of complexity, and chaos. The more unfathomable a situation is, for example, the less you are able to rely on the logical, rational "plan, do, review" approach to decision making. It is in times of chaos and complexity, that creative thinking—both individually and in groups—becomes important.

CHARACTERISTICS OF THE CREATIVE PERSONALITY

One of the first questions when exploring the creativity concept is: What constitutes a creative person? In his seminal book "*Creativity–Flow and the Psychology of Discovery and Invention*" (1996), the creativity and "flow" guru

Mihaly Csikszentmihalyi identifies ten characteristics of the creative personality, which we could also regard as tensions:

1. Creative individuals have a great deal of energy, but they are also often quiet and relaxed.
2. Creative individuals tend to be smart, but simultaneously naive.
3. Creative individuals show a combination of playfulness and discipline, or responsibility and irresponsibility.
4. Creative individuals alternate between the extremes imagination and fantasy, and a rooted sense of reality.
5. Creative people seem to harbor opposite tendencies on the continuum between extroversion and introversion.
6. Creative individuals are simultaneously remarkably humble and proud.
7. Creative individuals avoid rigid gender-role stereotyping to a certain extent, and have a tendency towards androgyny.
8. Generally, creative people are thought to be rebellious and independent.
9. Most creative persons are very passionate about their work, yet they can be extremely objective about it as well.
10. The openness and sensitivity of creative individuals often expose them not only to suffering, but also to a great deal of enjoyment.

Most of the creative people, thus, have and actually use their mental flexibility. In addition, as early as 1991 onward, Thorne & Gough's research into MBTI[i] and creativity suggested that creative individuals tend to be more extroverted ("E") rather than introverted ("I"), more intuitive ("N") than sensing ("S"), more thinking ("T") than feeling ("F"), and more perceiving ("P") than judging ("J"). This suggests that the stereotypical marketing type (ENTP) would tend to self-select into a creative role. However, as the people acquainted with MBTI know, whichever type you are you can venture out of your "home base" and access other preferences— it just takes a little time and effort, using a bit more energy and is initially somewhat unfamiliar. There is no truly fatalistic situation for personalities with a different letter combination.

ABOUT LEADERS AND MANAGERS

As the world turns into an ever-changing and increasingly complex place, the resulting demands on individuals and managers in all organizations are increasing at similar rates. The external drivers of change—from the political, economic, societal, technological, legal, and environmental

Table 20.1.   Managers versus Leaders

Managers	Leaders
Administers	Innovates
Is a copy	Is an original
Maintains	Develops
Focuses on systems and structure	Focuses on people
Relies on control	Inspires trust
Has a short-range view	Has a long range perspective
Asks how and when	Asks why
Has his eye on the bottom line	Has his eye on the horizon
Imitates	Originates
Accepts the status quo	Challenges the status quo
Classic good soldier	His own person
Does things right	Does the right thing

Source: Based on Bennis, 1994.

drivers to the need to improve internal organizational strategies, systems, structures, skills, and so forth—all require people to do things in different ways. The old adage "keep on doing what you are doing, and you will keep on getting what you get' is still true—but the results may no longer suffice in a world with increasing demands and expectations. To help you reflect on your role, Bennis (1994) offers an often reproduced list of the differences between a manager and a leader. You will note that the leader seems to be the one, who is increasingly taking over the creative role.

Currently, a large part of managers' role is actually delivering the objectives they set, at the beginning of a year. Creativity comes into play when they have to deliver in more innovative ways, or when they need to become more imaginative in terms of developing future strategies. This is supported by Pascale's insight that "... managing is helping to make happen what is supposed to happen anyway; leadership is making happen what is not going to happen anyway" (1990, p. 3). To sum up, if you do not hone your creativity skills, you cannot qualify for more leadership assignments.

CREATIVITY AND ITS ROLE IN MANAGING AND DEALING WITH COMPLEXITY AND CRISIS

What can be done to instil creativity into the process of managing crises or complexity? Firstly, depending on the context, there is no dearth of consultants or facilitators who could help with creative processes. It is not failure or a loss of face to ask colleagues or coaches for support. Secondly, the other chapters on complexity and crises have already presented check-lists and orientation points, regarding where to start. Would you like to cut through complexity? You were offered four simplifiers. You also learned that complexity is sometimes good. The latter holds, for example, when customer or the company draws special benefits from complexity. Besides these four pointers for simplification and the advice to involve a good mod-erator or facilitator, a well-managed, diverse team which brings different perspectives to the table, offers a creative process through which to apply these points.

Organizing for the right process support (in the form of a facilitator), orientation points and "letting lose" the right people to take on the chal-lenge, can already entail major progress. Research tells us, though, that only two out of 350 important new ideas come from structured meetings. Tight schedules, different or packed agendas, and the lack of an open-minded organizational culture can impede improved statistics. Hence, we need to ensure that additional factors function smoothly to prepare our working environments for more creativity.

Two more ingredients are needed for the recipe for more increased crea-tivity. One is to create the right culture and to know the key creativity tech-niques well. The list below provides you with ideas to put into practice to help you become more creative in future. Not all of these ideas work for everybody. Choose the ideas that work the best for you, or at least use them as a basis for reflection on what could work for you, and what would not.

- Start with a brief reflection on yourself, your team and superior— some of them work best under great pressure. These people's motto is: When the going gets tough, the tough get going. A deadline and additional assignments create the conviction that finding a solution can no longer be put off. For example, the solution must be present-ed at 3pm on Friday. All of those involved are convinced that this is the ultimate deadline it is therefore just a question of working out the solution. It may actually be quite helpful to increase the time and workload pressure of these Type 1 people, thus ensuring that no time or energy unit is wasted. Projects often take all the time they are given—they are elastic. Type 2 people become more rigid, and freeze mentally, when put under pressure. Trying to stop them worrying or mentally unfreezing them will actually destroy energy and time resources. Consider simplifying and dissecting the issues. To whom could you delegate a part of the core or peripheral tasks? What is the key battle that should be fought and won—the one thing that has to happen? Who is the main target audience? Do you really need a per-fect solution right from the start, or would rapid learning be necessary, anyway? The latter holds especially true for situations with multiple new-new-new combinations in which, for example, new customers should adopt a new product, sold in a new way with a new pricing model, and so forth. The "right" creative process is contingent upon those involved!

- Allow for tackling blind spots—the brain will often take short cuts in understanding the world around it, or the ideas within it. Because of the immensity of the sensory experience the brain selects certain things based on its previous experiences. It helps to simplify the world and make it manageable. However, it means that we can all miss things which are there, because they have always been there, or because something new has happened. One can start reading different newspapers or watching different TV news channels, to get a wider perspective. Or, one can decide to take different routes to work or a different mode of transportation. These changes, which you can force upon yourself, will open you to new experiences and insights.

- Allow for playfulness—many creative techniques are based on the notion that the brain itself is playful and can make associations between different matters. One matter can remind us of another. Tying a knot in a handkerchief was a traditional way of remembering to do something. But we can extend this idea by looking at an object, and thinking of another ten things we can use that object for. This exercise helps our creative juices, so that we can begin to generate more options than usual, in a specific situation. One strategy professor even provides executives with Lego bricks to illustrate problems and solutions—with amazing results.

- Allow for the use of the subconscious. We all have probably had the experience of having to "sleep on" a problem or issue that we need to resolve. The brain will continue to work on an issue, regardless of whether we are consciously thinking about it or not. For this to work, we do need to have consciously thought about the subject for a while, as well as thought around the subject. We can then consciously hand it over to our subconscious to work on overnight, or over a week or more. Doing a little preparation for a project and then returning to it a week later, will reveal more ideas and options than working on it non-stop.

- Plan for some exercise. A healthy body leads to a healthy mind, as the saying *"mens sana in corpore sano"* has been reminding us for millennia. Exercising has two significant benefits for creativity. Taking regular exercise or specific exercise before a "creative session" will prepare you for the psychological task, and put you in a relaxed, yet focused, mode. Furthermore, having worked on the issue consciously for some time, an exercise break—for example, a long meandering walk—can allow the subconscious to do its share of the work.

A number of executives have reported that they never come back from a run, without at least one good idea. Not being at the office desk or in a sterile meeting room with artificial light actually helps you move forward.

- Ensure that a facilitating environment has been created, which can start with very simple but effective actions. One technique is to merely ask a group of participants what other purposes the water bottle on the meeting table could be used for, before a meeting starts. Allow their thoughts to wander, and a positive energy to develop in the room. Set the right tone from the beginning. Break the ice between the participants. Alternatively, ask them to cast their minds back to a time, when they were noticeably creative and successful in tapping into their imaginations. Ask them to try to remember the things that helped them be creative at that time, and also some of the barriers that they had removed to give the creative process full rein. For some it might be a clean desk, an uninterrupted schedule, and total focus on the issue. For others it might be an exciting interaction with a group of likeminded, or even dissimilar, people. Sometimes one problem will suggest one way of generating a solution, and sometimes the problem will call for a totally different environment in which to solve it.

- Change your perspectives. Imagine you are a mentor or leader you know reasonably well, now ask yourself how he or she would go about solving the problem, but at all times, try to ascertain if such a solution is compatible with your values and current situation.

- Check your company's mainstream creativity techniques. You should know them inside-out, but you could at times suggest alternatives. Ensure you brush up your insights on techniques for idea generation and divergent thinking, such as the morphological box or de Bono's six hats thinking method. Learn to ascertain which tool works best: Simpler challenges or more advanced dilemmas for multi-dimensional, non-quantifiable problems, where causal modelling and simulation do not function well at all.

- Trigger single-loop, double-loop, and deutero-loop learning. This ensures continuous improvement of your ways of working, as well as providing more confidence to face the next challenges. What do these learning loops comprize of? According to Argyris & Schön (1996), we can distinguish between the three levels of learning:
  - **Single-loop learning:** This is also known as adaptive learning and it focuses on incremental change. It occurs when you applied creativity (techniques) successfully to a challenge. This type of

learning solves the problems, but ignores the question of why the problem arose in the first place.

o **Double-loop learning:** This is generative learning, focussing on transformational change that modifies the status quo. Double-loop learning uses feedback from past actions, such as the creativity exercises, to question assumptions underlying current views. When considering feedback, managers, and professionals should not only question the reasons for their current actions, but also what they should do next and, even more importantly, why alternative actions should not to be implemented. The possible consequences could be, that selected team members need to be sent on a creativity training course, or you could determine clear-cut, but different, rules for facing the next creativity challenges.

o **Deutero-learning:** This is focused on how to learn better by seeking to improve both single and double-loop learning. Teams learn the most about themselves, at this level.

Learning about your creativity and the creativity evolution process are vital when climbing the career ladder. Make it a habit to identify inspirations for creativity and learning, possibly like the one portrayed in the following case study, and consider constantly, what the best way of currently inspiring creativity and learning should be.

CASE STUDY 1

Twyla Tharp's Insights on Being Creative

Twyla Tharp is one of America's greatest choreographers, having created more than 130 dances, having won two Emmy awards, and one Tony. She wrote *"The Creative Habit"*, which is based on her life-long immersion in the creative arts, and her experiences of developing creativity, whether the muse is with you or not:

"I was 58 years old when I finally felt like a "master choreographer" … for the first time in my career. I felt in control of all the components that go into making a dance—the music, the steps, the patterns, the deployment of people onstage, and the clarity of purpose. Finally, I had the skills to close the gap between what I could see in my mind, and what I could actually get onto the stage."

(Continued)

CASE STUDY 1 (*Continued*)

She begins by addressing "the task of starting with nothing and working your way toward creating something whole and beautiful and satisfying." Creativity is for everyone, not just 'artists", but also engineers, parents, children, and business people.

She writes: "In order to be creative, you have to know how to prepare to be creative. It involves deliberate and conscious preparation including the use of daily rituals and habits, which focus the mind on the creative process." She asks powerful questions of herself, and of you—what you fear most, mockery, rejection, or incompetence? And what you allow to distract you. One key is discovering "the one tool that feeds your creativity and is so essential that without it you feel naked and unprepared." Another is practicing going a week, without one of the things that you know will distract you (the TV, newspapers, and so forth.).

She suggests getting in touch with when you were previously creative by writing a "creative autobiography" and, with many other creative people she stresses, how observation and memory—muscle memory, virtual memory, sensual memory, and so forth—can be harnessed. For those of us who think that the creative person is not organized, there is a wonderful chapter illustrating the exact opposite: "*Before you can think out of the box, you have to start with a box.*" That is a box in which to organize your project!

She is constantly on the lookout for ideas; she calls it "scratching" and generates ideas from all parts of her awake state and, indeed, her sleeping life–from reading, conversation, observations, nature, and dreams. But she is always open to that stroke of luck, whether good luck or bad luck, when "[a]ccidents will happen" and things do not turn out as perfectly as planned, but other ideas emerge. Or, as Leonard Cohen sings: "*There is a crack in everything. That's how the light gets in ...*"

CONCLUSION

Albert Einstein suggested that if we do not change our mindsets, we cannot solve the problems that we created with our current patterns of thought. Since "times are a-changing", we have to embrace our lives and careers with a tremendous readiness, to learn or unlearn. Life-long learning is generally as essential as honing one's creativity skills. While there are, of course, the lucky geniuses with break-through ideas, Edison reminds us that genius is 1% inspiration, and 99% perspiration. He needed more than a thousand attempts before he invented a light bulb that worked. But he retained a positive mental attitude, as he was said to comment that this long journey of discovery had successfully taught him a thousand ways of how NOT to build a light bulb.

This chapter shared insights into why creativity matters significantly in these times, what makes a person creative, what expectations we have of leaders and managers' creativity, and how to pool all the thoughts on creativity to combat complexity and creativity challenges.

Your Activities for Enhanced Creativity Skills

Activity 1: Reset your brain! The do-it-all-differently day.

Our brain is trained to work and function in specific ways, and only by interrupting our daily routines, are we able to challenge ourselves into new ways of thinking and behaving. One way of doing this is by picking a day in the week, in which you will have the freedom to do things differently from your accustomed way of doing them. To start off, we suggest you pick a Sunday as this new behavior may have some risk if applied in the workplace. On this day, try to do everything that you usually would not do—there are no limits to challenging yourself. Make different phone calls, dress differently, walk and speak differently, stay in bed all day.

If you work in an environment that constantly challenges you to put on a friendly face to fit in, do not do this on the Sunday if you do not feel like it. Be authentic—express (almost) everything that comes to your mind. Look around you, choose a familiar object, and study it. Touch it, pick it up, smell it. Keep studying it until you have learned something about it that you did not know before. Perhaps it is how even the smoothest paper varies in thickness, or the fact that your cat only has four toes on each hind foot. If you do this honestly, you will probably notice two things:

1.   You will feel very refreshed.
2.   You will notice that your way of looking at the world and interacting with it can be easily changed, to new ways of acting and thinking.

This is what it means to think outside the box. The box is what you know.

Activity 2: Think in terms of OPTIONS in decision making.

Now you have to learn to think outside the box all the time, not just within your isolated creativity exercise. This time you have to come up with a list of 10 alternatives to consider, before making a certain decision. What the decision or situation is, it is up to you. It can be the approach you should take when speaking to your superior about a relevant working issue, or about deciding on a holiday location, but you have to brainstorm this decision to build confidence in what you want. An important decision might be easier to tackle, but this is not really necessary. The important point is to establish a habit of thinking in alternatives, options, and possibilities. Make it a hobby. Think about this each day. Try to come up with just one more alternative, one more option, whenever you are about to make a certain decision.

You are not going to have 10 alternative options for every decision you take without becoming rather unrealistic at times. And that is fine, because here the walls of the box consist of your belief of what is acceptable and correct. To think outside the box, you might have to start taking aspects into consideration that you initially considered wrong. However, if you establish this new habit firmly, it can transform you into a creative and much more flexible professional, within months.

Activity 3: How to find your next brilliant idea.

Sometimes big ideas come to us in a moment. However, the most brilliant ideas have a history behind them, a history of people working consciously towards building up something new. In the following, you will find a few recommendations, on how you can bring more creativity into your life:

- **The creativity box:** Buy a box for your office and one for your home where you can collect ideas that you have jotted down throughout the day.
- **Use smart phone apps:** Use the camera on your phone to take pictures of interesting articles.
- **Magazines and newspapers:** When you have read an interesting article/headline, or whatever that refers to your next big idea or next big project, store it in your creativity box.
- **The great inventors of our times** have all had interesting networks with which they discussed their ideas. Get together with people from very different walks of life to discuss your ideas.

> The more alike the people in your network, the less likely it is that you will come up with something genuinely new.
> - **Take a reading and research sabbatical**—this can be a weekend, a week or a month—whatever suits your life.
>
> A great idea sometimes needs time to cultivate. So do not think of yourself of not being creative—invest time in brainstorming, in searching for ideas, revisit your creativity box, mingle with new people, and, over time, you might become more skilled at **connecting the dots**—as Steve Jobs rightly put it.

NOTE

i. See our previous chapter on personality for an overview of the MBTI concept and its explanations.

REFERENCES AND FURTHER READING

Argyris, Chr., & Schön, D. (1996). *Organizational learning*. Reading, MA: Addison-Wesley.

Bennis, W. (1994). *On becoming a leader*. Reading, MA: Perseus.

Csikszentmihalyi, M. (1996). *Creativity–Flow and the psychology of discovery and invention*. New York: HarperPerennial.

de Bono, E. (1985). *Six thinking hats: An essential approach to business management*. New York: Little, Brown & Company.

Gardener, H. (2006). *Five minds for the future*. Boston, MA: Harvard Press.

Pascale, R. (1990). *Managing on the edge*. London: Penguin.

Snowden, D., & Boone, M. (2007). A leader's framework for decision-making, *Harvard Business Review*, 85(11), 69–76.

Tharp, T. (2006). *The creative habit—learn it and use it for life*. New York: Simon & Schuster.

Thorne, A., & Gough, H. (1991). *Portraits of type: An MBTI research compendium*. Palo Alto, California: Consulting Psychologists Press, Inc.

CHAPTER 21

KEY LESSONS ON LEADERSHIP AND PERSONAL DEVELOPMENT

Katja Kruckeberg, Wolfgang Amann, and Mike Green

Making the right choices in a world of opportunities and complexities is not an easy task. Investing heavily in personal development will enable you to make more balanced decisions. In the following, we distil the essence of this book.

THE POWER OF FOCUS AND REFLECTION

We have provided you with what we consider to be most desirable parts of the "buffet" of leadership and personal development. While we hope that you actually consider trying out all of these parts, we encourage you to be selective when it comes to your focus areas, as each person has individual development needs. We believe that we all know that time is one of our most valuable assets in life, as it is one of the few assets that are not yet recy-

Leadership and Personal Development: A Toolbox for the 21st Century Professional, pp. 357–363

clable. Once it is spent, it is gone forever. Therefore, invest your time and efforts wisely. Ask yourself:

- Which leadership and personal development goals will give me the greatest return?
- Which achievements will give me the greatest personal reward?

If you look at what differentiates good leaders from great leaders, you will quickly notice that the latter make time for purposeful, strategic thinking in their busy schedules, in order to make smart decisions. Great leaders and high performers take time to think purposefully and strategically—not only about their business, but also about their development as a person and leader.

DELIBERATE, EFFECTIVE AND ENJOYABLE ACTIONS

Once you have made good choices for yourself, you have to activate these choices through the right actions. The Pareto Principle maintains that 20% of your actions will get 80% of your results. While we might query this principle's figures, we all know that there is some truth in the principle. In order to take the most effective action, you need to focus your attention on activities with high returns. Leave the other activities for a later time, or think about delegating them if this is at all possible.

The most effective actions are usually those which play to your strengths. Think of the activities that you enjoy - those that give you energy instead of draining you. Then you do not have to worry about burn-out so much. The development journey should be rewarding in itself, while still leading you to your goal.

FROM GOOD TO GREAT THROUGH CONSCIOUS PRACTICE AND FEEDBACK

You may already have a substantial skills in all the areas we discussed in this book. However, to move from good to better to excellent takes deliberate thinking and acting. We are building on the age-old debate of quantity versus quality. It is about becoming more systematic and effective at using one's development time, about reflection and—more than anything else—about being mentally and physically focussed while practicing. From a strength-based approach, we recommend that in order to achieve excellence and to excel in your field, you should identify areas for improvement in your greatest strengths. This does not, of course, mean that you should ignore the areas in which you are weak, but they should not be at the center of your development efforts. Another integral element of conscious practice is to continuously seek feedback from others on your performance and improvement. Beyond a certain level of competence, it is difficult to improve any further without this rich pool of information, which allows you to look at yourself through other people's eyes.

DEVELOP A GENUINE 21ST CENTURY WIN-WIN NETWORK ATTITUDE

A 21st century win-win attitude towards leadership and personal development is so crucial, that everything in this book could have been centered on finding and applying win-win solutions. A win-win attitude does, however, require a certain level of maturity, which relates to your ability to pursue your goals in a balanced manner, with consideration for other's thoughts and feelings. When it comes to achieving your goals through a relationship, the win-win mindset requires you to regard your goals, from the perspective of others. When understanding what others wish to achieve, one has the best opportunity of finding a way to fulfill both parties' needs.

Thinking win-win is about adopting a new paradigm—the paradigm of creation instead of competition as the famous Stephen Covey puts it. Once an individual thinks win-win, he or she will most certainly create deals where there may not have been any. Such a mind-set makes people opportunity creators, rather than opportunity receivers. A win-win attitude creates trust. People are interested in others who have something to offer, and are happy to help in return when the time and opportunity are right. Win-win builds lasting partnerships that nurture our network, and thereby our development. Like creativity, learning occurs primarily in social settings. Opportunities arise mainly through interactions with others, and not when you work isolated from others.

THE RESPONSIBILITY FOR LEADERSHIP AND PERSONAL DEVELOPMENT IS CLEARLY ALLOCATED—YOU DRIVE IT

The responsibility for leadership and personal development lies mainly on your shoulders. Currently, training budgets may be cut and companies may not really know what your most urgent training requirement is. A superior may also have an interest in keeping highly effective people in their current positions. Not all superiors have understood that–ethically, as well as a part of a true leader's responsibility–developing talent is part of their job portfolio. In addition, while downsizing—or "rightsizing"—the companies require fewer people to accomplish the same number of tasks, often in less time, and with fewer resources. This enhances your responsibility to drive your development, and to have it on your and your superior's radar.

MODESTY BEATS ARROGANCE

Self-confidence paired with modesty is the best combination for the future. Failure will happen. Crises will hit you. Hence, your readiness to embrace trouble and complexity is as much needed, as your willingness to constantly unlearn the old things and adopt new skills and knowledge, whenever new tasks await you. The good news is, however, that never before have there been more opportunities to prepare yourself for what awaits. Coaches have never been more affordable. The Internet offers a great variety of material. Nevertheless, if you have a "tough guy" attitude, are arrogant and careless about how you treat people while on the way up, they will remember this.

THE POWER OF KNOWING THE CONCEPTS AND SEMANTICS

Simultaneously, we encourage you to familiarize yourself with the key concepts and semantics of what we have to offer. There is tremendous power in knowing how to label and, thus, communicate problems more easily. The reason for many of the recent management and personal development books' success does not lie in break-through, simple recipes for success, but in the vocabularies they gave us to understand the challenges and solutions, better than before. The more detailed and proactively developed is your awareness of the tools and semantics offered in this book, the better off will you be since you may not always have sufficient time to reflect on how to phrase the issues.

YOU KNOW WHAT TO EXPECT—IT IS YOUR CONSCIOUS CHOICE

We have outlined the tremendous challenges that your career will face in future. There will be more system shocks, crises, new technologies, and new competitors from different backgrounds. Besides having to face tougher competition, the higher you climb the corporate ladder, the greater the likelihood that you will have to face political games and the lonelier your battles may become. The potential risks increase, but so do the rewards. At all times, it is your choice whether to reach higher, to follow your ambitions, to chase glory, and resources. If you decide to go further, ensure that you match career advancement with an effort to adapt your skills. What brought you there may not get you further. We thus explicitly warn you of the "Peter Principle". People are often promoted above their main areas of competencies. Engineers and natural scientists suddenly need to lead and understand financial numbers and interdependencies. Leading people to carry out work is very different, from doing the work yourself. This tends to happen to many white collar staff members, which is where many problems commence. This also explains why so many employees have issues with their superiors. It is therefore important to remain in your development channel, at all times.

Since you are now aware of these patterns, you can make more conscious choices. We have offered you, and based this book on, the philosophy of strengths-based development. It is the emerging paradigm in career management, strongly calling for a focus on your actual strengths. It does not, of course, mean that you should completely ignore your weaknesses. You still have to know them, and ensure that you achieve a minimum level of performance in the most crucial ones, say, soft skills. But rather than trying to become somewhat good at too many dimensions, focus on your strengths. In some cultures, working on compensating for one's weaknesses is still a time-honored activity, and much overrated. In our fast-paced world there may not be enough time to be an all-rounder, and these personalities may not be as competitive, as those who have focused for years, on organizing their work around their main strengths.

UNDERSTAND AND MANAGE COMPLEXITIES

Embark on understanding the main drivers of complexity in your business challenges or life with the right attitude, and immediately look for the right simplifiers. The latter can come from guiding principles, values, and strategies, and certainly include created awareness and clear-cut proactive decisions. These simplifiers allow you to drive development instead of being driven by it. Reflect on a generation Y representative's traits—this person may have had up to 14 jobs by the age of 38. It is all about 1) learning, 2) growth, 3) avoiding boredom, 4) fun, and 5) driving things yourself. The other side of the coin prescribes flexibility, mobility, and high mental speed. Some people make it a clear principle to focus fully on gathering experience, not earning money until the age of 40. What they want from the company is the right learning and development opportunity. Why? The highest income opportunities are not generated in one's 30s. Playing it too safely may impede fast progress on the learning curve and in career advancement. We do, however, acknowledge that such a philosophy is not for everyone. Some prefer crisp plans, others go with the flow. The generation Y's approach may conflict with the other priorities, such as the wish to have a family, to continue to be rooted within one's family and circle of friends, and so forth. Therefore, the diversity of characters amongst you, our readers, forces you to "know thyself," and proactively find the simplifying logics yourself.

In this book, we have provided you with the most important concepts for leadership, and personal development. We have aimed to share the following:

- What is it all about? Why is it important?
- How does it work on the conceptual level?
- How can you actually apply the concepts and tools to a number of practical activities and exercises?
- What does it mean for you personally?

We hope to have achieved our goal to help you embark on a proactive journey of personal development. Choose where, when and how to take your journey further. Experiment with the content and processes we have offered in this book. Some concepts may be understood quickly, but the implementation and transformation may take additional effort.

ACCEPTING LARGER RESPONSIBILITIES

We want to close this book by ensuring we have sent the right message concerning what leadership and personal development are all about—also from an ethical point of view. We believe that we are currently experiencing a world, in which humans and their fundamental needs are at least partially classified into too many materialistic necessities. Rather than human beings, we are seen as customers or "human resources". This "economization" of everyday life may actually be supplanting long-standing humanistic ideals. These ideals have been the foundation of free, liberal, and democratic societies, focussing holistically on human nature and its potential. As authors, we therefore believe, that turning market economies into evermore efficient and effective "market societies" may well, to some extent mean, biting the hand that feeds us, as we put the very foundation of social peace and cohesion, which is fundamental for a thriving free-market economy, at risk.

Consequently, as a current or future manager, or business leader, you have important choices ahead. Will you generate and sustain prosperity for more members of the global society? Will you enjoy the benefits of "markets within societies"? On your way up, reflect on how to use your positions, projects, and enhanced soft skills. With greater powers come greater responsibilities. As a final exercise or activity, we encourage you to reflect on what you could possibly do, either now or later, to protect and enhance human dignity in our economic systems, organizations, and teams. Orient yourself according to the question: What would happen if more managers and leaders were to follow your approach? Would companies and societies become fairer? Would we work at more fun places? At places where 75% of the staff members do not suffer from inner withdrawal? At places where human dignity is constantly respected, and is not relegated to a back seat? At places where people constantly grow, evolve, and contribute their best skills? We leave such value considerations up to you as the choice is solely up to you. Our book on personal development for the 21st century professional would not be complete, without having raised these crucial, final questions.

We wish you good luck on your further journey.

Katja, Wolfgang, and Mike
August 20, 2011

ABOUT THE EDITORS AND AUTHORS

Katja Kruckeberg

Dr. Katja Kruckeberg, MBA (USA) is an international consultant and conference speaker, who specializes in strength-based leadership development, executive coaching, and personal excellence. Katja has designed and delivered management and leadership development programs for various top companies across the world, working with senior and middle managers from diverse cultural and industrial backgrounds. Before founding her own consultancy company (KKC–www.kruckeberg.de), Katja acted as Client Director and Senior Consultant for Mannaz, a Scandinavian consulting firm working internationally with organizations to focus on real achievements in business life. During this time, Katja worked with clients such as ABN AMRO, Canon Europe, EADS, Fujitsu, Deloitte and Pirelli (*et al.*), adopting innovative adopting innovative and efficient learning methods to enable people development and business success. Prior to that, Katja worked in various capacities for Henley Business School, which is ranked first class in its field. After leading Henley's Executive MBA programme in Frankfurt and London, Katja became a fulltime faculty member of the School of Leadership, Change and HR. As an expert on Leadership and Personal Development, she teaches managers academic as well as corporate

programs in these fields. Today, Katja still collaborates with Henley and acts as a Visiting Academic and Executive Fellow. Furthermore, her many years of experience in management education and management consultancy include several roles and activities with other leading companies in the sector, such as the Frankfurt Business School, St. Gallen Business School (Switzerland), Ashridge Consulting (UK), and the Akademie für Führungskräfte (Germany). Katja lives with her family in Wiesbaden, where she spends much time outside with her daughter, and enjoys practising outdoor sports all the year around.

Wolfgang Amann

Dr Wolfgang Amann graduated from Harvard University's Institute for Management and Learning in Higher Education. He developed his research skills at the Wharton School in Philadelphia, and his executive education skills at IMD in Lausanne. After years in top management consulting, he has been marketing, designing, directing, and delivering executive education seminars for more than a decade. He previously directed the Henley Centre for Creative Destruction, and was the Vice-Director of the Executive School at the University of St. Gallen, where he was the Executive Director of a variety of international programs, including all activities along the program innovations, marketing, admission, operations, career services, and alumni management "value" chain. He has also been a visiting professor in the field of international strategy and sustainability at Hosei University in Tokyo, Tsinghua in Beijing, The Indian Institute of Management in Bangalore, ISP St. Petersburg, Warwick Business School, and Henley Business School in the UK.

He now serves as the Executive Director of Executive Education at the Goethe Business School of the University of Frankfurt. He has written a variety of books, such as *The Impact of Internationalization on Organizational Cultures* (2003); *Building Strategic Success Positions* (2005); *The Private Equity Investor as a Strategy Coach* (2005); *Humanism in Business* (2007); *Managing Complexity in Global Organizations* (2007); *Work-Life Balance* (2008); *Corporate Governance—How to Add Value* (2008); *Humanism in Business: Perspectives on the Development of a Responsible Business Society* (2009); *Complexity in Organization—Text and Cases* (2011); *Business Schools Under Fire–Humanistic Management Education as the Way Forward* (2011); and *Humanistic Management in Practice* (2011).

Mike Green

Mike is the Managing Director of Transitional Space, which has been helping individuals, teams and organizations manage change for over 20 years. He is the author of *Change Management Masterclass* (2007), and co-author of the top-selling book *Making Sense of Change Management* (2009), and *Making Sense of Leadership* (2008). Underpinned by extensive research and based on practical organizational experience they are all guides to the models, tools and techniques of individual, team, and organizational change. Mike is an Economics graduate from the University of Bristol, a qualified psychodynamic psychotherapist, and also has an MBA from Henley Business School. His career has spanned finance, HR and management consultancy. Mike is a Visiting Executive Fellow at Henley Business School, tutoring in Leadership and Change, People and Performance and Personal Development on MBA and corporate programs. He also works extensively in both the public, private, and not-for-profit sectors, helping senior and middle managers manage change more effectively. He has been a consultant to a number of international financial services companies as well as IBM and Deutsche Telekom, and both central and local government. He has also written practitioner guides for middle managers (Emerging Leadership), top teams (Inside Top Teams) and political leaders (Politicians and Personality). Mike is an accredited executive coach

AUTHORS

Chris Dalton

Chris Dalton is the Subject Area Leader for the Personal Development module on the Henley Business School MBA. Prior to this role, he was the Director of Studies for the Flexible (Distance) Learning MBA program. Before coming to Henley, he has worked at the Central European University Business School in Budapest, Hungary, where he directed the fulltime MBA programs. During his time in Hungary, he also acted as a consultant in Budapest, with the experiential team-building company Concordia Outdoor Training. He has been a member of the faculty at the Weatherhead School of Management at Case Western Reserve University in Cleveland, USA. From 1992–1997 Chris was Director of International Relations at IMC. He also worked for 3 years on international business development for

Hungary's largest integrated marketing communications company. He has experience working on projects in Romania, Macedonia, Czech Republic, South Africa, Switzerland, and Austria. Chris holds a Henley MBA, and is an accredited executive coach. He is currently studying toward a PhD in Management Learning and Leadership with Lancaster University.

Christoph Nedopil

Dr. Christoph Nedopil is the Managing Director of the award-winning innovation consultancy (YOUSE). Christoph Nedopil has previously been a research associate at IMD for more than 3 years, and has been engaged in academic and business research, as well as in the development of numerous executive education programs, with a focus on corporate governance and complexity management. During his tenure at IMD, he wrote more than 40 case studies and has worked with numerous companies and institutions around the globe, such as the Malaysian Directors Academy, Daimler, Holcim, and WWF. Since 2008, Nedopil has also worked on several projects, and delivered executive education programs for the World Bank Group and the Dutch FMO. He finished his PhD on the topic of corporate governance in emerging economies at the Technische University in Berlin. In 2008, he received the Best Doctoral Paper Award at the European Academy of Management Conference. His publications have been translated into a number of languages, including Russian and Chinese. He is also the author of the text book on Manging Complexity in Organizations.

Claire Collins

Claire is a Development Fellow at Henley Business School, actively involved in research on and teaching of Leadership, Leadership Development, and Coaching. She previously enjoyed a 20 year career in the National Health Service, formerly as a Haematology Scientist and latterly in senior manager positions, and finally as the Assistant Director of Planning of one of UK's largest Trusts. As if working with doctors was not enough, Claire then went on to be the CEO of a leading London law firm. During this time, she undertook her MBA at Henley, and qualified as a business coach with Meyler Campbell. Following this, Claire spent a period working as a consultant for many organizations, including some of the largest law firms in the UK, and acting as a Research Fellow at the Royal College of Nursing. Besides leading Leadership at Henley, Claire is also undertaking doctoral research on using coaching within leadership development, specifically studying the progression of the coaching relationship.

Daniel F. Pinnow

Daniel F. Pinnow, CEO of the Academy for Leadership GmbH in Überlingen, Germany, is known as a pioneer of systemic leadership, and counted among the leading experts in management and leadership in German speaking areas. The management trainer and leadership coach has been on the board of directors of the Cognos AG, one of Germany's biggest private providers of further education and has gained extensive leadership experience as a manager in international companies such as EADS and E.ON Ruhrgas AG. He is a lecturer on Human Resource Management at the Technical University of Munich, and an associate Professor at the Capital University of Economics and Business in Beijing, China. Pinnow is the author of numerous publications on leadership, management, and ethics; his book *"Führen–worauf es wirklich ankommt"* (4th edition 2009) has been published as one of the first German management books in China.

Didier Gonin

Didier Gonin is the Managing Director of *Didier Gonin & Associates,* an international network of senior coaches and facilitators, who specialized in executive coaching and leadership development. After teaching at Paris and Bangkok universities, he joined IBM-Europe, where he managed the Management Development function for EMEA. He was the Managing Director of the Center for Creative Leadership before starting his own company in 1999. During his career, Didier has developed more than 60 seminars for managers and executives and has conducted hundreds of coaching sessions and leadership seminars globally. He is the author of several books including: *"The Learner Within"* (IBM), *"Innovation in Leadership Development"* (Mannaz), and *"Réussir sa vie avec le Tao"*(Albin Michel).

Denis Sartain

Denis is a consultant and conference speaker based in the UK, where he designs and delivers group or individual coaching. He is an Associate Client Director at Henley Business School, University of Reading, and a member of the External Faculty. In these roles, he co-ordinates the MBA programs and tutors on the Coaching Certificate program, and is also responsible for the management and delivery of Henley's programs in parts of the Middle East. Denis has a multi-cultural background, being half Chinese and was born in Hong Kong. He has lived and worked in the UK,

Australia, New Zealand, Singapore, and worked in many other countries, and brings his multi-cultural perspective to much of his coaching and leadership development work. Originally from a background in ship-broking, working in the Far East, London, and Australia, Denis returned to the UK in 1990. He holds a postgraduate diploma in Clinical Hypnosis, and also works as a hypnotherapist, stress, and change management consultant. His latest book with Patricia Bossons and Jeremy Kourdi, is *Coaching Essentials* (2009). His new book, *Under Pressure*, will be released in 2011.

Erich Barthel

Erich Barthel is Professor of Corporate Culture and Human Resources Management at Frankfurt School of Finance and Management, one of the leading Business Schools in Germany. Among others activities, he teaches Leadership and Change Management, Intercultural Management and Human Resource Management. Before he joined Frankfurt School he was the Head of Human Resources in a German bank, and a member of the management team in an international consultancy. He is a co-editor of several books on competency building, in which individuals' competencies are regarded as the ability to self-organize behavior in changing organizations, rather than skills or qualifications in a given context. In order to develop these competencies, teams and organizations' supporting cultural and structural elements have been identified. Within Frankfurt School, he is a scientific advisor of different programmes, such as the School's Excellence in Leadership and the Executive MBA program.

Franklin Vrede

Through his work, Franklin has specialized in Change Management and Leadership Transitions. He regularly speaks on these topics at international conferences, and acts as an executive coach to individual leaders. Besides his work at the European School of Management (Berlin) and INSEAD Business School (Fontainebleau), Franklin leads his own international Executive Coaching and Leadership Development firm. Franklin has worked with leaders in Finance, Manufacturing, Oil & Gas, Information Technology, Consulting and Government. In his last corporate role, he was responsible for developing the Global Top Executive Group at a major European Bank. Franklin is an alumnus of INSEAD business school, where he completed the Executive Master: Coaching & Consulting for Change. Besides his Bachelor in Human Resources, Franklin has also earned a Master's degree in Learning and Developmental Sciences from the University of Tilburg, The Netherlands. Franklin is qualified to use a variety of psychometric tools, such as MBTI and FIRO-B. Franklin is a Dutch citizen and currently lives close to the beach in The Hague with his wife and two teenage daughters.

Helen Stride

Helen began her career in London as a stockbroker for one of UK's leading banks. In 1990, she was awarded a sabbatical to be a small business advisor to an international charity in South America. She subsequently joined the charity sector where she worked in conservation, adult disability and overseas development. While she was the head of Donor Recruitment at Christian Aid, one of UK's largest aid organizations, she developed a keen interest in the area of developing and leading values-based organizations. Helen is now a member of the faculty at Henley Business School, where she teaches Reputation and Responsibility. She is also an executive coach and team facilitator on a range of MBA and leadership development programs. Helen's expertize lies in the impact that individual and organizational values have on behavior, performance, and well-being. Helen is also an NLP practitioner.

Inger Buus

Inger Buus is the Executive Vice President, EMEA of Mannaz A/S. Inger started her career in operations management with Rank Xerox UK, and gained her management experience before specializing in leadership development. Over the past 12 years, she has designed and delivered customized leadership development to a broad range of global clients in Europe, US, South America, and Asia. Inger is particularly interested in developing individual and organizational leadership capability in large global organizations. She is an accredited executive coach and facilitator. Inger has published in the national and international HR press, is an awarded conference speaker and holds an MA in French from Copenhagen Business School (1992) and an MBA specialized in Strategic HR from Cranfield School of Management (1997). She is a Chartered Member of the Institute of Personnel and Development. Inger is a Danish national, who lives in the UK with her family.

Patricia Bossons

Dr Patricia Bossons is the Director of the Henley Centre for Coaching and Facilitation at Henley Business School, University of Reading, in the UK. She set up the Henley Centre in 2004, as part of the Executive Education

School in the Business School, and created its flagship programs: the Henley Certificate in Coaching and the MSc in Coaching and Behavioral Change. Over 700 students have now been through these programs and Patricia is focused on developing new development initiatives in this field to keep the Center at the cutting edge of coaching practice. Before joining Henley in 1998, Patricia worked as the Director of Training and Assessment at Financial Times Management, part of the Pearson Group. She is a Chartered Psychologist and has worked as a business psychologist in several countries in Europe and the Far East, as well as in New Zealand and South Africa over the last 25 years. Her first book, *Mentoring: A Henley Perspective*, was published in 2004, and her second, *Coaching Essentials*, in 2009. She is a resident of both Britain and New Zealand, and is particularly interested in how coaching is developing in the global business world within different cultural contexts. Her original doctoral research was in the area of personality and adult learning, and this continues to influence her work and her coaching practice.

Philip Cullen

Philip Cullen is an independent consultant, writer and executive coach. He has a background in Operations Management regarding leading large teams, and has successfully led his business unit to Investors in People, one of the most important awards for outstanding people management practise. For over 10 years he has worked as a management consultant, implementing and delivering Leadership and Management Development programs in a variety of organizations. He has written widely in the field of management and contributed to a variety of Master's level programmes. Phil is a Visiting Executive Fellow at Henley Business School where he specializes in Personal and Leadership Development, and was one of the core writers of their Personal Development module, which has been ranked No.1 in the World for Personal Development. He has coached managers from a variety of organizations. He is an NLP Practitioner and a Certified NLP Coach Practitioner. He is currently researching for a Doctorate in Business Administration.

Shiban Khan

Shiban Khan's expertise is in theories and cultural implications of CSR, and sustainable business strategies. This includes sound crisis management. She is a visiting tutor at Henley Business School and also teaches on the BRIC countries at the University of St.Gallen, St.Gallen, Switzerland. She has been a visiting scholar at the Indian Institute of Management,

Bangalore, and Hosei University, Tokyo. Shiban holds a Master's in Environmental Studies from the University of Pennsylvania, and a Doctorate from the University of St.Gallen.

Ulrich Steger

Professor Ulrich Steger has worked for IMD, leading the research and educational programs in the disciplines of complexity management, sustainability management and corporate governance. Since joining IMD, Professor Steger has directed various top management programs, including the Board Program. He has published extensively on all the three subjects. Since 2005 alone, he has co-authored nine books on these topics, including *Managing Complexity in Global Organizations* (2007), *Corporate Governance—How to Add Value* (2008) and *Sustainability Partnerships: The Manager's Handbook* (2009), as well as publications and cases in the developing world. His books have been published in German, English, Russian, Japanese and Chinese, and his articles have been translated into more than ten languages.